INSTITUTE OF ECONOMIC GROWTH

Studies in Economic Development and Planning No. 53

General Editor: T.N. Madan

STUDIES IN IRRIGATION AND WATER MANAGEMENT

Institute of Economic Growth, Delhi
Studies in Economic Development and Planning

For a list of titles in this series published by the Institute of Economic Growth, see at the end of this book

STUDIES IN IRRIGATION AND WATER MANAGEMENT

B.D. DHAWAN

Commonwealth

Studies in Irrigation and Water Management

ISBN : 81-7169-027-0

Edition : 2024

Published by :
COMMONWEALTH PUBLISHERS (P) LTD.
4831/24, Govind Lane,
Ansari Road, Darya Ganj,
New Delhi - 110002
Ph. : 23272541, 23242541
e-mail : commonwealthpublishers2016@gmail.com

Distributed by :
ARJUN PUBLISHING HOUSE
4831/24, Govind Lane,
Ansari Road, Darya Ganj,
New Delhi - 110002
Ph. : 23272541, 23242541
e-mail : arjunbooks2001@gmail.com

Laser Typesetting by :
Dimple Computers
Delhi

Printed at :
Milan Enterprises
Delhi

DEDICATED TO

THE CHERISHED MEMORY OF MY MATERNAL GRAND FATHER

L. KAHAN CHAND CHOPRA (1889-1959)

PREFACE

This volume is a collection of papers. These papers were written over the last three years after the completion of my major work on impact of irrigation on the Indian economy. These emerged out of two research projects, 'Irrigation and Water Management in India' and 'Interlinkages among Irrigation Sources', undertaken by the author at the Institute of Economic Growth. Needless to add, both these projects are extremely topical.

The papers in this collection are largely published already. As these are published in diverse journals, they are not readily accessible to interested readers. In view of their topicality, the attempt to bring them together in a single volume hardly needs any explication. Yet, it may be pointed out that these have been duly revised, modified and expanded wherever felt necessary. This has also been done in respect of some papers which either constitute parts of the proceedings of seminars/workshops at which these were first presented, or were put in restricted circulation by the author for eliciting comments. While doing so, some smaller papers have been consolidated into one. Also, individual 'References' at the end of each paper have been dropped. Instead, a unified Bibliography has been prepared from these paper-wise references. Towards this end, we now follow mostly the American system of referring to a cited author's name and year of publication (page number, or other identifying reference, wherever felt necessary).

Admittedly, the subject of water management research is both exciting and quite boundless in disciplinary domain. It therefore interests scholars from diverse disciplines. Economists as well as irrigation engineers/administrators are, unlike social anthropologists, soil scientists and agronomists, are rather late comers to this area of research and enquiry. Anyway, this underlines the multi-facet character of the subject matter. My principal concern in this book is with the issues of over-irrigation, groundwater depletion, underutilisation of irrigation capacity, optimal crop mix with given water resources, drought-proofing of Indian agriculture, conjunctive irrigation, the big dam controversy, and water-logging in canal commands. Some of these issues are explored at chapter length level also.

The book consists of fourteen chapters. The first chapter is in the nature of an overview to the problems of irrigation and water management.

Gradually, the scholars' interest is getting more focussed on issues of water management, with a corresponding reduction in the issues of irrigation expansion. The ultimate objective of irrigation management is to maximise the productivity of our limited resources of land and water, simultaneously minimising (a) adverse ecological consequences like groundwater depletion and waterlogging, (d) instability in agricultural growth and (c) inequality in income and wealth in the countryside.

India's natural endowment of water is looked into in chapter 2 from the specific angle of its irrigation potential. How groundwater resource can be used as a sort of buffer during drought time is highlighted. For discharging this drought proofing role it is imperative that groundwater is not in a state of over-exploitation in drought-prone areas. Measures for preventing over-exploitation of groundwater resource are outlined in chapter 3, wherein we look at some empirical evidence on the state of exploitation of groundwater in various states of India.

There is a widely-shared feeling that farmers in India, thanks to area-related water tariff in public irrigation works, tend to over-irrigate their crops. The empirical data in this regard, however, is rather scanty. Whatever data is available is sifted in chapter 4. In chapter 5 we take up the issue of big dam controversy. The way out of the Narmada imbroglio is suggested. Also, the myth of groundwater irrigation vis-à-vis major irrigation in the matter of cost advantage is exploded. Both surface irrigation and groundwater irrigation need to be developed in conjunction because of their strong interconnectedness in hydrological realm. The external economies of canal irrigation on groundwater-based agriculture in water-short regions like Maharashtra, Punjab and Tamil Nadu are measured in chaper 6.

Chapters 7 to 12 are more project specific than thematic in nature. Promoting private well irrigation within the commands of public canals is an important objective of Indian irrigation planning now. Results of a case study from western U.P. are discussed from various angles in chapter 7. A comprehensive impact analysis study of a major irrigation work located in a very high rainfall area of the Konkan region of Western India is carried out in chapter 8. Water use within the Mula command in western Maharashtra is probed in chapter 9.

Several hypotheses about Indian irrigated farming are tested in chapter 10. For this purpose, the survey data from an NCAER study for the states of Andhra Pradesh, Gujarat and U.P. are used. Likewise, ORG survey data for ten major irrigation works are reanalysed in chapter 11, the focus being on the issue of comparative productivity of water. To what extent irrigation in general and private tubewell irrigation in particular can alleviate poverty of the small and marginal farmers in the east Gangetic plains is sized up through three case studies in chapter 12. Finally, a short comment on the New Water Policy is offered in chapter 13. An integrated view of the principal results of the book is presented in the concluding chapter 14.

Needless to say, very many other issues of water management in India are left untouched in this volume. Some noteworthy omissions are: slow diffusion of water-economising devices like sprinklers and drip irrigation; watershed management; flood control and drainage; farmers' participation in the management of largescale irrigation works; etc. It is hoped that the author would have an opportunity to say something on these omitted aspects in a later study.

Acknowledgements are too many to be enumerated here individually without committing very many errors of omission. Still, I must make a special mention of Mr. K.J.S. Satya Sai. He did much more than the normal assignment for a research assistant at the Institute of Economic Growth. Evincing keen interest in my research endeavours, he undertook the added responsibility of being co-author in three papers, two of which are reproduced in chapter 6 and chapter 10. Likewise, I am thankful to Mrs. Rama Sethi for typing-and retyping ungrudgingly - a major portion of the manuscript.

The author is grateful to both the Indian Society of Agricultural Economics, Bombay, and the Editor, Economic and Political Weekly, Bombay, for readily granting permission to reproduce, partly or wholly, portions of my papers that were already published earlier in their journals.

Finally, I must put on record my high appreciation of the encouragement received from Dr. T.N. Madan, who, as Director of the Institute, provided excellent support in the completion of this volume.

May 1989 **B D Dhawan**

CONTENTS

	Pages
Preface	
Chapter	
1. Goals and Problems of Irrigation Management	1
2. Indian Water Endowment and its Drought Proofing Potential	18
3. Measures for Preventing Groundwater Over-Exploitation	34
4. Over-Irrigation by Indian Farmers	48
5. The Big Dam Controversy: Major Versus Minor Irrigation	62
6. Measurement of Linkages between Surface and Groundwater	81
7. Rise of Private Tubewell Irrigation in Canal Commands	95
8. Irrigation's Impact on Farm Economy in High Rainfall Areas	117
9. Water Management in the Mula Command	136
10. Analysis of Survey Evidence on Irrigated Farming in Andhra, U.P. and Gujarat	155
11. Productivity of Irrigation Water in Ten Canal Commands	176
12. Eradicating Poverty in Water abundant Eastern India	194
13. Towards a New Water Policy	215
14. Salient Recapitulations and Some Reconsiderations	226
Bibliography	237
Index	243

Chapter 1

GOALS AND PROBLEMS OF IRRIGATION MANAGEMENT*

The multifarious wants satisfied by water resources can be divided into two categories, namely, consumptive and non-consumptive. While in consumptive use water is literally consumed, it is more or less unaffected through its non-consumptive usage e.g., hydel power generation, navigation, fisheries, recreation etc. The consumptive use of water in an economy is primarily in the three sectors of agriculture, industry and household. Within agriculture sector, it is mainly used for crop activity.

As crop production is increasingly taking place under irrigated conditions, demand for irrigation water is steadily rising. Though this agricultural demand is not growing as fast as the other consumptive demand from industry and urban centres, yet the overall demand for water would preponderantly continue to be from agriculture sector. Thus the major issues of water resources management pertain to irrigation. In this chapter, I propose to focus on some of these issues. But before taking up these issues, a few observations are necessary.

First, we need to be clear about the ultimate goals of irrigation management. Are these of a universal nature, that is, are they the same everywhere? At first thought, the answer is in the affirmative. After all, every community would unexceptionally subscribe to the following goals of irrigation management:

... maximising farm production along a stable growth path;
... realising full utilisation of created irrigation potential;
... minimising over-irrigation and ecological degradation;
... attaining cost-effectiveness and reliability in irrigation service;
... achieving high water conveyance and storage efficiencies;
... promoting sustainable irrigated farming

* Revised and enlarged version of my IJAE article (Dhawan, 1986b).

At the stage of operationalising these goals, each community's larger goals of development have to be duly reckoned with. Since there is no universality about these developmental goals, the aforesaid goals of irrigation management get duly tempered with the community specific goals of development. Often, the emphasis on balanced regional development and on inter-personal equity in income and wealth varies from nation to nation. Thus considerations of balanced development between states within a large federal structure like ours may necessitate sizable transfer of water from water-abundant to water-short states. Likewise, the twin-imperative of equity and healthy polity in a water-short region like Maharashtra can be realised in an irrigation system in which water is allocated on egalitarian principles and with maximum coverage of farmers and arable land. It is for a community to decide to what extent it can go in for bearing extra costs and foregoing some production opportunities (if any) in designing irrigation systems that are in harmony with its avowed development goals.

Second, water is probably the most complex among the natural resources. As it is not amenable to simplistic conceptions and elemental measurements, ample scope for confusion and puzzlement exists for the unwary. In the Indian situation, the data limitations further add to misunderstandings, more so when one set of irrigation-related data is married with another one. To illustrate, the promoters of the minor irrigation cause, utilising Five Year Plan statistics on outlays and irrigation potential, have erroneously argued that the cost of minor irrigation works, area for area, is a small fraction of the corresponding cost for major irrigation works. Their error stems from ignoring the elementary fact that the plan statistics on outlays are exclusive of private outlays on minor works.

Third, India is a country of continental diversity. Here, the ground reality is bound to be quite varied. One has, therefore, to be very circumspect in making generalisations from limited experiences from few tracts/states. The compulsion, if not temptation, for generalising is all the greater when good data on various problems of water management are lacking in spatio-temporal coverage.

Problem Areas

The problems of Indian irrigation arise both in the construction and the operation phases. The serious problem of time and cost overruns in completing public irrigation projects is one of the construction phase. The causes of these two inter-related overruns are not yet fully understood, though inadequate project funding by state governments is widely mentioned as a single most important factor. What are the reasons for inadequate funding. Resource crunch? Too many project starts under political compulsions? Whatever be the reasons, the inevitable consequence of short funding is real resource cost of developing irrigation shoots up. This is not healthy for the viability of irrigation activity whose cost structure is already dominated by capital costs.

Many of the ills of Indian irrigation are of the operational phase, though some of them are due to inefficiencies of the construction phase. For instance, the ticklish problem of farmers in tail reaches of a canal not getting due share of canal supplies is largely traced to the fact that farmers in the top reaches get accustomed to excessive use of canal water because of a lag in construction of water distribution network vis-a-vis the construction of storage reservoir. Owing to this lack of synchronisation in construction stage, there is a natural tendency to allow the stored waters to be used profusely on the limited command area already covered by distribution network in the head reaches. Afterwards, these top-end farmers are disinclined to give up the excessive use of water for raising heavily-irrigated crops like paddy and sugarcane, thereby affecting the farmers' interest in the lower reaches.

My attempt here is to throw light on the following problems of irrigation management in India.

1. Underutilisation of irrigation capacity;
2. Inequity in irrigation;
3. Dependability of irrigation;
4. Wastage of irrigation water;
5. Financial losses;
6. Sustainability of irrigated farming.

In what follows each of these problems is examined one by one. Needless to add, these are inter-linked problems. Also, some of them are pursued in detail in other chapters. Thus, the problem of groundwater depletion, which is a threat to the thriving groundwater-based agriculture, is taken up in depth in chapter 3. Likewise, the problem of wastage of irrigation water by the Indian farmer is probed in chapter 4.

The Phenomenon of Underutilisation

Capacity utilisation is a fascinating area for industrial economists. In the case of irrigation activity, it is a tricky thing that needs to be handled with extreme caution. It is imperative to appreciate the true nature of our much-talked about problem of underutilisation of water resources.

Its two distinct aspects need to be distinguished, namely, the problem of exploitation of water resources as against the problem of full utilisation of the exploited resources. In either case, the picture that may emerge from analysis is affected by the units of measurement, namely, whether the progress is viewed in terms of area statistics or volume of water. In terms of area statistics, it would appear that the three-fourths of the national groundwater potential is already tapped. But the volumetric approach, that is usually adopted by the Central Groundwater Board, would yield an entirely different picture, namely, nearly three-fourths of the groundwater potential is yet to be tapped.

Mercifully, both the approaches yield similar results in respect of surface irrigation development, that is, six-tenths of the exploitable potential has been developed. Here, however, the picture of utilisation of the created potential is sensitive to the approach chosen for analysis. Generally, the area approach, which is normally used by scholars and to which we revert later in this section, yields lower rate of utilisation than does the other approach by volume of water. This may be attributed to two reasons. Firstly, while translating volume of water available in reservoirs/streams into their area irrigable counterpart, there creeps in overoptimism with regard to (a) water losses in conveyance and (b) curbing the cultivation of water intensive crops like sugarcane and paddy in canal commands. As the conveyance losses turn out to be higher and the farmers get away with greater proportion of their crop area under water intensive crops, the utilisation in terms of area statistics becomes lower than that indicated in project reports. The important thing to realise about this unutilised potential is that the water may neither be remaining in the reservoir nor wholly flowing to the sea.

Secondly, the very basis for computing created irrigation potential has been somewhat questionable. Potential is said to be established when the canal network owned and maintained by the irrigation department is completed. Field channels, the last bit of the canal system, are supposed to be set up by farmers. Evidently, farmers' failure to do so would give rise to underutilisation of created potential. Lately, attempt is being made, mainly through the Command Area Development programme, to construct field channels as part of the project.

Irrigation being a capital intensive activity, periodic reports of gross underutilisation of capacity of new irrigation projects become a source of dismay. Such estimates of underutilisation of irrigation capacity, derived as these are from a simple juxtaposition of actual area irrigated (*A*) against area potentially irrigable (*P*), need to be interpreted with caution lest erroneous inferences should arise. A low value of this utilisation ratio (A/P.100) does not necessarily mean that lot of costly water is flowing to the sea. For, the ratio tends to recede below 100 as the actual crop pattern tends to tilt in favour of heavily-irrigated crops (like sugarcane and paddy). Since Indian farmers have shown much stronger preference for paddy and sugarcane than what has been contemplated in irrigation project reports, this imparts an inherent downward bias to the utilisation ratio. Likewise, a high value of this ratio does not imply a near-capacity utilisation situation if each irrigated hectare receives much less irrigation water than what is contemplated in the capacity estimate 'P'. Since Indian irrigation system is believed to be delivering to farmers water much less than the provision made while designing the system, some perceptive scholars have rightly perceived an element of upward bias in the utilisation ratio on this count.

To what extent this upward bias is counterbalanced by the downward bias due to the deviation in crop pattern is not possible to figure out. Given these limitations, one cannot conclude much about the true extent of underutilisation of irrigation in India by a simple recourse to the utilisation ratio. Apparently, for the irrigation sector as a whole the official statistics of irrigation potential and benefitted area reveal a picture of 'good utilisation' that compares favourably with the level attained in the Indian industry sector, that is, above 85 per cent.[1] Much of this 'unutilised capacity' is in the surface irrigation works.

Given the pitfalls of the utilisation ratio as a measure of performance, some critics have taken recourse to alternative ways of judging the extent of underutilisation in Indian irrigation. Since the principal objective of irrigation is to augment agricultural production, they appraise the performance of Indian irrigation by comparing the crop yields of irrigated lands with some normative levels. These normative values are not drawn from the expected values used in the irrigation project reports (while computing the ex-ante benefit-cost ratio for a project) but are derived from two data sources, namely, (1) crop yields observed prevailing on well-managed irrigation systems elsewhere and (2) yields realised

1. Some observers have discerned a downward tendency in the ratio. This tendency has partly emerged because of a change in procedures in the sense that in recent years statistics of utilisation are no more computed on the assumption of full utilisation of minor irrigation potential.

on national demonstration plots. In terms of foodgrains, Indian yield on irrigated lands averages about 20 quintals/ha, which is far below the level of 50 to 60 quintals/ha in the Far East, and also substantially below the level of 35 to 40 quintals/ha obtaining on the demonstration plots. Evidently, in such reckonings the performance of Indian irrigation emerges in poor light. But one may question the relevance of such an approach to the problem of underutilisation of capacity on two counts. Firstly, irrigation by itself is expected to enhance rainfed or unirrigated crop yield (varying from 4 to 8 quintals/ha) by 3 to 5 quintals/ha only. The high crop yields in the Far East, as also on the demonstration plots, are based on very intensive application of bio-chemical inputs. Thus the lower yields may be partly traceable to the less intensive application of fertilisers and pesticides. The question is: What are the determinants of input intensification in agriculture?

Secondly, much of the Indian public irrigation is deliberately designed not to encourage very intensive farming but to promote irrigated farming in as much areal extent as possible. In other words, canal water is rather thinly deployed by fixing large command area in relation to availability of irrigation water. (In technical terms, 'water allowance' is kept low, or 'water duty' per unit volume of water is kept high). Whatever be the motives[1] behind such 'underirrigated' farming, in which irrigation needs of plants are not met upto the point at which maximum yield potential of a crop is attained, such farming effectively brings about maximisation of crop output per unit of irrigation water. Then, why judge its performance in terms of crop output per unit of area?

In passing, I would like to mention another route via which performance of Indian irrigation has been berated in India. In this route, the ratio of gross irrigated area to net irrigated area is used to judge utilisation of irrigation. Erroneously adopting a norm of 200 percent for this ratio, the observed ratio of 125 percent is used to infer that 75 percent of irrigation potential is unutilised in India.[2]

Equity in Irrigation

It is useful to keep a distinction between spatial and interper-

1. During the British colonial rule irrigation works were taken up in tracts where land was more abundant than irrigation water. Among the motives behind developing unduly large command area with low intensity of irrigation were (1) maximisation of revenue per unit of investment in irrigation, (2) containing waterlogging due to seepage of canal water, and (3) maximisation of protective cover during the event of a drought.
2. For more details, see Dhawan (1985).

sonal/inter-class inequity in gains from irrigation. Official statistics of distribution of land holdings by size and area benefitted from irrigation do not lend support to the impression that irrigation resource in India has been disproportionately appropriated by large farmers. For, the irrigation ratio (irrigated area as a percent of size of holding) is not found to rise with farm size. In the pre-HYV era, it decisively diminished with farm size, an important explanation for the well-known inverse relation between land productivity and farm size. Well irrigation, though an indivisible investment more undertaken by large than small farmers, has not still resulted in the emergence of a positive relation between farm size and the overall irrigation ratio. What has been reported by scholars is more an emergence of a positive relation between farm size and income or productivity gains from each unit of irrigated area. Though there are noteworthy exceptions, the new relation arises primarily due to a positive variation in access to farm resources (including irrigation) with farm size (Dhawan, 1988, chapter 9). It is the positive relationship between income gains and farm size that is now weakening the inverse farm size-productivity relation of the pre-HYV days. Evidently, this implies further widening of disparities of income and wealth between small and large farmers. And thus becomes a cause for concern among students of political economy.

In the matter of spatial equity within a state, as also within the command of an irrigation work, major irrigation works of North-Western India have to be accorded a high rating. By adopting a policy of under-irrigation, the spatial coverage of the benefits has been extended maximally. And by creating the institution of *warabandi* (a time-shared system of taking canal water by turns) in the tertiary part of the canal system (that is, below the canal outlet) - and successfully enforcing it - the farmers in the tail-ends of the canal system have not suffered unduly from undue appropriations by the top-enders.[1] Elsewhere, the undue appropriations by the top-enders have not only drastically curtailed the due share of the tail-enders but also led to substantial shrinkage in benefitted area vis-a-vis the planned irrigable area. This is partly an outcome of notoriously large time over-runs in completing irrigation projects. As dam work is completed much ahead of the construction of distribution network, the farmers in the upper reaches are temporarily

1. It is reported lately that the discipline in water-sharing in some of the canals in U.P. is now breaking down to the verge of anarchy, especially during a year of drought when demand for water is far more than the canal supply.

allowed to raise heavily-irrigated crops on a far greater scale than that contemplated in the project plan. In the absence of adequacy of fund allocation for completing the distribution network, the top-end farmers get used to raising heavily-irrigated crops. As these crops are, acre for acre, generally far more remunerative than lightly-irrigated crops, these farmers stoutly resist giving up the unwarranted cultivation of such crops, thereby depriving farmers in the lower reaches from practicing irrigated farming as per project planning. Many empirical studies have drawn attention to such gross inequity in income and yield benefits within canal commands. How do we rectify this situation?

A preventive solution to the problem is to eliminate altogether the growing of heavily-irrigated crops on canal waters in areas like the Deccan plateau where water is an extremely scarce resource in relation to arable land. In the particular case of Maharashtra where cultivation of sugarcane absorbs bulk of the canal capacity (in terms of volume of reservoir water), one drastic recommendation is to allow the operation of a canal system for only 8 months in a year so that no farmer in the canal system can raise sugarcane by depending exclusively on canal irrigation. With this restriction, irrigation capacity in Maharashtra (measured in terms of irrigable area) can be substantially enhanced. This will mean a substantial improvement in spatial equity in gains from irrigation–its beneficial consequences for groundwater development are explored in Dhawan (1986a).

In passing, I would like to refer to the emergence of a wide inter-state disparity in irrigation. Since water endowment is highly variable across states, inter-state disparity in irrigation is inevitable. The minimum that the planners at the Centre must strive to ensure is that the actual disparity in irrigation from Plan to Plan is not out of alignment with the disparity that would ultimately prevail when all water resources are fully tapped. But we must realize the limited role of the Centre in this regard. Irrigation being a state subject, its development hinges vitally on the plan priority accorded to it by the state planners/politicians.

Dependability of Irrigation

Public irrigation in India has been widely criticized for its failure to meet farmers' irrigation needs on time and in requisite quantum. Because of this, some observers have dubbed public irrigation in India as protective one that is ill-suited for sustaining intensive farming based on the HYV seeds which have exacting water requirements as compared to local seed varieties. Analytically, it is useful to discuss timeliness (a measure of quality of irrigation) and quantitativeness of irrigation separately though the two are indeed inter-linked.

From the viewpoint of timeliness in completing irrigation operation, public irrigation works compare quite unfavourably with the ones owned individually by farmers, especially tubewells and dugwells fitted with pumpsets, a fact that emerged forcefully in numerous field studies about the suceess in propagating HYV technology since the mid-sixties. Thus the problem of timely irrigation is basically one that pertains to public irrigation systems, more so to largescale works with huge commands. When land holdings of beneficiaries are tiny (in comparison to large holdings in the USA), the irrigation system is bound to be operated rigidly according to predetermined time schedules, and not on demand from the individual farmers in the system. In the Indian conditions, it is well nigh impossible to cater to irrigation needs of an individual farmer according to water stress being experienced by his different crops. Yet, a brief discussion of two following hypothetical cases that promise timely irrigation in a major irrigation work is quite instructive as it provides an important clue to a well-managed irrigation system.

Each farmer in a large public irrigation command can complete on time his irrigation operations for all crops during a given crop season, say, rabi season, in two alternative schemes of things. In one scheme, water is allowed to flow continuously throughout the distribution system (constructed right upto each farmer's field) during the whole of rabi season, with the result that each farmer feels as if he is situated by the side of a river from which he draws water whenever a crop on his field exhibits signs of water stress. In the second scheme, each farmer is allowed to store canal water sufficiently enough to meet his irrigation needs till fresh canal supplies arrive. The feasibility of the first scheme of water distribution hinges on abundance of water availability, as a good deal of water is bound to flow down the drain in this scheme. Likewise, the feasibility of the second scheme is dependent on farmers' willingness and capacity to bear the added cost of on-farm storage of canal water.[1]

Quantitative inadequacy of surface irrigation works has two aspects. One, many works are designed on the scarcity principle, namely, in water-scarce regions irrigation water is so shared that each farmer gets water per unit of his land holding much less than the requisite optimum

1. Dryland farming experts are advocating the harvesting of rain water in small farm ponds which can provide 'life saving' irrigation in the event of a long break in monsoons in regions of highly uncertain rainfall.

for crops recommended by agronomists. For example, in the northern wheat-belt the optimum number of irrigations (each of 7.5 cm depth) for realizing the full yield potential of non-HYV wheats was considered to be four. Yet, the canal systems here provided for about two irrigations. The second aspect pertains to the periodic water shortages that are traceable to either reduced inflow in reservoirs due to drought in the catchment area, or to a rise in irrigation requirements of crops due to drought conditions prevailing in the command area. This periodic shortage, super-imposed on a basic system design of underirrigation, is certainly not conducive to intensive farming, especially with HYV seeds which are truly sensitive to situations of water stress. This has led to fervent pleas for abandoning the scarcity principle in designing distribution network for public irrigation works, and instead go in for productive irrigation that can meet full irrigation needs of HYV seeds.

Instead of raising 'water allowance' — that tantamounts to shortening the command area[1] — it is better to persist with the scarcity principle and simultaneously promote the establishment of wells by the beneficiaries. In fact, the beneficiaries have already done so on an extensive scale in northern canal tracts, in the tail-end areas of canals elsewhere, and in tank-irrigated tracts. In more than one sense, such supplementary wells play a vital role in Indian irrigation. First, these have improved total availability of irrigation water to irrigators, both in terms of quantum and quality. Second, the dependability of irrigation has risen to the extent farmers' own wells can be relied upon for providing additional water during drought years.[2] Third, the wells that extract canal seepage incidentally provide the much-needed drainage in drainage-deficient Indian canal networks, thereby effectively mitigating waterlogging and soil salinity problems of canal irrigation.[3] Thus, such conjunctive use of surface and ground waters, in which ills of the public sector are rectified by the merits of the private enterprise, has radically improved the quality of irrigation in India, especially in North Western India. As a result, HYV technology has been profitably adopted in such canal tracts. Of course, the level of crop yield, though rising over time,

1. In the latter half of the sixties, the government of Uttar Pradesh decided to drastically curtail the command area per public tubewell with a view to promoting productive farming. Such curtailment in command area in existing surface irrigation works is infeasible.
2. This flexibility of groundwater irrigation during drought, which usually curtails irrigation capacity of tanks and canals that depend on surface water run-off only, tends to drought proof groundwater-based farming. For more details, see Dhawan (1988 a, chapter 8).
3. For empirical evidence in respect of the state of Punjab, see Chopra (1989).

is still below the potential yield level. But there is no doubt that overall farm output from the available resources of land and water is much greater — and more equitably shared — than would be the case if canal irrigation were developed so as to meet full irrigation needs of crops as per the agronomists' recommendations.

Wastage of Water

Water conveyance efficiency, as also efficiency in field application, is indeed quite low in Indian surface irrigation works. The overall efficiency, defined as the ratio of irrigation water used by a crop (for evapo-transpiration purpose) to the water released from the headworks, is alleged to be as low as 20 per cent only. Since such statistics are not routinely compiled by irrigation project authorities, it is difficult to vouchsafe for the veracity of the above estimate.[1] It is imperative to understand the nature of such losses of irrigation water so as to correctly appreciate their significance from the viewpoint of project performance.

Bulk of the loss is due to (*a*) seepage from canal network (including field channels below the final outlet) and (*b*) water percolation below the crop root zone at the farmer's field level. Since this seepage-cum-percolation loss is a very large proportion of the irrigation water released from the headworks, surface irrigation works become an important source of artificial (i.e., man-made, as distinguished from natural recharge from rainfall, snow, floods etc.) recharge to groundwater table. Evidently, such continual recharge raises both the water table and the groundwater availability underneath.

Whereas rise in groundwater table in areas of high depth to water table reduces the intolerably high cost of groundwater lifting, the greater water availability enhances water-yield of wells in areas of poor natural recharge (e.g., in much of the Deccan plateau that is in the rain shadow of the Western Ghat mountains). Thus, the so-called canal losses become a beneficial external economy to the users of groundwater, thereby improving returns to investment in well irrigation. And one should not worry unduly on account of such losses so long as these are recouped through groundwater withdrawals for irrigation, for industrial use, for drinking purpose etc. The real issue is whether this way of recouping the 'lost' water is more advantageous than investing in techniques that prevent such seepage/percolation in the first instance. The current thinking

1. To the extent water in conveyance is stolen or used unauthorisedly — not an uncommon occurrence both in India and Pakistan — the estimate of conveyance efficiency gets unduly biased downwards.

favours canal lining of the main and branch canals only — lining of the whole canal network is recommended in arid areas having soils of high permeability and underlain with saline waters.[1]

As for wasteful use of irrigation water at farmer's level, four aspects of such wastage need to be distinguished for a proper appreciation of this phenomenon. One pertains to escape of water to drains during the course of its transit from the outlet to the field because of lack of channel supervision by an irrigator. The second wastage arises because of recourse to field-to-field irrigation in the absence of field channels that connect individual fields to the canal outlet. The third aspect of wastage is the surface run-off of irrigation water because of lack of field levelling. And the fourth is the problem of over-irrigation. The wastages of the second and the third types are being eliminated through the on-going Command Area Development Programme that commenced in the early seventies. The first one being a minor problem, we better concentrate on the wastage due to overirrigation, and explore if it can be curbed by appropriate pricing of irrigation water.

What do we mean by overirrigation? Is it confined to users of public irrigation service only? How does one account for the phenomenon of overirrigation in a canal system operated on the scarcity principle viz underirrigation, in which farmers usually complain of lack of canal supplies? As far as scientific water management experts are concerned, a case of overirrigation arises if an irrigator, during a **single irrigation operation,** applies more water than is retained in the crop root zone from where the plant ingests nutrients in soluble form - the excess water percolates mainly to the groundwater table that is well below the crop root zone. Thus if a watering of 7.5 cm depth is needed for wetting the crop root zone fully, but an application of 10 cm is made, an overirrigation of 2.5 cm arises. If two such waterings are given as compared to five such recommended waterings for a crop for attaining its full yield potential, there is overirrigation to the extent of 5 cm from the technical viewpoint of the water experts but a situation of underirrigation from the farmer's angle — his actual use comes to 20 cm which is almost half of the recommended application.

A farmer's practice of overirrigating his field is understandable because of (1) uncertainty about his next turn for irrigation from a system that is outside his control and (2) his inability to correctly assess the full

1. It may be pointed out that seepage is not altogether eliminated in a lined canal. The extent of reduction in seepage depends also on the nature of material used for lining.

wetting of the crop root zone. Evidently, if he has not to pay for irrigation by volume of water, some overirrigation is inevitable. Such eventuality is all the more if the optimal doses of irrigation depth for a crop are highly variable with (*a*) the stage of plant growth,[1] (*b*) weather conditions and (*c*) soil characteristics. The role of price instrument in curbing such over-irrigation appears to be rather very limited in the given circumstances. So long as the basis of pricing is not somehow linked with the volume of water, the simple pitching up of area-cum-crop linked water rates offers no pecuniary incentive to the farmer to avoid over-irrigation — the problem is further probed in chapter 4.

Financial Performance

Financial health of public irrigation works in India has always been low. But in recent years it has deteriorated rather rapidly. The irrigation administrators, as also many an economist, attribute this deterioration to a policy of gross underpricing being pursued by the state politicians. Close observers of state run irrigation systems link this financial mess with the inefficiencies in the execution and management of irrigation projects. Knowing as we do know about the poor quality of administration in all public departments, the causes of the poor management of public irrigation works are quite complex.

As per the latest published records of public irrigation works in India, the picture of operational costs (excluding interest charge on capital) is as follows. The operational expenditure for the multipurpose river projects amounted to about Rs. 279 millions during 1980-81. In respect of major and medium irrigation projects the same totalled around Rs. 1083 millions.[2] Thus overall operational costs of canal irrigation may be reckoned at Rs. 1362 millions, of which Rs. 530 millions was accounted by establishment cost alone. The maintenance and repair expenditure stood at about Rs. 844 million, just about 15 per cent below

1. For instance, optimal dose for HYV wheat at crown root initiation stage (about 21 days after sowing) is about one inch compared to about 3 inches later on (4 to 5 inches in the pre-sowing stage).
2. Strictly speaking, this is not an all-India figure. It is derived by aggregating data for 15 states, namely, Andhra Pradesh, Bihar, Gujarat, Haryana, Jammu and Kashmir, Karnataka, Kerala, Madhya Pradesh, Maharashtra, Orissa, Punjab, Rajasthan, Tamil Nadu, U.P., and West Bengal. Data on maintenance and repairs is not reported for M.P. and West Bengal.

Source: Government of India, *Combined Finance and Revenue Accounts of the Union and State Governments in India,* Annual publication of the Comptroller and Auditor Generlal of India, New Delhi.

the revenue income (Rs. 986 millions) from the canal system in 1980-81. Adopting a figure of 23 million hectare for area actually irrigated (as against a created irrigation potential of 28.6 million ha) by major and medium works for the year 1980-81, one obtains an approximate estimate of Rs. 60/ha as operational cost for canal irrigation in India. This is well below the requisite level (about Rs. 100/ha) needed for good maintenance work.

The investment cost is rising much faster than the general price level, adding to the interest cost burden. Not to speak of interest cost on capital investment, even the operating expenses (which constitute a small proportion in the total cost of irrigation) are not being recovered from the farmer beneficiaries. To have shifted the focus from departmental income receipts (from sale of water) to social income gains in project appraisal is undoubtedly a contribution of economists in public welfare area, with the result irrigation investments are possible at an accelerating rate in the face of mounting financial deficits of the existing projects. One unintended consequence, however, has been a pathetic disinclination on the part of state politicians to let irrigation authorities recover from beneficiaries substantially, if not wholly, the project costs through appropriate pricing of water. Politicians simply do not realize the myopia of their policy of gross underpricing of water that ultimately lowers the quality of irrigation service. For, a project authority that is short on maintenance funds, which accrue primarily from revenue receipts, cannot undertake timely repair work, not to mention of preventive maintenance work that is vital for good service — this is particularly true for public tubewells and surface waterlifting schemes based on mechanical pumping.

This author does not favour that the entire cost of public irrigation be recouped from the beneficiary farmers. In support, he can advance several arguments. However, before spelling out some of these, he may clarify he is not rationalising or defending the present position in which the beneficiaries of Indian public irrigation works hardly pay one-tenth of the nominal resource cost of such works. Among the arguments that militate against the idea of total recoupment, one may mention the following ones.

First, a sizable part of the reported investment in all public works (including irrigation works) in India is of a fictitious nature as it comprises bribes and kickbacks paid by contractors to construction engineers, administrators and political bigwigs for obtaining contracts for public works on an open bidding basis. Even in the departmentally executed works, the expenditure on account of inflated muster rolls and leakages of construction material, such as cement and steel, are of considerable magnitude. Second, there are real inefficiencies in project execution—the notorious time over-runs leading to cost over-runs. Why should the beneficiary farmer be asked to defray such portions of irrigation project costs due to corruption or inefficiencies in the system as a whole? Why not let this part of the cost be set off against the increase in revenue income of the state and the Central governments in the wake of increased economic activity due to the introduction of irrigation in rainfed agriculture?

Sustainability Question

Demand for farm products continues to grow, partly because of a steady increase in population and partly due to rise in incomes due to planning. Since the income elasticities for food products are not likely to approach zero for many, many decades, we have to so exploit our land and water resources that these meet our growing food needs on a sustained basis. It is in this context of long-run sustainability of our agricultural growth that anxiety is now and then expressed by concerned citizens about irrigation-related adverse developments: siltation of reservoirs, waterlogging, soil salinisation, groundwater depletion etc.

Setback due to excessive siltation of dams and reservoirs is becoming a new question mark on the sustainability of irrigated farming. Siltation is an inevitable process of damming a river and dam builders do reckon with this by providing 'dead' storage (space for silt accummulation without affecting the irrigation capacity during the life of a dam). The cause for worry arises when the soil erosion in the catchment area rises, resulting in (*a*) filling-in of the dead storage more rapidly than envisaged and (*b*) siltation spreading to 'live' storage area of the reservoir. Preventing deforestation and increasing afforestation in the river catchment are the only effective ways to cope with the siltation problem. Presently, irrigation authorities are not taking active interest in the catchment areas which are left wholly to the care of other departments (forest and agricultural departments). Since (1) the dam sites are quite scarce — this is the major argument advanced for building big instead of small dams — and (2) desiltation of reservoirs is not a feasible proposition, the sustainability of irrigated farming within the commands of such reservoirs hinges on our controlling the siltation process.

Setback to agricultural growth in the case of surface irrigation works due to waterloggging and soil salinization is well recorded in the world history of canal irrigation. This twin danger is all the greater in arid regions like Rajasthan where seeped-in canal waters bring saline groundwater to the land surface before long. Therefore, it is a major challenge to human ingenuity to practice irrigated farming in arid regions. As of today, sprinklers and drippers are the best, though very expensive, methods for controlling soil salinity in such areas. Construction of a network of drains, another expensive proposition, is another alternative route to keep water table as well as salts below the crop root zone.

A system of conjunctive irrigation is a good insurance against waterlogging. Waterlogging arising from impeded drainage from developmental works like roads and railways requires adequate investment in cross drainage works. Investment in drainage system, as also in flood control through storage reservoirs, is of vital importance in high rainfall areas with flat topography. Possibly, greater emphasis on groundwater vis-a-vis surface irrigation in such areas is required to keep the problem of waterlogging under control

A declining water table in not conducive to a growing agriculture on two counts. First, groundwater resource may be rendered unfit for irrigation purpose if saline and brackish waters from adjacent tracts intrude into the voids created by the receding water table — this danger is great in the coastal plains and the states adjoining Rajasthan desert. Second, resource cost of raising groundwater is an increasing function of depth to water table. Indian hydrogeologists have been repeatedly urging the planners to enact groundwater regulation laws so as to prevent (*a*) permanent lowering of water table and (*b*) mutual interference among well owners while tapping a common pool of groundwater. These laws have yet to be enacted — a model bill on this aspect was prepared by the Centre in the early seventies for the guidance of the state legislatures. The ticklish issue is explored in detail in chapter 3.

Concluding Remarks

As irrigation in India is increasingly becoming a sort of infrastructural input, it is imperative that its management by both farmers and the concerned government agencies is firmed up for the realisation of main goals of irrigation development. Awareness about these goals need wider propagation, both in the context of endowment of natural resources and the socio-political imperatives of this country of continental dimensions. While most goals of irrigation development are of universal nature, some may be quite community specific. To illustrate this important point, the objective of equity in gains from irrigation development is far more a community specific goals, emphasis on which may vary from nation to nation.

Since the beginning of the Second Five Year Plan, the problem of unutilised irrigation potential established with large capital outlays has engaged attention of both the planners and the critics of Indian irrigation. As this area of analysis is full of pitfalls, it is no wonder that definitive results are lacking. Therefore, simplistic findings in this regard need not be taken at their face value. Because of definitional deficiencies of the available data on irrigation potential and its utilisation, neither the rising trend in the rate of underutilisatioh of irrigation capacity nor this rate bring greater for major than for minor irrigation works is a truth that is beyond the pale of doubt. Recourse to indirect methods, so as to overcome the shortcomings of the direct methods, is equally unsatisfactory. For example, comparing observed crop yields under irrigated conditions with normative yields expected under good agronomical practices visualised by the farm experts can be a questionable method of appraising irrigation utilisation for protective canal commands, like those of northern India, which are not designed to promote intensive farming.

In contrast to the colonial period, the pace of irrigation development in India has been very rapid: the gross addition to irrigation capacity over the last 35 years has been more than twice the level of 22.5 million hectares in 1951. In the light of the current priority for irrigation in Indian planning, the national water resource potential for irrigation may be fully tapped during the coming 25 years. With such rapid expansion in capacity the management problems become more onerous, especially when the managerial skills at the State level are not so well endowed. It is high time that the political leadership in each State should show as zealous a commitment to proper management of irrigation projects as it has shown in the matter of starting new irrigation schemes.

Chapter 2

INDIAN WATER ENDOWMENT AND ITS DROUGHT PROOFING POTENTIAL*

Since ages, development of irrigation has helped man in insulating his crops against the ravages of a drought. Though this protective motive has been somewhat overshadowed lately by the productive motive aimed at hastening the rate of growth of agricultural output/income, yet there is no doubt that as more of the water resources are tapped for irrigation purpose the protective goal continues to be realised, partially or wholly. Since the commencement of planning in 1951, there has been impressive expansion in irrigation facilities in our country. Yet, hardly one-third of our crop area has the protective benefit of irrigation. In this context, two questions arise: have we enough water for attaining 100 per cent irrigated farming, and are we investing sufficiently in irrigation sector? To answer the first question we need to have a critical look at our endowment of both surface and ground waters, one task that we hope to fulfil in this chapter.

Even in a wholly irrigated agriculture, drought does make a dent in crop output. The extent of the dent is positively related with the severity of a drought, as also with the vulnerability of an irrigation source to drought itself. For instance, while tubewell-irrigated lands are known to suffer the least, the tank-irrigated lands in India fare rather badly during a drought. This differential in the protective role of irrigation is mainly due to a hydrological reality, namely, the lower layers of groundwater, which feed a tubewell, are comparatively immune to drought which otherwise reduces markedly the surface water inflow into a tank. This suggests that if tank-irrigated lands were to have some access to groundwater irrigation also, these could withstand a drought better. This brings us to the vital question of using our groundwater

* Revised and expanded version of paper, entitled 'Groundwater as a Buffer during Drought' presented at the Symposium on Water Management held at the Central Soil Salinity Research Institute (CSSRI), Karnal, in February 1988.

resources in conjunction with our surface water resources so as to improve the dependability of our irrigation system during the trying drought time.

Of course, inter-linking two surface water sources also adds to the irrigation reliability. In fact, some of the tanks in Tamil nadu are linked with rivers or canals. As these tanks, known as system tanks, receive inflows both from their own small catchments (in the shape of rainfall runoff) and from rivers/canals, farm areas under their commands have much better chance of escaping from the rigours of a drought. Extending this interlinking idea, one may rightly ask: how about inter-linking Indian rivers? Such inter-linking of two rivers may augment diminished water flow in one river due to drought in its catchment provided (*a*) there is no simultaneous drought in the catchment area of the other river and (*b*) water can be moved by the force of gravity from the latter to the former river.

In the two-fold exposition that follows our main concern is with sizing up our bounty of water resources and examining how the reliability of our irrigation can be enhanced for meeting the periodic challenge of a drought. The central aim is to explore the buffer role that can be played by our groundwater reserves in the event of a drought. Needless to say, this has bearing on alternative ways of coping with a drought, e.g., the maintenance of either buffer stocks of grains or of foreign exchange reserves for grain imports for drought years. The signal advantage in droughtproofing agriculture through irrigation is that it obviates the need for organising relief measures as farm incomes of the countryside, alongwith farm output, get protected through a reliable system of irrigation.

OUR BOUNTY OF WATER

The mighty rivers of India, especially when they are in spate during the monsoon period, do give rise to an impression of Nature having been too bountiful to us in the matter of water. Though the impression does receive a jolt when the periodic drought stalks the land, yet it lingers on as the following appealing idea crosses the mind. The idea is one of harnessing the flood waters, now flowing to the seas, for use in drought-prone regions of the country. Unfortunately, there is much more romantic vision about Indian water endowment, and much less awareness about harsh realities in this regard. The principal harsh reality is two-fold: low rainfall in regions having good exploitability of resultant water resources, and high rainfall in regions lacking exploitability of water resources.

India being a country of continental size, the annual rianfall, which is the ultimate source of both surface water and goundwater, is variable across its land mass. While peninsular and North-Western India have large areas of rainfall less than half the national average of about 1150 mm, few states in the far eastern India and the narrow strip of western coast (Konkan down to Malabar) have more than twice the national average. Thus the picture of abundance of water is confined mainly to these high rainfall tracts. The mean flow in the Brahamputra and Barak rivers of the east amounts to about 59 million hectare-metres (MHM), about one-third of the combined flow of all the the rivers put together. As hardly 5 per cent of this flow is exploitable as per the present expert assessment, this brings down the overall utilisability of the Himalayan flows to 32 per cent. Likewise, the exploitability of the short, coastal rivers originating from the high rainfall mountains of the Western Ghats is quite low, namely, 16 per cent. Thus the rivers, which are very bountiful because of either high rain or snow precipitation in their catchments (i.e. the Himalayan and the western coastal rivers of the Western Ghats) have utilisable flows to the extent of about one-fourth only.[1] On the other hand, the less bountiful rivers of the peninsular India, because of the rocky terrain through which these flow, have comparatively high proportion of utilisable waters. Statistics of river flows are shown in Table 1.

Table 1

Water Flows of Indian Rivers and their Exploitability

S. No.	*River*	*Annual flow MHM*	*Exploitable portion MHM*
	River Categories		
I.	Himalayan Rivers	116	32.0 (27)
II.	Deccan Rivers	44	31.8 (74)
III.	Western Ghat Coastal Rivers	18	3.0 (16)
IV.	Inland	1.5	1.5 (99)
	Total (I to IV)	180	68.4 (38)

1. This fraction is comparable with the recoverable fraction for petroleum oil resources in the world. In general, only a fraction of the mineral resources of a nation are exploitable for economic use.

Table 1 Contd.

S. No.	*River*	*Annual flow MHM*	*Exploitable portion MHM*
	Main River Basins		
1.	Ganga	50.16	25.00 (49.8)
2.	Brahmaputra	49.99	
3.	Barak and other rivers	9.08	] 2.40 (4.1)
4.	West flowing coastal rivers below Tapi and upto Kanyakumari	18.29	3.00 (16.4)
5.	Tapi	1.70	1.45 (85.5)
6.	Narmada	4.30	3.45 (80.2)
7.	Mahi	1.18	0.31 (26.3)
8.	Sabarmati	0.29	0.19 (65.5)
9.	Luni and others of Saurashtra and Kutch rivers	1.51	1.50 (99.2)
10.	Indus	7.33	4.60 (62.8)
11.	East flowing rivers between Ganga and Mahanadi	4.70	2.51 (53.4)
12.	Mahanadi	6.69	5.00 (74.7)
13.	Godavari	11.90	7.63 (64.1)
14.	Krishna	6.78	5.80 (77.4)
15.	East flowing rivers between Krishna and Pennar and between Mahanadi and Godavari	1.69	1.31 (77.4)
16.	Pennar	0.69	0.69 (100.0)
17.	Cauvery	2.07	1.90 (91.8)
18.	East flowing rivers below Cauvery	1.77	1.67 (94.0)
	All–India	180.11	68.41 (38.0)

Source: Government of India (1987)
Notes: (1) Figures in parentheses are percentages to annual flow.
(2) MHM = million hectare-metre. Orignal data are in Km^3 (thousand million cubic metres). One hectare-metre equals 10,000 cubic metres, or nearly 100 acre-inches.
(3) Earlier, the author had published a similar table in *Mainstream* of 26 December 1987. That was based on data given in Chaturvedi's book (1976).

Before sizing up ultimate irrigation capacity of our rivers in terms of crop area these can irrigate, it is imperative to mention two infirmities in our knowledge about our surface water flows. Thanks to a long, investigative pursuit that commenced with the appointment of the First Indian Irrigation Commission at the turn of this century, our knowledge about the mean annual flows in our rivers is quite firm. But the firmness of this knowledge is deficient in two respects, one having a bearing on the magnitude of our ultimate irrigation capacity and the other on the intrinsic, or designed, reliability of an irrigation project — the two are somewhat inter-linked. The first one pertains to the proportion of the flows that are considered unexploitable for techno-economic reasons, and the second one is about the year-to-year fluctuations in the annual flow of a river.

Given the assessment that only 38 per cent of our surface flows can be tapped for irrigation purpose, the ultimate irrigation potential from this source would suffice for crop area to the tune of 74 million ha only. This potential can rise if the exploitable fraction can be enhanced somehow, say due to inter-basin transfer of surplus river waters, a subject that we take up in the chapter 13. The late Dr. K.L Rao, an erstwhile Union Minister of Irrigation and Power, thought that this fraction could be raised to over 50 per cent. In that case, the magnitude of the irrigation potential might be nearer 97 million ha. This additional irrigation capacity of about 23 million ha compares well with the estimate of additional potential of 25 million ha anticipated as a result of inter-basin transfers in the Seventh Plan document (para 3.5, p. 72).

There is scope for enlarging our ultimate irrigation potential by constructing irrigation works of lower 'dependability', as there is an inverse relation between 'dependability' and volume of water flow available in a river. An idea about the extent of this inverse relationship can be obtained from selected river data in Table 2. Irrigation schemes in India are usually designed on 75 per cent dependability. So, if we go in for lower dependability works, as recommended by Dandekar et al (1979) for Maharashtra, we can increase our ultimate irrigation potential from our surface water resources. Since the protective value of irrigation is less when the designed dependability is lower, the purpose of extending irrigation benefit to a greater area may be realised more in a productive sense than in a protective sense. A more prudent course would be to design projects of lower dependability, say, 50 per cent, but keep their area coverage on a higher dependability, say, 75 per cent. Its practical implication would be enlargement of reservoir size per unit area to be irrigated, thereby enabling reservoir managers to store more water for carryover purpose in years of abundant inflows which

Table 2

Annual Water Yield of Some Major Rivers of Different Dependability Level*

S. No.	*River (location)*	*Estimated volume of water flow per year (MHM)*		
		dependability level		
		50%	75%	90%
1.	Narmada (Garudeshwar)	4.1	3.4	2.4
2.	Godavari (Dowalaishwarm)	11.8	7.1	N.A
3.	Cauvery (Mettur)	1.44	1.28	1.17
4.	Ganga (Allahbad)	12.1	9.6	7.2
	(Patna)	27.3	24.4	16.6

Source: Government of India (1987, Table 7).

* Dependability level means the number of years out of a 100-year period (expressed in per cent) that an irrigation works would have water at least equal to the volume as per the project design.

can be deployed in drought year. This gain in protection during drought comes partly at a higher capital cost and partly at a greater submergence of the land.

Since the investigative work on the irrigation potential of India's groundwater resources commenced in the latter half of the sixties, it is no wonder that our estimates of groundwater potential lack firmness. The delay may be condoned on two counts. First, the real emphasis on developing groundwater-based irrigation came in the early sixties when the rural electrification programme for the specific purpose of pump energisation began, to be soon reinforced with a massive programme for institutional credit for installing wells and pumpsets. Second, to a large extent the estimates of river flows were inclusive of groundwater recharge, the reason being that the 'base' flows of the non-monsoon period are the result of sub-terranean discharge of groundwater into a river. Thus Raju, while commenting on Dr. Khosla's estimate of 1949 (167.4 MHM) for mean annual flow of Indian rivers, observes: "However, the concept adopted by him does not indicate the relative proportion of the surface and ground water resources" (Raju, 1987).

If we contemplate drawing upon our groundwater reserves during a drought, it is imperative that we know the size of these reserves and their characteristics such as their depth and quality. Such information is lacking. Even the estimates of annual groundwater recharge are not yet firmly established, ranging between 26.50 MHM and 42.29 MHM for the country as a whole. (These are in net, and not gross terms. The gross magnitudes corresponding to these are of the order of 42 and 66 MHM, respectively, that is, about 60 per cent higher).[1] While the lower estimate is being reckoned by the Planning Commission, the higher estimate is due to the Central Groundwater Board (CGWB) and is officially adopted by the Central Water Commission in its document, entitled *Water Resources of India* (Government of India, 1987). This CGWB estimate is in close proximity to the one arising out of a summation of individual state-wide estimates worked out by the state groundwater directorates. But some noteworthy divergence is observed in respect of some states, notably Punjab, Gujarat, Rajasthan, Tamil Nadu, M.P. and Maharashtra (vide Table 3).

Table 3
Comparative Estimates of Groundwater Recharge

S.No.	*State*	*CGWB estimate (MHM)*	*State directorate estimate (MHM)*	*Excess of col.3 over col.4 (%)*
(1)	*(2)*	*(3)*	*(4)*	*(5)*
1.	Andhra Pradesh	3.660	3.989	(–) 8
2.	Assam	1.650	1.673	Neg.
3.	Bihar	2.860	2.880	Neg.
4.	Gujarat	2.030	2.569	(–) 21
5.	Haryana	0.880	0.814	8
6.	H.P.	0.067	0.060	12
7.	J & K	0.189	0.180	5
8.	Karnataka	1.300	1.390	(–) 6
9.	Kerala	0.690	0.680	Neg.
10.	M.P.	5.950	5.081	17
11.	Maharashtra	3.450	2.970	16
12.	Manipur	0.008	0.008	–
13.	Meghalaya	0.028	0.020	40
14.	Nagaland	0.003	0.003	–
15.	Orissa	2.150	1.915	12
16.	Punjab	1.310	1.815	(–) 28
17.	Rajasthan	1.830	1.365	34

1. The whole of the gross recharge is not considered utilisable for irrigation because (1) a substantial part of this gets naturally discharged into rivers and nallahs and (2) utilisation of groundwater by trees and other deep-rooted shrubs.

Table 3 Contd.

S.No.	*State*	*CGWB estimate (MHM)*	*State directorate estimate (MHM)*	*Excess of col.3 over col.4 (%)*
18.	Tamil Nadu	2.690	2.140	26
19.	Tripura	0.059	0.060	Neg.
20.	U.P.	9.270	7.861	18
21.	West Bengal	1.640	1.960	(-) 14
	Total	41.714	39.433	6

Sources: For column 3, Government of India (1987).
For column 4, S.P. Sangal (1987).

Notes: (1) MHM = million hectare-metre.
(2) Neg. = negligible.
(3) CGWB = Central Groundwater Board.

At the national level, the author is quite inclined to the higher estimate of groundwater potential, with the proviso that this ultimate groundwater potential would be materially relevant on full development of our surface irrigation resources. Even then, our endowment of groundwater is much less plentiful than our endowment of surface water. In terms of utilisable levels, our surface irrigation potential of 68.4 MHM exceeds our groundwater irrigation potential of 42.3 MHM by nearly 60 per cent. Assuming additivity of the two potentials, the national irrigation potential in volume terms becomes 110.7 MHM, of which a little less than two-fifths is from groundwater.[1]

Needless to say, the relative share of groundwater varies from region to region, being much less than the national percentage in the Deccan plateau and well above the national average in the case of the Indo-Gangetic plains. In the absence of state-wise estimates of surface irrigation potential by volume, a broad picture of th regional differential in the relative endowment of groundwater vis-a-vis surface water is formed by using the irrigation potential statistics by irrigable area. This picture is depicted in Table 4.

The paucity of our groundwater resource can be viewed from another angle, namely, its availability in relation to our crop land. We have a net sown area of the order of 140 million ha. The groundwater

1. The share of groundwater in total irrigation would amount to less than one-third if lower estimate of groundwater potential of 26.5 MHM is used.

Table 4

Region-wise Groundwater Share in Total Irrigation Capacity

S. No.	*Region*	*Ultimate potential (000 ha)* by groundwater	*Ultimate potential (000 ha)* by all waters	*% Share of groundwater*
(1)	*(2)*	*(3)*	*(4)*	*(5)*
1.	Southern	5,200	19,800	26
2.	Northern	17,200	37,935	45
3.	Eastern	8,742	30,087	29
4.	Western	5,500	17,200	32
5.	Central	3,000	10,200	29
	All-India	40,000*	113,475*	35

* includes Union Territories data.

Sources: 1. For column 3, state-wise statistice given in Government of India (1980, Annex. III).

2. For column 4, state-wise statisics given in Seventh Plan document (Annex. 3.2 and 3.6 of Volume II).

potential per unit area thus amounts to hardly 30 cm per year. This amount would just suffice for 4 waterings of the land in the whole year. The region of the acutest paucity is Western India (Rajasthan,

Table 5

Region-wise Groundwater Availability per Unit of Land Area

S. No.	*Region*	*Annual ground-water recharge (MHM)*	*Net sown area (m.ha)*	*Groundwater availability (col . 3 ÷ 4) (cm)*
(1)	(2)	(3)	(4)	(5)
1.	Northern	11.36	26.51	43
2.	Southern	8.27	29.69	28
3.	Eastern	8.52	23.25	37
4.	Western	7.20	43.72	16
5.	Central	5.52	18.84	29
	All-India	40.86	142.00	29

Source: For column 3, the average of the estimates of groundwater potential prepared by CGWB and state groundwater directorates.

Gujarat and Maharashtra) where groundwater availability per unit of land area is almost two-fifth the level found for Northern India (vide Table 5).

The actual state-of-the-art in Indian irrigation being what it is, the area potential of our water resources may be placed somewhere between 113.50 and 148 million crop hectares. The lower estimate is rather more firmly established, whereas the upper one is not. Anyway, the scarce nature of our water endowment gets underlined by the fact that, while the lower estimate of irrigation potential is about one-fifth less than our net sown area of the order of 140 million ha, the upper one is marginally higher than our arable land under plough. In this context, let us explore the scope for double cropping our land with full development of our irrigation potential.

The higher estimate of 148 million ha is based on an optimistic assessment with regard to inter-basin transfer of river water that has been hitherto considered unexploitable within its own basin. Even the irrigation resources based on such optimistic considerations are patently insufficient for enabling Indian farmers to practise double cropping under wholly irrigated conditions. In view of the uneven endowment of water in the country, the tantalising prospect of such double cropping of our limited farm land can at best be visualised for some water-abundant tracts, like East U.P., Gangetic North Bihar and West Bengal. Elsewhere, water is so scarce in relation to farm land in some regions, like the Deccan plateau, North Gujarat and much of Rajasthan, that one begins doubting even the realisation of more modest goal of double cropping, whereby one crop is raised under rainfed conditions and the other with the aid of irrigation. The dimensions of our unevenness in water bounty are aptly conveyed when we relate the ultimate irrigation potential of a region to its farm land. Going by the lower but more firmly estimated irrigation potential, we find that irrigation resources appear adequate for 39 per cent of the net sown area in Western India (Rajasthan, Gujarat and Maharashtra); 54 per cent in Central India (Madhya Pradesh); 66 per cent in Southern India (Tamil Nadu, Andhra Pradesh, Karnataka and Kerala) 129 per cent in Eastern India (Bihar West Bengal, Orissa, Assam and other eastern States) and 143 per cent in Northern India (Punjab, Haryana, U.P., H.P. and J & K). Thus while northern and eastern India are above the national average, the other three regions are below the national level as per the following data:

Region	*Ultimate irrigation potential as per cent of net sown area*
North	143
East	129
South	66
Central	54
West	39
All-India	80

Evidently, our irrigation potential, when viewed in terms of its area capacity, can undoubtedly be enhanced if irrigators can accomplish some economy in water use at the field level. This economy can come in two ways, namely, (1) investments in water-economising devices,e.g., sprinklers and drippers and (2) greater adoption of on-farm irrigation methods being recommended on the basis of scientific researches in water management. Likewise, improvement in conveyance efficiency of water distribution system can enhance our crop coverage with given amount of tapped water resources.

Investment in sprinkler mode of field application of water reduces irrigation requirements by 25 to 33 per cent (the requirements are measured at the field gate level, and not canal headworks). However, two limitations of this mode of field application of irrigation water need mentioning. One is about its unsuitability for paddy crop, our single most important irrigated crop that claims presently almost 40 per cent of our total irrigated area. The other is about its lack of adaptability to tank and canal irrigation; it has been best adapted to wells equipped with pumpsets. Likewise, drip irrigation, which can economise water use to half the earlier level, is best suited to fruits and vegetable crops which presently occupy a low position in our crop mix. Canal lining and piped channels are a must in arid regions where seeped-in waters are difficult to recover through groundwater development. But canal lining in low and medium rainfall regions would not truly enhance our irrigation capability if groundwater irrigation receives a setback as a result of reduced groundwater recharge in the absence of canal seepage.

To conclude this section on our bounty of water, we have compiled a comparative picture of water availability of each main region. This availability consists of (1) rainfall water, (2) exploitable surface water by volume and (3) exploitable groundwater by volume. The estimates of irrigation potential, by volume and per unit of our land resource, are listed in Table 6. Both in terms of rainfall and irrigation water, Western, Southern and Central India are poorly endowed. It is here we need to make our best effort in promoting (*a*) the use of water economising devices, (*b*) the diffusion of modern knowledge about on-farm management of water and (*c*) the cultivation of crops having lower water requirements.

Table 6

Estimates of Water Availability by Regions

S.No.	*Region*	*Rainfall (cm)*	*Exploitable water by volume (MHM)*			*Exploitable water per unit area (cm)*		
			surface water	*ground water*	*total*	*surface water*	*ground water*	*total*
(1)	(2)	(3)	(4)	(5)	(6)	(7)	(8)	(9)
1.	North	86	18.7 (62)	11.4 (38)	30.1 (100)	70	43	113
2.	South	102	13.1 (61)	8.3 (39)	21.4 (100)	44	28	72
3.	East	162	19.2 (69)	8.5 (31)	27.7 (100)	82	37	119
4.	West	718	10.5 (61)	7.2 (39)	17.7 (100)	25	16	41
5.	Central	119	6.5 (55)	5.5 (45)	12.0 100)	35	29	64
	India	115	68.4 (62)	40.9 (38)	109.3 (100)	48	29	77

Notes: (1) Col. 3 is normal rainfall, obtained by weighting normal rainfall for each state by its net sown area.

(2) Col. 4 is derived by multiplying ultimate surface irrigation potential in area terms (lower estimate) by 0.90.

(3) Col. 5 is the mean of the two estimates by CGWB and by state groundwater directorates.

(4) Columns 7, 8 and 9 are obtained by dividing columns 4, 5 and 6 by net sown area of a region.

This multi-prong effort would provide maximal security to crop acreage in the event of a drought.

GROUNDWATER AS A BUFFER DURING DROUGHT

When supplies of a good are prone to wide fluctuations over time, prudence demands a policy of buffer stocking of such a good. Thus, for sustained and smooth production process industrial firms resort to some stockpiling of their raw materials. Likewise, a welfare state may maintain buffer stocks of foodgrains to tide over a period of serious shortfall in grain supplies, say, due to a severe drought. This reqires investment both in buffer grains and in the necessary storage capacity for them. Alternatively, the state may maintain requisite foreign exchange reserves to import grains from abroad to make up for the deficiency in domestic grain output. This option is recomm-ended by the American (U.S.) circles (e.g. the World Bank) for the Third World nations like India.

Prior to India's Independence, the official policy leaned on some development of protective irrigation, alongside development of transport and communications, and famine relief works in the event of a drought. The policy has been pursued with greater zeal in the post-Independence period, leading to the creation of new irrigation capacity equal to four times the one added during the entire British rule in the country. In the latter phase of this period, the Centre has evinced interest in building grain stocks, first with a view to running the public foodgrains distribution system and later on for building the real buffer stocks. Thanks to the buffer stocks, the country could cope with the drought of 1987-88 when foodgrains output fell about 15-20 million tons below the likely level under favourable weather conditions.

Besides the problem of foodgrains, drought is now raising the serious problem of drinking water for both men and livestock and also a fodder problem for the survival of the animals in states like Gujarat, Rajasthan and Himachal Pradesh. It is generally perceived that the brunt of the drought this year (1987-88) would be borne by our livestock. Evidently, a stockpiling policy in respect of drinking water and fodder is rather infeasible for meeting a situation arising out of drought. Instead, it would be better to create capacity to produce the needed quantities of drinking water and fodder during the drought itself very near the points of consumption. Earmarking surface irrigation water for drinking purpose on a priority basis, as recommended in the National Water Policy document, is a step in the right direction. Yet, it can entail substantial expenditure on transporation to distant consumption centres, that is, towns and villages — the lead increasing with the onset of summer when reservoirs tend to deplete.

I think groundwater resources can be effectively used to cope with the exigencies arising out of drought. For one reason, groundwater is far more ubiquitous in natural occurrence than is surface water in the shape of rivers and lakes (Dutt, 1986 and 1987B). Thus it can be tapped for local use (near farm fields, village sites and towns) much more effectively than surface water which normally entails considerable transportation from the tapping point to the point of use (tanks and ponds are an exception). Secondly, we have natural stocks of groundwater, which are several times the rate at which replenishment occurs annually to these stocks from rainfall infiltration, canal water seepage, field percolation of irrigation water etc. By nature, the stock of groundwater is much bigger than the surface water flow per year.

Thirdly, groundwater, being underneath the land, does not suffer from evaporation losses which mount up during drought year in the case of surface reservoirs, tanks, ponds and lakes. While groundwater table may recede because of lack of infiltration due to drought, the technology of bore hole can remain quite cost effective over a considerable range of water table. Of course, two or three consecutive droughts can make groundwater scarce in low and medium rainfall regions having poor development of surface irrigation works that are an ideal source of artificial groundwater recharge.

If groundwater has to play its role of a buffer during drought time, it is imperative that it is not in a state of depletion at the drought time. That is to say, in normal times we do not overexploit it for purposes of irrigation, drinking water, industrial use etc. It is only when groundwater resource is underexploited in normal times that we can afford to draw on it for meeting extra demand for water owing to a drought. One policy implication of this is that we must reduce the demand for groundwater in normal years. For this, we must emphasise the development of surface irrigation works, and not groundwater-based irrigation, especially in areas of poor natural endowment of groundwater such as western and southern India.

As a result of surface irrigation availability, the demand for irrigation from groundwater source is *ceteris paribus* diminished, thereby reducing pressure on the groundwater reserves. Simultaneously, seepage of water from tanks and canals handsomely enhances groundwater availability in areas of poor endowment of groundwater. These external economies of investment in surface irrigation works have not been properly reckoned with by scholars/planners while evaluating benefits from investments in surface irrigation works in the Indian sub-continent. That these are very substantial has been demonstrated by the author elsewhere (Dhawan, 1986b and 1987a, and Dhawan and Satya Sai, 1988) — these are also explored in chapter 6.

In my view, the key to the efficient utilisation of our groundwater resource lies in the appropriate development of our surface waters, more so in the water scarce regions of India. To being with, we must provide a little more cushion for extra storage of water in reservoirs for express use in drought years. Secondly, surface water must be distributed more on a protective basis so as to maximise productivity and spatial equity in sharing gains from public investment in surface irrigation — this will also maximise the areal coverage in artificial groundwater recharge. We must realise the danger of waterlogging/salinity when an irrigation system tries to provide intensive irrigation, because under such a system farmers have no incentive to invest in groundwater irrigation that serves the purpose of vertical drainage. Without life saving irrigation, dry farming technology is not going to yield much in the Indian agro-climatic conditions. That such irrigation can do wonders is aptly demonstrated by data in Table 7.

A Summary View

There is some sort of romanticism about India's water resources that is totally out of alignment with ground reality. The irrigation capability of our water resources is rather modest. Except in the east Gangetic plains and the Konkan-Malabar coastal plains below the Western Ghats, we are short of water.

Droughts are inevitable. Their ill effects are best minimised by expanding the irrigation cover on the one hand and maintaining buffer stocks of foodgrains and edible oils. Dips in crop output due to drought can be moderated through the following measures. Firstly, we should start building surface reservoirs with extra capacity for storing excess rain water of above-normal rainfall years *for use during* following drought years. Secondly, we may adopt a policy that underemphasises the use of groundwater during normal times. If groundwater reserves are underexploited in normal times, we can overdraw on them during drought time for meeting our irrigation and drinking water needs, as also for raising green fodder specifically for meeting feed needs of the livestock.

Thirdly, we should pursue the goal of protective irrigation to the point that life saving irrigation is available to dry lands.

Table 7

Effects of Critical Irrigation (5 cm) on Yield of Crops

S.No.	*Crop*	*Research Station*	*No. of trials*	*Yield (q/ha)*		*Per cent increase*
				without irrigation	*with irrig-ation*	*due to life saving irrigation*
1.	Wheat	Dehra Dun	4	21.4	35.5	66
2.	Wheat	Ludhiana	4	19.2	41.1	114
3.	Wheat	Agra	2	21.9	27.4	25
4.	Wheat	Rewa (M.P.)	4	5.7	18.8	230
5.	Barley	Varanasi	2	26.0	33.6	29
6.	Sorghum	Bijapur	5	16.5	23.6	43
7.	Sorghum	Bellary	4	4.3	13.7	219
8.	Upland rice	Rewa (M.P.)	4	16.2	27.8	72
9.	Sorghum	Solapur	5	9.8	18.2	86
10.	Native tobacco	Anand (Gujarat).	4	12.1	18.1	50
		Mean		15.3	23.8	56

Source: Singh and Vijaylakshmi (1987).

Chapter 3

MEASURES FOR PREVENTING GROUNDWATER OVER-EXPLOITATION*

Thanks to heightened awareness of environmental aspects of economic development, there is now a wider, if not universal, concern with regard to excessive exploitation of natural resources of land, water, forests, fisheries etc. Over-exploitation of any resource creates anxiety both among its users and the non-users, the latter being often more forceful in giving vent to their apprehensions as to how the larger interests of the community may be adversely affected by such over-exploitation. Given such a milieu, one cannot but take some note of alarm bells being sounded by concerned citizens in the popular media about the hazards of over-use of groundwater for obtaining enhanced productivity of land. Recently, N.S. Randhawa, the ICAR chief, in an interview to the press, expressed his fear that Punjab may become desert again if the state farmers persist in using groundwater for growing heavily-irrigated paddy in the semi-arid conditions of Punjab. Similar forebodings have been made earlier for Meerut district of West U.P., another semi-arid area, where the extensive use of tubewell water for raising sugarcane, another heavily-irrigated crop that needs copious irrigation throughout the year, led to continuous decline in water table in Daha block.[1]

Now that groundwater occupies a signal position in the rural as well as the metropolitan economy of India, its depletion over time is bound to give rise to serious problems. Every summer one reads pathetic accounts of insufficient supply of groundwater for civic uses in big cities like Madras, Hyderabad, Ahmedabad, Chandigarh etc.[2] Since long, groundwater has played a vital role in meeting drinking

* Enlarged version of my EPW paper (Dhawan, 1987c).

1. For a brief account of over-exploitation in this block, see Dhawan (1982, p. 155).

2. Almost all over the globe, groundwater table has been receding in major cities due to excessive withdrawals for drinking and industrial uses.

water needs of both villages and small towns during drought time when availability of surface water in rivers and ponds is poor, more so during the summer season.

As a source of irrigation, groundwater has become particularly important in the Indian farm economy. In areal coverage, it now compares well with major and medium surface irrigation works which can presently cover 30 million ha of crop area of the nation. In fact, Indian agricultural development since the mid-sixties has come to be identified far more with development of private wells and shallow tubewells than with canal or tank irrigation. As the crop yields on groundwater-irrigated lands are higher than those on canal or tank-irrigated lands, one has to admit that the productive role of groundwater is indeed substantially more than its two-fifths share in total irrigation capacity of the country. Furthermore, with six-tenths of the national grain output originating from irrigated areas now, any setback in the availability of groundwater for irrigation purpose can slow down, if not undermine, the trend rate of expansion in our foodgrains supply.

Our focus in this chapter is primarily on groundwater regulations for irrigation purpose only. The serious problem of over-exploitation of groundwater in city areas is a local phenomenon arising out of a basic imbalance in demand and supply forces. Urban demand for water, when viewed in terms of the land mass of a densely-settled as well as industrialised pocket, is inherently excessive in comparison to poor infiltration rate of rainfall due to high portion of the city land surface becoming impermeable because of pucca roads and high density of dwellings. Without import of surface water from another place, the groundwater in cities is bound to remain in perpetual siege.

It is not our purpose to dwell here on the consequences of groundwater overdrawal, nor identify areas of the country where the stage of such overdrawal has been reached by now. In what follows, we first offer a brief elucidation of the concept of over-exploitation of groundwater resource. Our main effort is to draw a line between a short phase of overdrawal and a permanent state of over-exploitation that is practically irreversible. This distinction is necessary for understanding the sharp drop in water table during drought years. To what extent decline in water table or in rate of water discharge from a pumpset, is a clear sign of over-exploitation of groundwater is commented upon. Next, we sift the available empirical evidence on the extent of exploitation of our groundwater resources, so as to unearth the pockets of over-exploitation in different regions of the country.

Lastly, we come to the core of this chapter, namely, the array of direct and indirect measures for preventing over-exploitation of groundwater. Our main effort is to draw attention to the limitations of groundwater regulation through legislative measures being suggested by our groundwater experts.

CONCEPT OF OVER-EXPLOITATION

Like surface water, groundwater too has its origin in rain water. Rainfall, including snowfall, being a periodic phenomenon of some regularity, its infiltration well beyond the crop root zone is the source of groundwater replenishment every year. Owing to the downward pull of the force of earth's gravity, the infiltrated water gradually penetrates deep below the land surface — in the Indo-Gangetic plains at places groundwater is found at a depth of 30,000 feet (i.e., upto the point one encounters the alluvial deposits brought by rivers from the mountains of the Himalayas, the Vindhyas and the Arravalis). Since in the distant past our groundwater withdrawóls were persistently a fraction of the annual replenishment from rainfall, from flood waters and from few surface irrigation works, the stock of groundwater rose continually. (This cumulative process is substantially halted as the top of the accumulated groundwater 'reservoir' rises above the bed level of nearby rivers and nallahs).

This *stock* aspect of groundwater resource needs to be duly distinguished from the annual replenishment or *flow*, dimension. When groundwater by nature is said to be far more plentiful than surface water,[1] the reference is to its stock dimension whose comparison with the flow dimension of surface water is of questionable relevance in the context of water resource utilisation for a sustainable irrigated agriculture. Anyway, the stock of groundwater is usually many times the annual amount of replenishment, called recharge in hydrogeologists' parlance.

The concept of over-exploitation of groundwater resource is essentially normative in character. The resource is deemed to be in a state of over-exploitation when the withdrawals for irrigation and non-irrigation purposes *tend* to exceed the annual recharge. This normative definition is based on the 'safe yield' principle of groundwater hydrology. According to this principle, the withdrawals should match the recharge

1. "If the 94 per cent of the earth's water that rests in oceans and seas at high levels of salinity is removed from consideration, then groundwater accounts for about two-thirds of the fresh water resources of the world", observes D.K. Dutt, the present Chairman of the Central Groundwater Board (CGWB). See Dutt (1987c).

so as to keep the stock of groundwater intact.[1] In case an imbalance arises, the depth to water table, a critical parameter both in the economics of groundwater irrigation as well as groundwater hydrology, is affected.

Introduction of surface irrigation in general and canal irrigation in particular alters groundwater regime. Seeped-in canal waters become a new substantial source of groundwater recharge. If farmers do not undertake to step up their groundwater withdrawals, the stock of groundwater begins swelling, bringing up the water table. In the absence of seeped-in waters, any excessive use of groundwater decreases the stock of groundwater, resulting in a decline in water table. As the rising water table reaches the crop root zone (generally taken as 1.5m of the upper soil), the pernicious phenomenon of waterlogging commences. In the converse situation of a receding water table, the process of groundwater depletion ensues, with its attendant consequences, such as, land subsidence in alluvial regions and likely damage to aquifers from the intrusion of saline waters.[2] The only circumstance when a lowering of water table is a matter of welcome relief is when this happens in waterlogged regions e.g., in the Punjab during the sixties and the seventies.

It may be clarified that a transitory decline in groundwater table due to some transient imbalance in groundwater recharge and withdrawals is a short-lived phenomenon. Such decline could be due to either a seasonal or a cyclical factor. After the cessation of monsoon period, water table keeps receding, touching the lowest level of a year during the summer season — rising again with the onset of the next monsoon rains. Similarly, decline in water table during a drought year is of a cyclical nature, as there is recovery during the following above-normal rainfall years. Even though these seasonal and cyclical changes in water table have some economic implications,[3] these are ignored here

1. D.K. Dutt remarks that "although the concept of safe yield has been widely used in groundwater resource evaluation, there has always been widespread dissatisfaction with it." (Dutt, 1987c, p. 2.9).
2. This intrusion problem exists in coastal regions and in semi-arid regions where saline and brackish water bodies are found by nature. It is said that as a result of over-exploitation of groundwater in the coastal areas of Saurashtra, sea water has ingressed upto 10 kms inland. When such saline waters are inadvertently pumped for irrigation, they create soil salinity that lowers crop yields.
3. While seasonal fluctuations in water table may force farmers to relocate their pumping sets according to crop season, a severe drop in water table during drought might entail much more effort to maintain irrigation supplies to crops. The Punjab government compensated its farmers in 1987-88 with a bonus of Rs. 18 per quintal of paddy which is mainly grown on tubewell water, on the assumption that the severe drought (rainfall 50 per cent below normal) substantially enhanced the cost of watering paddy.

because these do not lead to a permanent lowering of water table. Thus a phase of short-run over-exploitation of groundwater due to a row of drought years needs to be distinguished from a long-run over-exploitation leading to a downward tendency in groundwater table.

Neither a decline in water table nor a reduction in the rate of water discharge of a pumpset is an unmistakable indicator of over-exploitation of groundwater resource. In a drought year, the recession in water table reported by farmers is certainly not wholly due to over-exploitation. In a region where groundwater is already in a state of over exploitation, this recession gets magnified as the transitory decline superimposes itself on the trend element in downward movement in groundwater table. Likewise, in a region where wells are not properly distanced from one another, there is mutual interference among them when these are used simultaneously with the aid of power pumps. As a result of this mutual interference, the water discharge becomes less than the rated one, especially during a long break in monsoon when working of pumps by their owners accentuates this problem of mutual interference. In such a situation, farmers' reports of reduced flow of water from their pumpsets are no clear evidence of over-exploitation of groundwater in that tract.

AREAL EXTENT OF OVER-EXPLOITATION

The available data on groundwater development does not lend much credence to stories of over-exploitation or depletion of groundwater that appear in the media now and then. This disparity could be for two reasons. First, our estimates of groundwater potential and its use still lack firmness. Here it would suffice to mention that the two sets of data available on the subject reveal a very divergent picture of the present level of exploitation of our water resources. While the area-based statistics of groundwater potential and its utilisation indicate that nearly three-fourths of the ultimate groundwater irrigation potential of the country is already tapped, the same information in volumetric terms indicates that a little over one-fourth of the groundwater resources have been tapped. This disparate picture, though considerably narrowed when we adjust for difference in the estimates of groundwater potential in the two data sets,[1] should caution us against being categorical while

1. Estimates of groundwater potential, when expressed in volumetric terms, have risen sharply over time. While the estimated area that can be ultimately irrigated by our groundwater resources remains underpinned to an earlier estimate of groundwater viz. 26.50 million ha-metres (MHM), the new estimate in volumetric terms, as per the norms laid down by the Groundwater Estimation Committee in 1984, is of the order of 42 MHM — this is not yet officially accepted.

disputing claims of over-exploitation of groundwater in certain regions of the country.

Second, the available evidence on the level of groundwater exploitation is rather very aggregative in its areal extent. The area-based data are at State and Union Territory level only. While the volume-based data of the CGWB are of similar coverage, the same data gathered by the state Groundwater Directorates are usually recorded upto the block level. However, this latter data set is not readily available. Fortunately, NABARD, the apex body for promoting groundwater development with the aid of institutional finance, has access to this data, and one of its senior groundwater experts has published a paper that gives some glimpses of a disaggregative picture of the state of groundwater exploitation in June 1986. Yet, enough details are not available to ascertain the veracity of stories of groundwater depletion in certain tracts, such as Coimbatore district in Tamil Nadu, Mehsana district in North Gujarat, coastal districts of Saurashtra, Karnal district of Haryana etc.

The Planning Commission carries out its water planning exercises through the area approach, whereas expert water bodies like the Central Water Commission (CWC) and CGWB conduct their work mainly through the volumetric approach. Undoubtedly, the volumetric approach is superior, although in the present case it indicates as if there is enormous scope for developing groundwater-based agriculture in the country. However, we begin with the area approach first.

The groundwater resources of India, on full development, are deemed capable of irrigating about 40 million ha of crop area. By the time the planning era commenced in 1951, a groundwater potential of the order of 6.50 million ha had been established through nearly 4 million dugwells, 3 thousand private tubewells and 2400 government-owned, deep tubewells of large capacity (1.50 cusec). At the beginning of the Sixth Five year Plan (i.e. 1979-80 end), a further addition of nearly 4 million dugwells, 2 million private tubewells and 34 thousand government tubewells raised the national groundwater potential to 22 million ha.[1] According to the 7th Plan report, an additional groundwater potential of 7.4 million ha was established during the Sixth Plan period. So, by the mid-eighties a little over 29 million ha of groundwater potential had been created. Assuming that the 7th Plan

1. The numbers quoted in this para so far are from the report of a study group constituted by the Planning Commission. For details, see its report (Government of India, 1980).

target for groundwater development of 7.1 million ha is moving on course, we may say the total groundwater potential is now (1987-88) somewhere between 33 and 34 million ha, about 6 to 7 million ha below our ultimate groundwater potential. Much of this untapped potential is found in high rainfall areas, such as, Orissa, West Bengal, Assam, Bihar, East U.P. and Madhya Pradesh.

For 1982, the volumetric data is the handiwork of CGWB, whereas for 1986 the data is compiled by the state groundwater investigation organisations. According to these sources, hardly 24 percent of the national groundwater potential had been tapped in 1982 (Government of India, 1987, Table 9), and 27 per cent in 1986 (Sangal, 1987, Table 1). Interregional variations in the level of exploitation are listed below:

	1982 (%)	*1986* (%)
1. North India	38	43
2. West India	24	25
3. South India	24	28
4. East India	14	16
5. Central India	8	13
all-India	24	27

At a more disaggregative level, Punjab and Haryana among the states and Delhi and Chandigarh among the Union Territories have witnessed comparatively high rate of groundwater exploitation. Their percent rates are as follows:

	Punjab	*Haryana*	*Delhi*	*Chandigarh*
1982	73	70	88	116
1986	86	60	NA	NA

According to S.P. Sangal, half the blocks in the state of Punjab have now been declared as 'dark' areas where further promotional work for groundwater development is to be halted as over 85 per cent of the groundwater irrigation potential is said to have been attained in these blocks. In Haryana, one-fourth of the blocks are labelled 'dark'. In all, 5 per cent of the blocks of the country are characterisable as 'dark', with Punjab and Haryana together accounting for over two-fifths of these. Region-wise, the 'dark' blocks were comparatively more in Northern and Western India than in other regions, as shown below.

	% blocks of 'dark' category
North India	9
West India	10*
South India	4
East India	2
Central India	0
All-India	5

* Excluding Maharashtra where 2 per cent of the 1481 micro watersheds were 'dark.'

Assuming for the moment that 15 per cent of groundwater potential needs to be earmarked for drinking and other non-irrigation uses, one may say that the phenomenon of over-exploitation of groundwater in India is primarily confined to big cities and to about one-twentieth of the 5000 rural blocks of this country. The level of exploitation and the extent of 'dark' category areas of the hard rock regions of the Deccan plateau, Rajasthan and Gujarat are probably much more than indicated by the official groundwater data in volumetric terms whose limitations are taken up in the chapter 2.

PREVENTIVE MEASURES

Limitations of Legislative Means

Year after year, Indian groundwater experts, notably the hydrogeologists, have been giving clarion calls for groundwater regulation through legislative enactment. Water being a state subject in the Indian Constitution, the Centre has been commending the need for such regulatory mechanism to the state governments. In order to expedite such enactments at each state level, the Centre prepared a model bill in 1974 and circulated it among the states.

While a few states like Tamil Nadu and Gujarat initiated some action in this regard, no state has as yet prepared a legislation on the subject of groundwater regulation. While this has dismayed Indian associations of water experts, this author does not entertain any great expectations from such a legislative measure even if enacted. For, there is little hope for effective implementation of such laws which are inherently difficult to enforce in the Indian conditions of small land holdings, inadequate administrative set-up in the countryside, and eroded state of ethics. In view of this perception about the implementability of such regulations, one can appreciate why the state legislators have baulked at the enactment.

Leaving aside the two special cases, namely, (1) inevitability of groundwater mining in arid areas of little recharge from rainfall and (2) need for over-exploiting groundwater in waterlogged regions, the essential task of groundwater regulation is two-fold: one of controlling overcrowding of wells and the other of containing aggregate groundwater withdrawals well within the limits of total recharge. A little reflection would show that this would require groundwater regulation on the lines of our industrial licensing scheme, necessitating some statutory control both on well location and on groundwater withdrawals by each well owner.

While the need for groundwater quotas is self-evident, the case for well location requires enunciation. The problem of well location must be distinguished from the problem of its proper siting in a field. The siting issue for a farmer is mainly one of covering maximum of field area by gravity flow but at minimum length of setting up water distributing network. On the other hand, the location aspect alludes to avoiding crowding of wells in a given aquifer. Overcrowding gives rise to the problem of mutual interference among wells when these are operated simultaneously. In technical terms, the 'radii of influence' of wells overlap, that is, a well is located within the 'radius of influence' of another well. Due to mutual interference the operational cost of waterlifting rises: as the discharge of waterlifting mechanism diminishes, the duration for completing an irrigation operation rises. Needless to add, the well owner with a small waterlifting capacity is disadvantageously placed, and in the extreme case he may not be able to lift any water till the well owner with larger pumping capacity stops the irrigation operation. In general, owners of traditional wells suffer when modern wells equipped with power driven pumpsets come up in their vicinity.

When land holdings are large (as in the South-Western U.S.A.), spacing between wells can be ensured by calling upon farmers to site their wells outside the radii of influence of their neighbours' wells. But when these are small and fragmented in space, suitable distancing among wells cannot be ensured without denying permission to some late comers whose proposed wells may come within the radii of influence of the existing wells in an aquifer/watershed. This kind of groundwater regulation becomes inequitous in the light of the fact that farmers with comparatively smaller land holdings often decide to dig their own wells after the bigger farmers have installed their own wells. If two shallow tubewells are not to interfere with each other's working, these must be located 200 metres apart (CSSRI, 1985, p. 4). If these were sited at the centre of two square fields, each field must be above 10 acre size for the interference problem not to arise. This should bring home why spacing regulations, if strictly enforced, will discriminate against small farmers.

In contrast to the problem of mutual interference, the problem of over-exploitation of groundwater resource is far more intractable and with far more serious consequences in certain situations. If decline in water table in a tract continues unabated, the rising cost of groundwater irrigation may prove inadequate to arrest the process of decline in water table. In fact, even before the depth to water table reaches a level where marginal cost of exploitation equals the marginal benefit from a unit of water, groundwater resource may be damaged due to intrusion of saline/brackish waters from the neighbourhood. This is a real danger in shallow aquifers near the sea coast and in semi-arid regions underlain with brackish waters unfit for farming.[1] Since well owners seldom subject the pumped water to periodic check-up for salt content analysis, they come to learn of the intrusion of saline water into their aquifer rather late (usually when white crusts appear in the fields).

Electricity Pricing

In a way, rural electrification has enhanced pressure on groundwater resource. To begin with, electric pumpsets are best suited for continuous pumping of water from any depth.[2] Secondly, electric

1. In some semi-arid tracts one may encounter the phenomenon of layers of sweet water interspersed with layers of brackish water.
2. A manually operated waterlift becomes dysfunctional when depth to water table exceeds 15 feet. The same limit for an animal-operated, persian wheel is around 35 feet, and about 50 feet for 'mhot', a traditional animal-operated lift of southern, western and northern India. A diesel pumpset is only a shade less than an electric pumpset in the matter of depth to water table.

power for agricultural pumpsets is heavily underpriced both in comparison to its resource cost and the alternative sources of energy for lifting water. Thirdly, the linking of power tariff with horse power of a motor instead of actual consumption of power in many states makes well owners behave as if the marginal cost of pumping water is zero. Thus the structure of power tariff, as also the pitch of electricity price, badly needs due modification. Though the need for rectifying these weaknesses in the electricity pricing are emphasized by many scholars, implementation is becoming problematic, more so in view of farmers' resistance to pay more for farm inputs in general and electricity input in particular. In fact, the structural distortion in power tariff came about because the state electricity boards failed to collect electricity bills from farmers who, in connivance with lower functionaries of the electricity department, began tinkering with electricity meters.[1]

Indirect Means

Attempts to control both the density of wells and well spacings in a tract through indirect means have proved rather ineffectual. Linking of the grant of electricity connection for a pumpset with prior certification that there is no other pumpset/well within a specified distance has been overcome by farmers procuring the needed certificate through bribing of officials — failing this they could opt for the next best solution, namely, the installation of a diesel engine. Likewise, stoppage of institutional finance when a tract has witnessed overdevelopment of well irrigation may have slowed down further over-exploitation of groundwater resource provided benefit-cost ratio based on funds drawn from non-institutional source is not found to be favourable by farmers in that tract. The trouble with this instrument, however, is two-fold: (1) coping with strong political pressures that prevent declaring a tract ineligible for fresh financing for well irrigation and (2) its invokation rather late in the day by which time over-exploitation has become a reality. Even when no new wells are coming into existence, the existing well owners tend to depress the water table as they enhance their withdrawals by gradually improving intensity of cropping, or altering crop pattern in favour of more resource-using crops which usually need more irrigation.It is only when some of them begin investing in water-

1. This tinkering with the meters — and occasionally deliberately felling them from their poles and getting away by laying the blame on wayward buffaloes or bulls - sums up our ability to enforce statutory regulations in the countryside, a fact that is better known to legislators and administrators than to scientists in city portals.

economising devices (sprinklers, drippers, lining or piping of channels etc.) that downward pressure on groundwater table begins to ease.

Short of total exploitation of groundwater resource under governmental aegis, one sees no ideal solution to the twin-problem of over-exploitation and overcrowding in groundwater utilisation. In point of fact, some scholars (including this author) subscribe to the view that groundwater exploitation in the east Gangetic plains through public tubewells instead of individualy-owned wells is a superior option, given the preponderance of small and highly-fragmented holdings for which individually-owned wells are not a viable proposition. However, this is not a region for which one should apprehend the prospect of over-exploitation of groundwater resource — even if the water table recedes it is likely to stabilize, without any danger of intrusion of saline waters, at a new level not much below the river-bed level. Even for much of the western portion of the Indo-Gangetic alluvium, which has witnessed an explosive growth of individually-owned tubewells during the last two decades, one need not worry unduly about over-exploitation of groundwater. Extensive development of surface irrigation works massively augment groundwater recharge in this region, not to mention that availability of surface irrigation *ceteris paribus* reduces need for groundwater irrigation. The existence of an extensive canal network and some perennially flowing rivers (fed by snow melt and water stored in the mountains of the Himalayan, Aravalli and Vindhyan ranges) would tend to prevent decline in water table below the river-bed level. Here, the danger is in areas adjoining Rajasthan state (south-west U.P. plains, south western Haryana, and southern Punjab) because of high occurrence of saline bodies of groundwater.

Outside the Indo-Gangetic plains, scope for direct exploitation of groundwater resource under state ownership is rather meagre. To begin with, groundwater formations here are mainly of the rocky type in which tubewell technology can play little role. Secondly, wherever tubewell technology is feasible, (e.g. in the coastal alluvium), large size tubewells are not a feasible proposition at very many places. Thus it is not a worthwhile proposition for the state to operate under its aegis innumerable dugwells. Yet, it is here that groundwater resource is under great pressure. This pressure arises because groundwater endowment is poor. Though water in relation to land resource is comparatively more scarce here than in the Indo-Gangetic plains, surface water resources vis-a-vis groundwater resources are more abundantly available.

Wisdom lies in paying more attention to the development of surface irrigation works, so that a sizable fraction of surface waters end up in groundwater table. But for such artificial recharge of groundwater table through extensive development of canal network in Punjab, Haryana and West U.P., intensive farming based on tubewell irrigation would have been decisively less than what it is today.

Role of people's participation in watershed management in areas of undulating topography and hill regions is quite well recognised, if not firmly established, in India. The problems of groundwater management are primarily those of plains regions where groundwater-based agriculture comes into vogue. It is not yet clear how people's participation can help in the resolution of the twin problem of over-exploitation and overcrowding in groundwater irrigtion in the vulnerable regions.In the matter of major irrigation works, the action belongs to the state. It is with regard to minor surface irrigation works that people's participation at the local level may prove helpful, thereby improving the fraction of rainfall infiltrating into the ground. In particular, community effort in properly maintaining irrigation tanks (desilting of tank bed; periodic strengthening of tank bund, proper maintenance of feeder channels if any) is good for recharging groundwater as well. Likewise, percolation tanks can be taken up through community effort as well provided good geological advice is forthcoming — otherwise these may become simply 'evaporation' tanks.

Summary View

Excessive groundwater exploitation has become a matter of concern, especially among hydrogeologists and financial institutions which massively support groundwater development in India. Direct, regulatory measures on the lines of the model bill suggested by the Centre, namely, 'The Groundwater (Control and Regulation) Bill' of 1974, have yet to be enacted by the state legislatures. And the indirect measures such as restricting institutional finance and electricity connections in the endangered areas have proved rather ineffecive. The author thinks that in the particular conditions of relatively small and fragmented land holdings in India legislative enactments are of little practical value, and therefore main reliance has to continue on indirect measures. And here we need to broaden the set of measures.

Evidently, there is some imperative to curb the excessive demand for groundwater created by low tariff for electric pumpsets, especially where it has been linked with pump capacity instead of actual consumption of power. More importantly, measures aimed at ehnancing the very quantum of groundwater resource should be taken for regions where groundwater endowment is much less bountiful than that of surface water. Due emphasis on investments in surface irrigation works in these regions would go a long way in augmenting groundwater supplies, as a tidy fraction of such tapped waters end up in ground below the crop root zone. And by enforcing the policy of extensive instead of intensive irrigated agriculture within the canal commands of such water-scarce regions the benefits of canal seepage can be spatially spread — this also minimizes the danger of waterlogging and imparts more spatial equity to the process of income growth. In the case of minor works, like construction of ordinary tanks, percolation tanks, nallah bunding and check dams and their adequate maintenance (especially desiltation of tanks and their feeder channels, if any), people's participation helps in raising the fraction of rain water going into the ground.

Chapter 4

OVER-IRRIGATION BY INDIAN FARMERS*

The Indian farmer's behaviour as a production and marketing agent has been a matter of some controversy since long. While social scientists by and large deem him now to be a rational person, many natural scientists and the urban elites still harbour doubts about his rationality. Widening the concept of farmer rationality for a tradition-bound society, the sociologists and the social anthropologists have succeeded in improving our understanding of him as a producer. The economists have resolved some puzzles about his actions by a rigorous application of economic theory, e.g., the identification of the income effect behind a backward sloping supply curve of a grain that dominates in the production as well as the consumption basket, and invocation of the concept of opportunity cost for explaining the over-use of labour in farm production process.

In the matter of over-irrigating the fields, every one, including the economist, is quite concerned — and considerably puzzled — by the Indian farmer's behaviour. This calls for a close look at the whole issue of over-irrigation, so that we may understand the limits of the measures which are being suggested now and then for checking over-irrigation in India. Among these measures are: (*1*) the abandonment of the government policy of low-cost, highly-subsidised irrigation from government owned irrigation works, (2) linking water rates to volume of water actually used by farmers, (*3*) giving up the flat power tariff for electric pumpsets and(*4*) undertaking massive extension work to educate the farmers both about efficient irrigation and the harmful effects of over-irrigation.

The main questions that we take up in this chapter are as follows. What do we mean by over-irrigation? This simple question has arisen

* A part of this chapter was presented, under the title 'The Puzzling Phenomenon of Over-irrigation' at the workshop on the Development and Management of Groundwater Resources in Eastern U.P., held in April 1988 at the Agricultural University, Faizabad.

because farmers continue complaining about the insufficiency of water supply from public irrigation systems, whereas irrigation administrators, water management scientists and perceptive visitors to the Indian countryside maintain that fields are being over-irrigated. Is over-irrigation confined to public irrigation systems only? This question arises because over-irrigation has been found on fields of farmers owning electric pumpsets (Singh, 1987). Will over-irrigation vanish if water is sold to farmers on a volumetric basis? We are raising this question because some scholars report over-irrigation by farmers buying water from public tubewells on a volumetric basis.

Nature of Over-irrigation

The neo-classical framework of production behaviour of the firm is not very helpful in comprehending the phenomenon of over-irrigation. In this framework, the optimality of an input use is determined by making reference to relative price of that input. If the input price relative to the product price is far in excess of the marginal product of the input, a case of over-application of that input is visualised. In agriculture, both the weather uncertainties of the production process and the price uncertainties of the farm product markets do reduce the applicability of the neo-classical framework to the problem of assessing optimal use of factors of production. In the particular case of irrigation input, this problem is further compounded by the unresolvable issue of aggregation.

This issue of aggregation is well known to scholars familiar with macro production function, especially in the context of the aggregation of capital of different vintages. Whereas the productivity of a machine diminishes with vintage (because of technical progress), no such simple, time-related association can be visualised for various water applications to a crop in its different stages of growth, each water application having its own unique role in the crop production process. That is to say, we encounter here the added problem of interdependence in different waterings given to a crop at various stages of its growth. So, to judge the phenomenon of over-irrigation via the neo-classical route is not a very meaningful thing,[1] and it is more instructive to go

1. This observation should not be construed as an adverse remark on the empirical work done by some water experts who are exploring water-related production functions with dated water application to a crop, say, a la Cobb-Douglas function being investigated by S.S. Prihar at Punjab Agricultural University — B.S. Minhas et al did similar work in 1974

by adopting a normative route, that is, judging actual irrigation against the level recommended by the water management scientists. Needless to say, serious conceptual issues still remain unsorted, two of these being the validity of the scientific norms on the one hand and the intractable issue of aggregation on the other.

As a result of several years of research work by dedicated scientists, we have now fairly good estimates of irrigation requirements of crops for major soil-climatic regimes of the country. For the state of Punjab, the Punjab Agricultural University gives such values for main crops of the state, which are listed in Table 1. The irrigation requirements vary from 180 cm for paddy, 150 cm for sugarcane, 100 cm for fruits and rabi fodders, to 45 cm for wheat and cotton, and

Table 1

Crop-wise Irrigation Requirements in Punjab

Kharif crop	*Irrigation requir-ements (cm)*	*Rabi crops*	*Irrigation requir-ments (cm)*
1. paddy	180	1 wheat	45
2. sugarcane	150	2 rabi fodder	100
3. cotton	45	3 barley	25
4. fodder	30	4 gram	25
5. bajra	15	5 mustard	25
6. maize	40	6 peas and lentils	25
7. groundnut	25	7 vegetables	60
8. arhar	25	8 potato	60
9. other pulses	20	9 fruits	100

Source: Gurcharan Singh (1987)

25 cm for mustard, gram, barley, peas, lentil, groundnut and arhar. There is no doubt that such norms are derived under normal rainfall conditions. This has two implications. First, the water requirements would rise in a drought year and would be below the recommended level in above-normal rainfall years. Second, these would be somewhat higher in the Punjab border areas adjoining arid Western Rajasthan and having lower rainfall than the normal level for Punjab — likewise, these would be lower in the border areas in proximity to the cool Himalayas and having more precipitation. Thus the norms are not invariant

with time and space of a state. In short, there is no absolute fixedness about them. These can vary with crop variety, as also with the mode of irrigation. In the case of paddy, abandoning the common practice of keeping land under submergence throughout the growth period reduces irrigation needs by 20 to 40 per cent (Rajput, 1988).

Table 2

Irrigation Schedule Recommended for Wheat after a Pre-sowing Irrigation for Punjab

	Second irrigation (7.5 *cm*)	*Third irrigation* (7.5 *cm*)	*Fourth irrigation* (7.5 *cm*)
	Days after previous irrigation		
1-7 November	36	43	26
9-21 November	41	38	25
22 November-5 December	44	30	15
6-20 December	35	25	15
21 December-4 January	30	20	14
5-15 January	28	18	12

Source: Prihar and Grewal (1988).
Notes: 1. The indicated intervals for irrigation can be varied by 2 or 3 days either side.
2. For each cm of rain, increase the interval for the next irrigation by 5 days upto the end of January and by 2 days after this period.
3. This time-table is not applicable for excessively sandy or saline soils and fields having hard impervious layer in the soil-profile within one metre from the surface.

Each norm of irrigation requirements is underpinned by a sequence of waterings of certain depths (usually 7.5 cm) at specific times. An illustrative, but rather complex, time table for scheduling irrigation for wheat in Punjab is shown in Table 2. Thus one can come across the phenomenon of over-irrigation even during a single watering of a crop, say, applying 12 cm of depth for wheat when 7.5 cm is recommended for the second irrigation. If this over-irrigation is counterbalanced by a like amount of under-irrigation in the third watering — and the fourth watering is still of the recommended depth — the partial phenomenon of over-irrigation in second watering gets concealed by the fact that the total application remains equal to the recommeneded volume of irrigation. In case the farmer is unable to do the number of waterings as recommended — let us say he misses the fourth irrigation because of non-availability of canal water —, his total use of water indicates under-irrigation. It is this situation of over-irrigation in single watering and under-irrigation in terms of number of waterings that mainly prevails on our public canals. The water scientists observes over-irrigation at individual watering stage by the canal beneficiaries who have a point when they complain of inadequate irrigation supplies (in our above example, one irrigation has been missed by the wheat grower).

Thus one has to bear in mind the two dimensions of an irrigation norm, one capturing the depth aspect of watering (*D*) and the other the frequency of irrigation (as reflected in the number of waterings N). So, the total irrgation delta (*H*) amounts to N.D. It is important to realize that for H = N.D there is no fixity in either N or D when H is given. That is to say, the frequency of irrigation can be raised by simultaneously reducing the depth of watering. So, some inverse relationship exists between N and D.An implication of this inverseness is that a correct view about over-irrigation by farmers may not be had simply by looking at the one dimension, which is often the number of actual waterings done to a crop.

Extent of Over-irrigation

The empirical literature on actual use of irrigation water by volume and depth of watering in each irrigation operation is quite scarce. This is mainly because of the tremendous difficulty of measuring volume of water in the field conditions of India. This measurement is a technical job requiring the use of appropriate instruments on the one hand and a lot of time on the other. The limited literature that does exist is either partial in nature — it gives data mainly on number of waterings only — or the estimates of water by volume are derived through questionable methods of indirect nature. Moreover, the sample size is often so small that the results cannot be confidently generalised, say, for the state as a whole. Anyway, the available evidence is analysed in what follows.

The Department of Economics and Sociology, Punjab Agricultural University (PAU), looked into the economics of irrigated farming of 40 sample farmers of Amritsar, Jalandhar, Kapurthala and Sangrur districts of Punjab. Analysing the data in respect of kharif paddy crop, which is being now cultivated on an extensive scale in the State but whose high water requirements have become a matter of concern, Prihar and Grewal (1988) find unmistakable signs of over-irrigation. Using an irrigation norm of 25 waterings for the crop (this norm would be 24 waterings if we divide by 7.5 cm the PAU norm of 180 cm for paddy given in Table 1), they conclude that over one-third of paddy area of the sample farmers had over-irrigation. More specifically, the number of waterings for the crop during 1983-84 averaged at 32, with most of the over-irrigation confined to samll farmers. In the absence of data on the depth of these waterings, one cannot comment on over-irrigation during each watering, nor be able to figure out by how much the paddy growers overshot the irrigation norm of 180 cm. On the latter aspect, we have some information for groups of crops, such as kharif crops (in which paddy dominates) and rabi crops from another small survey.

Table 3

Groundwater Draft by Electric Tubewells in Punjab

S.No	*Block (district)*	*Volume of water withdrawn per ha of land (ham)*			*Required volume of water needed per ha (ham)*			*Percent over-irrigated*		
		Kharif	Rabi	Total	Kharif	Rabi	Total	Kharif Crops	Rabi Crops	Total Crops
1.	Kapurthala (Kapurthala)	1.43	0.94	2.37	1.24	0.56	1.80	15	68	32
2.	Rayya (Amritsar)	1.54	0.69	2.23	1.25	0.53	1.78	23	30	25
3.	Dhariwal (Gurdaspur)	1.29	0.73	2.02	1.23	0.60	1.83	5	22	10
4.	Banga (Jalandhar)	1.42	0.74	2.16	1.25	0.57	1.82	14	30	19
5.	Garhshanker (Hoshiarpur)	0.91	0.98	1.89	1.19	0.54	1.73	(-) 24	81	9
6.	Nurpur Bedi (Ropar)	0.96	0.88	1.84	1.18	0.49	1.67	(-) 19	80	10
	Average	1.29	0.87	2.16	1.23	0.55	1.78	4	58	21

Source: Gurcharan Singh (1987).

Notes: 1. The sample size consists of 84 cases.

2. In case of serial numbers 2, 3 and 4, the measurement of water was done with water meters; for serial nos. 5 and 6, it was with hour meter; and for serial no 1, with the help of energy meter.

3. Required volume of water is computed for the observed crop pattern with the help of irrigation norms recommended by PAU, Ludhiana.

4. The last row and the last three columns are derived by this author.

This survey pertains to a sample of 84 owners of electrically driven tubewells whose groundwater withdrawals were contrasted by Gurcharan Singh (1987) with the water requirements based on the actual crop pattern and the PAU norms for irrigation for various crops. While for the year as a whole the over-use of groundwater was to the extent of 21 per cent, for the kharif season crops the over-irrigation was comparatively smaller (vide Table 3). Also, the margin of over-irrigation was lower in the case of tubewell owners located in the northern part of the state, namely, the districts of Ropar, Gurdaspur and Hoshiarpur, known to have better rainfall conditions.

A task force of the Government of Uttar Pradesh, under the chairmanship of V.K. Sharma, while examining the impact of energy in agriculture vis-a-vis industry, looked into the watering data reported by a sample of over 230 farmers owning electric tubewells. For the year 1982-83, this data, listed in Table 4, shows that for all irrigated crops taken together the sample farmers hardly applied three irrigations per crop —this average tended to decline as one moved eastwards in the state from

Table 4

Crop-wise and Region-wise Number of Waterings in U.P., 1982-83

S. No.	*Crop*	*Recommended no. of waterings*	*Actual no. of waterings*		
			West U.P.	*Central U.P.*	*East U.P.*
1.	Paddy	5	3.00	2.52	2.64
2.	Maize	3	1.77	1.25	1.33
3.	Wheat	5	3.66	3.47	3.27
4.	Sugarcane	7	4.62	3.96	3.53
5.	Others	–	1.25	1.20	1.10
	Weighted average	–	2.93	2.76	2.64

Source: V.K. Sharma (1984)
Note: The weighted averages are computed by this author from the crop-wise data given in the task force report.

low-rainfall West U.P.to higher rainfall region of East U.P. There was not a single crop for which the number of actual waterings was anywhere near the level recommended by the Agricultural University, Pantnagar.

For example, for wheat the number of waterings averaged 3.66 in West U.P., 3.47 in Central U.P. and 3.27 in East U.P., the recommended number being 5 (Sharma, 1984). Were one to apply the area weights to the four principal irrigated crops of the sample farmers, namely, paddy, wheat maize and sugarcane, the shortfall in number of waterings for these four crops turn out to be between one-third and two-fifths of the recommended level, as shown by the data given below.

	West U.P.	*Central U.P.*	*East U.P.*
1. Observed no. of weighted waterings for the four crops	3.3	3.1	3.1
2. Recommended no. of weighted waterings for the four crops	4.9	5.1	5.3
3. Extent of under-irrigation (1 minus 2 as % of 2)	33%	39%	42%

Some truly largescale surveys give useful, though limited, information about the use of irrigation water in India. The following ones readily come to mind:

1. An all-India survey of over 22,000 farm households, carried out by the National Council of Applied Economic Research (NCAER), New Delhi, for the mid-seventies;
2. An all-India survey of over 88,000 farm households, carried out by the National Sample Survey (NSS) for the mid-seventies.

Many a hypothesis about Indian irrigated farming were tested with the aid of data of the above mentioned NCAER survey (see Dhawan and Satya Sai, 1987). For the subset of 2600 survey farmers using irrigation in Uttar Pradesh during 1975-76, the number of waterings per irrigated ha averaged to only 2.4, and not varying much with the type of irrigation — for both public canals and private tubewells it was almost equal at 2.6 (owners of pumpsets reported a somewhat better average of 3.2). The actual number of waterings was hardly half the recommended level. This evidence is in conformity with the inadequate irrigation system of the state, the inadequacy arising partly from the chronic shortage of electric power for electric pumpsets.[1] The NSS survey,

1. Hydel power, which constitutes a substantial portion of the state electricity supply system, tends to drop sharply in drought years. But since 1975-76 was an above-normal rainfall year, the transitory shortage of power could not be considered a relevant factor for this year.

based on a state-wide sample of almost 17,000 households, further confirms the situation of under-irrigated farming in this state which accounts for almost one-fifth of the national irrigated acreage. According to this data set, one-fourth of the irrigated area received only one watering during 1975-76, and another one-fourth received two. Even a major cash crop like sugarcane could not get the requisite 7 waterings. While according to the NCAER survey this crop was watered 3.7 times only, the NSS survey reveals that 10 percent of the crop area received just one irrigation in the whole year, and another one-seventh got two waterings only. Similarly, a major irrigated crop like wheat, which accounted for more than half the state irrigated area, barely got 3 irrigations (against the recommended 5) - 17 per cent area getting only one watering and 28 per cent area receiving two. No wonder, then, that the land productivity under irrigated conditions is rather low in the state (Dhawan, 1988 a).

In Andhra Pradesh the sample farmers, numbering over 1800, applied little over 4 waterings to each irrigated ha as per the NCAER survey. Inter-source variations were considerable, the number of waterings averaging 6.4 for fields receiving water from private tubewells (which are otherwise of minor importance in the state irrigation system) and 3.4 for tank-irrigated fields — for canal-irrigated fields and for traditional wells the average was near the state average for all sources taken together. Were we to adopt a norm of 7 irrigations per ha on the assumption that fields under the command of private tubewells were adequately irrigated, a situation of serious under-irrigation emerges. In a state, in which paddy predominates in irrigated farming under medium rainfall conditions, an uncovered gap of 3 waterings can hinder the realisation of full potential of land productivity under irrigated conditions. According to NSS data, bulk of the paddy was raised with 3 to 4 waterings in this state.

The NCAER data for over 1200 farmers of Gujarat State reveals 3.3 waterings per irrigated ha, with foodgrain crops receiving 2.8 waterings on the average. These waterings are undoubtedly well below the requisite requirements of crops in this state of low rainfall conditions (N = 725 mm). For tanks and traditional wells the number of waterings was marginally above two; for canal-irrigated fields it was near 3.5 and was above 4 for pumpset-equipped wells. Farmers depending on purchases from fellow owners of pumpsets/tubewells did no better than those owning their own traditional, animal-operated wells. For a major irrigated crop like wheat which accounted for over one-third of irrigated acreage of the state, the average number of waterings were 3.1, well below the 6 to 8 waterings recommended by the scientists.

The NSS survey, based on 31st Round (July 1976 to June 1977), was large in size as it was designed to obtain state-wide estimates about several parameters of Indian irrigated farming. The state-wise coverage of this survey is shown in Table 5. The survey results were published in *Sarvekshna* in two parts (NSS, 1984 and 1985). It is unfortunate that the

Table 5

Number of Sample Villages and Number of Sample Households in 31st NSS Round.

Sl. No.	*State/Union Territory*	*No. of Sample Villages Surveyed*	*No. of Sample Households Surveyed*
1.	Andhra Pradesh	672	8,697
2.	Assam	456	176
3.	Bihar	712	7,819
4.	Gujarat	312	3,184
5.	Haryana	144	1,660
6.	Himachal Pradesh	248	1,451
7.	Jammu & Kashmir	440	4,477
8.	Karnataka	312	3,221
9.	Kerala	360	3,755
10.	Madhya Pradesh	640	4,691
11.	Maharashtra	528	4,547
12.	Manipur	120	373
13.	Orissa	304	3,116
14.	Punjab	342	4,842
15.	Rajasthan	360	4,117
16.	Tamil Nadu	672	8,230
17.	Tripura	111	266
18.	Uttar Pradesh	968	16,920
19.	West Bengal	488	5,549
20.	Delhi	24	355
21.	Goa, Daman and Diu	40	322
22.	Pondicherry	40	270
23.	All India	8,293	88,028

Source: NSS (1984 and 1985).

extremely valuable data on number of waterings were not published in a wholly satisfactory manner. The NSS analysts concentrated on giving details about crop area by frequency of irrigation but without any mean value of the number of waterings. It is not easy to work out this mean value from the frequency table because only 4 frequency classes employed, namely, one, two, three, and more than three waterings. For heavily-irrigated crops, like sugarcane in the Deccan or paddy in Punjab-Haryana region, the last, open-ended, frequency class is not very useful.

Dovetailing NSS and NCAER data for Andhra Pradesh, U.P. and Gujarat we have found that the average number of waterings for the open-ended fourth frequency class (more than 3 waterings) works out to be 4.20, 3.67 and 3.54, respectively. Utilising this limited knowledge, we conclude that the average number of waterings received by each irrigated ha in the country for 1975-76 ranged between 2.9 and 3.3 waterings only.[1] Assuming an irrigation depth of 3 to 4 inches per watering, the Indian farmer used hardly an irrigation delta of one foot per irrigated crop ha in the mid-seventies. By no stretch of imagination it can be characterised as adequate irrigation, not to mention of over-irrigation.

Illusion of Over-irrigation under Public Tubewells

To begin with, we briefly report on Patel and Patel's work. Next, we report in detail on the recent work of Datye and Patil. Our main effort is to draw attention to the use of indirect methods for assessing volume of irrigation, and how inferences based on such measurements can be totally off the mark.

On the basis of a sample survey of 31 farmers receiving water from public tubewells in Meerut district of West U.P., Patel and Patel reported for 1968-69 an average irrigation delta of 34 inches per irrigated acre, about 45 per cent above the corresponding level observed in the case of private electric tubewells. This was estimated by dividing the reported expenditure on public tubewell irrigation by the then-prevailing rate of Rs. 2 per acre-inch of public tubewell water. Probe of the data set revealed that the estimated irrigation delta should be somewhere between 13 and 20 inches, and not 34 inches (Dhawan 1982, pp. 129-31). In fact, Moorti, who made actual measurements with the help of V-notch, reported a delta of about 16 inches for sample farmers of the neighbouring Aligarh district for the year 1966-67. The reason for overestimation of irrigation delta through expenditure-tubewell rate approach is two-fold. One, the reported expenditure is inclusive of bribes extracted by the tubewell operator. Two, some of the reported expenditure is on account of occasional purchases of water made from fellow farmers

1. Because 1975-76 was a year of very favourable weather conditions, one may say that the estimates of number of waterings are somewhat biased on the downward side.

owning tubewells/pumpsets at a price far above the rate for public tubewell water.[1]

Gradual deterioration in the working of the public tubewell irrigation programme in U.P. has been a subject of concern and enquiry among the state administrators. For overcoming the basic shortcomings of this programme, the World Bank came forward to support the installation of 500 new tubewells having superior technological inputs: underground piped water distribution system, overhead tanks, independent electric power supply lines, automatic switch-on system to cope with the chronic problem of absentee tubewell operator etc. Datye and Patil report on the performance of such tubewells established in Lucknow district of Central U.P. They are baffled by two facts: (1) gross over-irrgation in each watering despite the prevalence of a water-linked tubewell tariff (2.2 paise per cubic metre of water for kharif period and 4.4 paise per cubic metre for the rabi season) and (2) marked underirrigation in terms of number of waterings given to irrigated crops in which paddy and wheat dominate. This has impelled them to make observations on the rationality of the Central U.P. farmer, which revived my old memories of many writers who ascribed the underdevelopment of the east Gangetic plains to the human factor. My feeling, after reading their evaluation report (chapter 8 of Datye and Patil), is that their data base is not strong enough to warrant the strong inferences they have drawn about the behaviour of the farmers.

Datye and Patel's estimates of depth of watering for crops of the kharif and rabi seasons are shown in Table 6. How they worked out these

Table 6

Season-wise Irrigation Depth per Watering in the Command of Public Tubewells in Lucknow District

Year	*Kharif season (inches)*		*Rabi season (inches)*	
	I	II	I	II
1983-84	5.8 – 12.1	10.1 – 11.9	4.1 – 6.3	6.2 – 8.0
1984-85	5.0 – 11.8	9.2 – 11.6	5.3 – 9.0	5.7 – 8.1
1985-86	6.7 – 13.3	7.2 – 14.5	5.3 – 8.6	6.0 – 7.6

Source: Table 8.7 of Datye and Patil (1987).
Note: I stands for the set of 7 sample tubewells with independent power lines and II stands for 3 sample tubewells with ordinary power lines.

1. Sometimes (e.g. in the Farm Management Studies), the data on cost of irrigation is inclusive of farmers' labour time spent in (*a*) maintaining field channels for bringing canal water from canal outlet to the fields and (*b*) in carrying out irrigation operation.

estimates is not clear from the published details. Since these pertain to all farmers served by the sample ten tubewells (numbering over 2900 vide their Table 8.6), these appear to have been worked from the office records maintained for billing purposes — the collection task is entrusted to the state revenue department. Evidently, the following information would be required for deducing irrigation depth per watering:

(1) Farmers' names and the plot areas to which they applied the purchased tubewell water;
(2) No. or waterings for each plot in each season and their time durations;
(3) The rate of discharge for each tubewell at different points of time in a year.

Scope for error in deducing the irrigation depth is not inconsiderable. To begin with, in the absence of data on actual discharge rate one is forced to make the assumption that it equals the rated discharge for all time periods. If the actual discharge is less than the rated, an element of overestimation in irrigation depth would creep in. Likewise, the discrepancy in plot area statistics can affect the final estimate, though one cannot say a priori which way the direction of bias would be. Finally, what is the reliability of plot-wise time durations maintained by the lowly-paid tubewell operator (Rs. 300 per month)? Suppose he is supplying water to some plots of some farmers for a consideration. As he is not to show this sale of water in the office records, he then decides to account for such running time by inflating the time durations of the farmers on record.

Summary

The empirical evidence on farmers' irrigation application by volume and depth of watering in each irrigation operation is scanty. The limited survey data that one comes across is usually unsatisfactory on two counts. Either information only on number of waterings for a crop is gathered from respondent farmers, or volume of irrigation water used is inferred from the reported expenditure on irrigation and the volumetric water tariff in force. Our examination of some survey data reveals the following facts.

Prihar and Grewal (1988), on the basis of a small survey of 40 Punjab farmers, report an average of 32 waterings of paddy crop during 1983-84 as against the recommended level of 24 waterings of 7.5 cm depth each. In the case of 84 Punjab farmers owning electric tubewells, Gurcharan Singh (1987) found over-irrigation to the extent of one-fifth above the recommended levels but with marked variations over kharif and rabi seasons on the one hand and across the agro-climatic regions of the state on the other. In contrast, V.K. Sharma (1984) found significant under-irrigation in the case of 230 private electric tubewells in Uttar Pradesh. This result is in agreement with the NCAER and NSS survey data for U.P. for the mid-seventies. Dovetailing the NCAER and the NSS data, it is found that each irrigated hectare of crop area in the mid-seventies in India received, on the average, nearly three waterings. Keeping also in mind that waterings from public irrigation works, like canals and public tubewells, were deficient in timing, this cannot be described as a state of adequate irrigation, leave aside over-irrigation.

Our scrutiny of the puzzling phenomenon of over-irrigation within the command of public tubewells of Uttar Pradesh, as reported by S.M. Patel and K.V. Patel (1969) and K.R. Datye and R.K. Patil (1987), reveals serious shortcomings in the methods of analysis of these scholars. If direct measures of estimating volume of water application were to be used, the puzzle of over-irrigation by farmers paying for tubewell water on volumetric basis would vanish. This is amply demonstrated by T.V. Moorti's (1970) work in Aligarh district of U.P.

Chapter 5

THE BIG DAM CONTROVERSY: Major Versus Minor Irrigation*

There is growing opposition to the idea of big dams, whether these are planned for irrigation or hydel power generation. This opposition is not peculiar to India but is somewhat of a global phenomenon. About five years back, Goldsmith and Hildyard wrote their book *The Social and Environmental Effects of Large Dams,* in which they painstakingly put together the untoward consequences of the specific dams built in various regions of the world.

Whereas major irrigation projects of the pre-Independence or pre-planning era were primarily of the river diversion type, now the emphasis is on impounding river water through big dams because the scope for river diversion with the aid of low-height barrages and weirs was largely exploited during the British rule. Of course, serious ill-effects, like waterlogging and soil salinisation, occurred within the commands of such diversion works. But in reservoir-based major irrigation works the domain of ill-effects has enlarged, mainly because of the submergence of fertile valley lands and forest cover on the one hand and the displacement of sizable populations subsisting on these submerged valley/forest lands on the other. This has naturally led to increased questioning about the usefulness of major irrigation works, and simultaneous pleas for greater emphasis on smallscale irrigation works (like tanks, wells and tubewells) and dryland farming. In respect of Narmada dams and Tehri dam on the Ganga the controversy has become acrimonious.

My attempt in this chapter is to restore correct perspectives on both big dams and groundwater irrigation. By nature water is a very complex resource. As and when its complexities are ignored, or simplified

* Parts of this have been published in more than one place (Dhawan, 1988d, 1988e, 1988f and 1989a).

by the critics of water planning, controversies can easily crop up. In view of the heightened public interest in this vital resource, some of these controversies can spill over to public fora like the daily press, weekly magazines and the Parliament. Given the ample scope for misunderstanding of crucial aspects of this resource, nonissues can become issues of great concern and attention. Even for a country like the U.S.A., Professor Charles Howe is constrained to remark in his book *Natural Resource Economics*, that water among the natural resources is most misunderstood.

Among the vocal critics who have utilised the popular media indefatigably, is B.B. Vohra, an erstwhile able administrator with keen interest in land and water managment issues. (As an irrigation economist, I have found it difficult to bring round persons to my point of view whenever my views are at variance with his standpoint). By and large, our irrigation planners have shied away from responding to critics like Vohra. No wonder, their silence, as also indifference to sharing vital information with the public, has turned may men of public concern receptive to criticism of big dam appearing in the popular media in a rather sustained manner. This one-sided view of the dams has been facilitated by a sort of media's commitment to any criticism of official thinking/planning —there are indeed some cases where counter viewpoints were deliberately discouraged, if not suppressed, by some media men.

The scope of this chapter is limited to the following three aspects:

1. the main parameters of the rising opposition to major irrigation works;
2. an in-depth analysis of the cost side of the controversy;
3. the way out of the big dam imbroglio

The major grounds on which the construction of big dams are being questioned are in no one single realm. Both the criticism and the backgrounds of the critics are quite varied. Among the persistent critics are both the hard ones and the soft ones. The hard ones comprise the environmentalists, the natural scientists, the social scientists etc. They raise objections on discipline-specific grounds. But the soft ones reveal a rather woolly understanding of the complex nature of water resources, or of ecological matters, although some of them are persons of eminence in their own right and well imbued with sense of purpose. We may begin with the environmentalists who constitute the vanguard of the critics. As I see it, their main worry is on two environmental counts, though many of them are no less worried for two other concerns:

(1) the rehabilitation of the dam oustees and (2) the excessive siltation of reservoirs that reduces sharply the life of a dam.

Environmental Angle

First, as the forest cover of the earth is receding at an ominous rate, they naturally worry about any development that causes deforestation. A dam can reduce forest cover in two ways. One, the reservoir behind a dam can submerge forest on the upstream side because the submerged area for a dam can typically vary from 5 to 15 per cent of the irrigation potential created by the irrigation project. Second, the dam-buliding activity can lead to removal of nearby trees for building project roads and housing colonies. As far as the submergence aspect is concerned, the damage on this count is a small proportion of the total damage to forests from all other causes listed below:

(*i*) illegal fellings of forest trees;
(*ii*) unauthorised ploughing of forest lands;
(*iii*) authorised allotment of forest lands to dam oustees or the landless people;[1]
(*iv*) increased pressure from graziers as the village commons and the culturable waste lands are diminishing.

According to one knowledgeable dam builder, the total forest area so far lost in India due to submergence by reservoirs created by all big dams amounts to about five percent of the total forest cover we have lost since Independence.[2] Evidently, this underscores an important fact: the problem of our vanishing forest cover is not going to be solved by calling a halt to the construction of big dams. But wherever the forest cover to be lost by a single dam is unduly high, e.g., in the case of Narmada Sagar, it is worthwhile to minimise such loss by reducing the reservoir size via a reduction in height of the dam. Such middle paths, which are well suited to a democratic society, can emerge through wider discussion and sharing of relevant data available with the planners.

1. Allotment of forest land to landless families have been made by state governments, though this is now forbidden under the new Forest Act of 1980 — the Centre alone is now empowered to do so. For instance, no less than 2.5 million ha of forest land in Madhya Pradesh state was allotted to the landless for purpose of crop production Source: Varma, p. 101.
2. The name of this dam expert in Bharat Singh, a former Vice-Chancellor of University of Roorkee which is renowned for its education in water engineering. He delivered a special lecture during the course of the First National Water Convention held in Delhi during 12 to 14 November 1987 under the auspices of the Central Board of Irrigation and Power, New Delhi

Their second major apprehension relates to land degradation due to waterlogging and rising soil salinity within canal commands served by big reservoirs. In the light of the historical experience of India, there is no denying that major canals do give rise to problems of waterlogging and salinity. but the statistics quoted in this regard are of questionable magnitude and relevance.[1] Quite often, the cited statistics are for the entire land area suffering from waterlogging and salinity, without any separation of the area affected due to canals and due to other causes, natural and man-made. In flat areas receiving high rainfall, lot of land is naturally waterlogged — the problem here is further aggravated when roads, railways and river embankments are built with poor provision for cross drainage. Similarly, in highly arid regions of western and southern India, soil salinity is a natural occurrence which undoubtedly gets aggravated by the introduction of irrigation, particularly canal irrigation.

Indian canal irrigation has significantly contributed to waterlogging and soil salinisation. For this, the blame has been squarely fixed on non-construction of drainage system within canal commands. One of the main reasons why the drainage component has been missing from our major canal networks is the paucity of investment funds. After all, the cost of drainage network, both in capital and maintenance terms, is no different from that of the canal network itself. Fortunately, the extensive rise of private groundwater irrigation within the canal commands has served the incidental purpose of drainage. It is this vertical drainage that needs to be fostered in canal commands. However, it is imperative to realise the limits of this route to containing waterlogging. In the arid areas underlain with brackish waters unfit for irrigation, groundwater irrigation is naturally inhibited. Here, one must strive to contain the seepage of canal waters through canal lining on the one hand and through the encouragement of water application via sprinklers and drippers. This preventive solution is again a very costly proposition.

The Seismic Angle

Another area of concern relates to damage from earthquake. There is an apprehension that the huge mass of water behind a dam

1. Now and then, one comes across the assertion that net irrigation addition from new irrigation works is usually nil because annual increase in waterlogged area happens to match the annual increment in irrigated area through new works. But this is mostly an experience of the arid Middle East countries like Egypt and Iraq, and not of the whole world.

may induce seismic disturbances in the neighbourhood area. Increased seismic activity in the Koyna region has been ascribed by some persons to the Koyna dam. This is an issue which can be best resolved by geologists and seismologists. What is of greater concern is when a dam is proposed on a dam-site situated in an already well-marked seismic belt of the earth, e.g., the proposed Tehri dam in the Garhwal Himalayas. In such cases, a major breach in a dam following an earthquake of severe intensity could be an instrument of utter disaster instead of economic development. Here, too, one has no choice but to go by the judgement of civil engineers as to how much earthquake proofing can be achieved for dams built in seismic zones. If there is no unanimity among them on the new technology of rock-filled dams, scaling down the dam height would go a long way in lessening the anxiety about damage from dam burst due to an earthquake.

Rehabilitation of Dam Oustees

Among social scientists, the social anthropologists have never been at ease with one most bothersome aspect of the water related development process - the uprooting of populations from the villages submerged by reservoirs created by damming rivers. Among the affected populations are often sizable number of tribal people whose very survival is already at stake in this rapidly changing world. According to S.C. Varma, a former Vice-Chairman of the Narmada Development Authority, the composition of the dam oustees in the four major Narmada Valley Projects in M.P. alone is as follows:

	Population affected
1. Narmada Sagar:	
Total	80,500
Scheduled Tribes	17,653
Scheduled Castes	11,432
2. Sardar Sarovar:	
Total	45,000
Scheduled Tribes	23,240
Scheduled Castes	3,650
3. Omkareshwar	12,295
4. Maheshwar	9,420

It is truly a stupendous task to rehabilitate and resettle such dam oustees, and our past record in this vital sphere, thanks partly to our insensibilities to the problems of our tribes, has been very dismal.[1] It is this human question of rehabilitation that is now worrying very many a sensitive soul from various walks of life.

The issues of displacement of people by dam construction is certainly not an environmental issue. But it need not be dismissed on the simple plea that environmentalists have no business to take up cudgels on behalf of the dam oustees. Nor should one adopt the questionable stance that the problem is taken care of once rigorous exercises have been carried out in cost-benefit analysis of an investment project. For, one intractable problem of cost-benefit technique, in spite of so many advances in thinking in this realm, is that of whose costs and whose benefits. If the Yojana Bhavan has truly resolved this irresolvable problem, then let us know what methods has it employed to weigh the various costs (psychic, social and financial) of the dam oustees against the benefits of the Gujarat farmers. (In the case of the Narmada Valley Project, the main beneficiary is the state of Gujarat while the non-financial costs would be mainly borne by the people of Madhya Pradesh.)

Furthermore, while maximising the objective of use of Narmada water for irrigation, one has to handle carefully other conflicting objectives of river planning. By simply enlarging the storage capacity of a reservoir through an increase in the height of its dam, one very conveniently achieves the objective of maximum harnessing of river flows. But the increase in dam height has disproportionate consequences on the land area submerged under the reservoir. Because of the topography of a river basin, addition to dam height aggravates the land submergence problem in an accelerating fashion. In the particular case of Narmada Sagar, the biggest reservoir in the Narmada Valley Project, the relationship between dam height and area submerged is said to be as follows.[2]

1. Dam height (meters)	190	210	230	244	261
2. Total submerged area (ha)	1000	2000	24000	46000	80340
3. Incremental area submerged per metre increase in dam height of Narmada Sagar (ha)		50	1100	1571	2020

1. The Government of Gujarat has lately evinced very encouraging response to the demands of the dam oustees and the activist groups fighting on their behalf. According to press reports, over Rs. 6000 millions are now earmarked for rehabilitation purpose by it. This would enhance the investment cost of the Sardar Sarovar Project by one-tenth or thereabout.
2. Based on data given by Varma (1985, p. 48).

The corresponding relationship between dam height and land area submerged in respect of other Narmada dams is not Known to this author. For Sardar Sarovar, S.C. Varma mentions the fact that in the first stage submergence at the dam height of 106.70 metres (350 feet) the number of affected villages would be 23 (with 84 affected families). This number of affected villages would rise to 182 when the Sardar Sarovar attains its stipulated height of 138.7 metres (455 feet). It thus appears that the problems of displacement of the people, which is now causing great anxiety in many quarters, can be substantially reduced in scale by adjusting the height of the proposed dams on the Narmada.

Other Angles

Finally, one has to reckon with sundry groups and individuals who object to investments in big irrigation schemes for one reason or another. Some are sore as these schemes gobble up, Plan after Plan, the limited cake of investment funds earmarked for the agriculture sector. This has a crowding out effect on other imperative schemes, such as soil conservation and dryland farming technology programmes, thereby incurring hostility from their proponents. While there is need to rectify this imbalance in resource allocation within the agriculture sector, it does not warrant an abandonment of major irrigation works programme altogether. If returns from such investments are incommensurate with the promises held out by their promoters, is the ground reality in respect of alternative programmes of soil conservation and dryland farming different any way?[1]

Then there is a motley group of individuals who are sold out on the philosophy that small is beautiful. They would prefer a river to be tapped by a row-upon-row of small dams instead of one or two big dams. If this turns out to be insufficient for meeting our irrigation needs, they would like to see a well, or a small tubewell, or a farm pond constructed on every farm. Their fervour for the minor irrigation cause is articulated primarily on one or more of the following grounds:

(1) Minor irrigation schemes, especially those based on ground water, add, acre for acre, much more crop output than do major irrigation works.

(2) On an area to area basis, the cost of irrigation from minor works is a small fraction of the corresponding cost entailed in establishing

1. The issue of dryland farming vis-a-vis irrigated farming is discussed in detail by the author elsewhere (Dhawan, 1988 c).

major irrigation projects and later developing their command areas.

(3) Irrigation potential is fully utilised in the case of minor schemes, whereas gross underutilisation of potential arises in the case of major irrigation projects.

(4) Minor irrigation works are completed in very short time, while the construction of major irrigation projects lingers on for decades. This means quicker returns on investment funds put in minor works.

(5) No environmental threats are posed by minor irrigation works.

(6) Big contractors, in collusion with irrigation bureaucracy and politicians, have much less scope for siphoning off investment funds in the case of minor than major irrigation schemes.

What is the veracity of each of the above mentioned propositions whose combined thrust is one of highlighting superiority of minor over major irrigation works from every angle? It is a pity that irrigation engineers have never seriously tried to counter these propositions. Being duly aware of the gaping holes in some of these propositions, they do dismiss them in a lighter vein at their own friendly get-togethers. Since they have shown little inclination to do homework to tell the rest of the world where does major irrigation actually stand vis-a-vis minor irrigation, they have failed to stem the rising tide of half-truths and myths about minor irrigation that are being vigorously propogated by their rivals. They may, however, fend off this accusation on the following two pretexts:

Their first pretext could be that to carry out comparative analysis in costs or benefits of various types of irrigation works is economists, and not their job. This is valid enough. As the economists' in the Yojana Bhavan do have a hand in our irrigation planning, they can, if they so desire, give a helping hand to their engineer planners in the Yojana Bhavan as well as the Central Water Commission to defend themselves from the onslaught of the votaries of minor irrigation cause. For this to happen, the initiative has to come from the engineers, who can also solicit the support of knowledgeable economists outside the portals of the Yojana Bhavan. What has prevented them from doing so? Their cocksureness of the rightness of their own position?

The second plea could be that because of strong linkage between different irrigation sources it is futile to talk of this or that mode of irrigation. To put it differently, minor and major irrigation works are somewhat like two sides of a coin, that is, we need both of them for a balanced development of irrigated farming. Thus it is quite possible that the high benefits from one source of irrigation are partly due to the investment in the other source with apparently lower benefits. For example, in areas poorly endowed with groundwater, good returns on investment in well irrigation are often contingent on replenishment of well water yield by a nearby percolation tank or a canal. Unfortunately, the irrigation planners have not used this line of argument to enlighten their critics or the public.

The author has attempted to quantify the beneficial consequences of major irrigation works for sustaining groundwater-based agriculture in low rainfall areas in chapter 7 and 8. In what follows the focus is on comparative costs of major and minor irrigation works. The pitfalls in comparing costs alone of the two categories of irrigation, let alone their comparative augmentation in farm production, are here dealt with. It is hoped that this will go a long way in exploding the myth about minor irrigation being a low-cost proposition for the Indian economy. The harsh truth is that modern irrigation is a costly proposition, irrespective of its being major or minor in character.

COMPARATIVE COSTS

Admittedly, our estimates of unit capital cost nor our estimates of operational costs of major and minor irrigation works are very firmly established. Also, these are in nominal terms. One must duly reckon with two aspects of investment costs of major irrigation works, namely, (1) the true cost of land (including forest cover) submerged by reservoirs and (2) the rent-seeking elements (i.e. kickbacks and fictitious expenditure) in reported costs of major irrigation projects. While the true cost of land submergence is likely to be far more than the nominal figures shown in project records, the exclusion of rent-seeking costs will substantially bring down the true resource cost of the major irrigation projects.

Prior to the Fifth Five Year Plan, investment outlay needed for executing an irrigation work was the criterion of categorisation of irrigation works in Indian planning. Now this categorisation is mainly on the basis of irrigation capacity of work. When the crop area to be irrigated from a given scheme is 2,000 hectares or less, the scheme is treated as a minor irrigation work. It is when the irrigated acreage exceeds the limit of 10,000 ha that the irrigation work is characterised as major work. For a scheme designed to irrigate between 2,000 and 10,000 ha there is the third category of medium irrigation works. Schemes under the third category being few, these are usually clubbed with the category of major irrigation works. And all groundwater-based schemes are invariably included in the minor irrigation category. Within minor irrigation segment, dugwells and tubewells dominate, accounting for almost three-fourthsof the capacity of this segment. In fact, most of the additions to minor irrigation capacity since 1951 are from groundwater sources.

The Pitfalls of Capital Costs

Comparisons are always hazardous, and the cost comparisons between major and minor irrigation works are no exception to this adage. The principal hazard in the present case is one of omission of costs of minor irrigation. This omission is two-fold. Firstly, the capital costs of minor irrigation are grossly underassessed by writers who are motivated to demonstrate the high cost of developing major irrigation in India. Secondly, the recurring costs of either irrigation are not altogether reckoned with, an omission that goes to the advantage of minor irrigation in whose cost structure recurring costs are far more onerous than found in the case of major irrigation works.

Nowhere in the Five Year Plan reports one comes across data on unit capital requirements for irrigation works of either category. The figures quoted in this regard, category-wise or plan-wise, are usually the handiwork of analysts who try to estimate them from the following two sets of statistics: (1) outlays for major and minor irrigation works for each plan period, and (2) planners' own estimates of irrigation potential created in each plan period for each category of irrigation.

Let us see how faulty estimates of unit capital cost are generated when plan outlays are divided by the corresponding figures of irrigation potential. To begin with, the plan statistics on outlays in respect of minor irrigation give a partial picture of capital required for developing minor irrigation capacity. The reported outlays are for the public sector only, thereby leaving out investments on private account.[1] In other words, the plan outlays for minor irrigation works are not inclusive of farmers' own investments in tubewells, dugwells, pumpsets etc. Since the plan statistics on minor irrigation potential are for the entire minor irrigation segment (i.e., both on public and private account), the collation of the area and outlays data given in the plan documents gives rise to seriously underestimated figures of unit capital requirements of minor irrigation. But a similar exercise for major and medium irrigation works yields an estimate of unit capital cost which is free from the element of

1. Sometimes, these outlays are exclusive of funds provided by institutions like NABARD and commercial banks. In more recent period, public funds for minor irrigation works earmarked under anti-poverty programmes are not included in the head 'outlays for irrigation.'

underestimation as the major and medium irrigation schemes are developed entirely in the public sector.

Secondly, there is some lack of compatibility between outlays on irrigation in a given plan period and the resultant addition to irrigation capacity in the same plan period. It is well known that the gestation period for a major irrigation project is about 10 to 12 years under efficient conditions of implementation - 20 to 25 years under less efficient conditions prevailing in India. As irrigation capacity of an ongoing project is not created in direct proportion to investment expenditures in a given plan, a lack of correspondence between plan outlays and created irrigation potential can exist for a given plan period. This can distort the estimate of unit capital cost, the distortion being more serious in the case of major than minor irrigation works like wells which can be usually constructed within a single year.

The third limitation of the plan outlays on irrigation arises from the fact that some of these are not meant to result in any addition to irrigation capacity. For instance, outlays on (1) research and investigation organisations like the Central Water Commission and the Central Groundwater Board, (2) remodelling of headworks, lining of channels and strengthening of drainage in old irrigation and (3) replacement of old works that have outlived their useful lives, are not envisaged to enhance irrigation capacity as such. Instead, these are meant more to improve the productivity of the irrigation system as such. Evidently, such outlays unduly raise the derived figures of unit capital costs, the rise being obviously higher for major works.

The foregoing exposition of the principal drawbacks of the plan data on irrigation sector brings out that the estimates of unit capital cost for irrigation works, when derived from such data, can be quite erroneous. Such derived estimates, as we shall demonstrate presently, could be grossly understated in respect of minor irrigation works, especially for wells and tubewells, and overstated for major and medium irrigation works. Evidently, inferences based on a comparative analysis of such unit capital cost estimates are erroneous.

Let me now give some illustrations of writings based on plan data. Arun Ghosh, who writes a regular column for the *Economic and Political Weekly*, examined the data for the first three years of the Seventh Five Year Plan and concluded that the outlay needed for developing minor irrigation was one-tenth of that required for major irrigation. J.S. Kanwar (1988), analysing the proposed plan outlays and irrigation targets for the same plan, thought groundwater development costs, acre for acre to be irrigated, were one-fourth of the corresponding costs for surface irrigation. The Secretariat of the Afro-Asian Rural Reconstruction Organisation (1987) has worked out that for the entire period of Indian planning the investment cost of unit irrigated area for major and medium irrigation projects was 118 per cent more than for minor irrigation.

Before I give the reader an idea of the absolute figures of comparative investments for major and minor irrigation, I would like to touch on two other aspects which need bearing in mind. In a capital-short economy like ours, the direct investment of each option has to be judged alongwith (1) its replacement period and (2) its indirect or supporting investments. Here again the scales are tilted in favour of major instead of minor irrigation. For, the time period for their replacement is four to five times longer than pumpset-based minor irrigation, with minimal of supporting investments which are substantial in the case of electric pumpsets - energisation outlay for an electric pump today is believed to be in the range of Rs 20,000-25,000.

The life of major irrigation works is reckoned at 100 years[1] after which the civil structures of the canal network need to be reconstructed. As far as the dam is concerned, its life is governed mainly by the number of years it would take to get the 'dead' storage of the reservoir to fill up with silt and debris brought by water inflowing into the reservoir. It is widely agreed that the rate at which reservoir siltation is occurring in India is much higher than the rate assumed by dam designers. Even then, reservoirs are expected to serve useful purpose for 100 years or thereabouts. This is far in excess of the corresponding period for tubewells which last for 20 years or so under good maintenance conditions. Pumpsets fitted on open wells need replacement investment in 15 years time. It is only the investmant embedded in dugwell proper that requires replacement after a much longer time, say, about 50 years in the case of masonry wells located in alluvial soils and 100 years or more for dugwells in hard rock regions.

Major and medium works use the natural force of gravity in their operation, while groundwater and minor surface water lift schemes need energy for countering the pull of gravity. Thus supporting investments in the energy sector are minimal for major and medium works but quite substantial for modern groundwater irrigation. In particular, electric pumpsets/tubewells need requisite investment in power generation

1. Dam-wise data for 22 large reservoirs (more than 0.5 million acre-feet storage) in Murthy (1977), when averaged, gives a life of 155 years (the range is 75-450 years).

equipment and rural electrification system. An average pumpset in India required about 4 KW of power during the mid-seventies when each KW of generating capacity cost nearly Rs 3,000 in capital outlay alone. In addition, one needs money for transmitting this power from the generating point to the consumption points in the countryside.

It is not known how much is the capital cost borne by the nation while meeting the energy needs of an agricultural pumpset. Nor do we have firm estimates of such supporting investment needed for each unit area of irrigation potential established through minor irrigation works. But some idea about the relative dimension of such costs vis-a-vis the plan outlays on minor irrigation can be formed by adopting the following procedure, which we apply to the Fifth Five Year Plan data. To begin with, we estimate that portion of the plan outlay on power generation as can be attributed to 0.870 million electric pumpsets added during the same plan period. To this we add the specific plan outlay earmarked for rural electrification. Finally, we estimate the investment in minor irrigation on farmers' own account. Adding these three costs on capital account to the direct capital outlay reported for minor irrigation, we obtain total investment needs of the minor irrigation segment, which on division by the corresponding addition to minor irrigation potential yields the estimate of total investment cost per unit area for minor irrigation works.

Assuming (1) each electric pumpset requires 4 KW capacity at the power generating point and (2) each KW capacity was established at Rs 3,500 during the 5th Plan, the Plan outlay for power generation for 0.870 million electric pumpsets would amount to about Rs 12,180 million. To this may be added Rs 8,420 million on account of expenditure on rural electrification programme during the Fifth Plan, making a total of Rs 20, 600 million on account of supporting investment in power for electric pumpsets. Against indirect investment of the order of Rs 20,600 million, the Fifth Plan figure of direct investment in minor irrigation was Rs 14,110 million, with the following breakup:

state governments	....	Rs 6310 million
institutional funds	....	Rs 7800 million

As pointed out earlier, the figure is exclusive of investment on farmers' own account. If we make an assumption that farmers' own funds amounted to just *one-fifth*[1] of the total direct investments in minor irrigation, the farmers' share would be arround Rs 3528 million. Thus

1. The Minor Irrigation Working Group for Sixth Plan assumed that 35% of the outlay on private wells would be financed by farmers themselves (Government of India, 1980).

aggregate direct outlays on minor irrigation for Fifth Plan add up to nearly Rs 17,638 million, still less than the corresponding indirect outlay of Rs 20,600 million on account of electric pumpsets. The sum of these direct and indirect outlays comes to about Rs 38 billion, which on division by 3.8 million ha of minor irrigation potential added during the Fifth Plan yields an estimate of nearly Rs 10,000 per ha. This unit capital cost is far above the corresponding estimate of Rs 3700/ha for minor irrigation derived from plan data by many scholars like Sachidanandan and Sinha (quoted in Kanwar's book). No less significantly, it is higher than the unit cost estimate of about Rs 6110 for major and medium works for the Fifth Plan.

In the above exercise for obtaining indirect investment requirements of minor irrigation, the author has admittedly erred on the higher side, as he has made no allowances for the fact that investments in the eletricity segment are not to be wholly attributed to the minor irrigation segment. Some of the rural electrification benefits accrue to rural industrial enterprises and domestic users. Likewise, hardly one-third of the power output from each KW of generating capacity is used by the rural pumpsets. The absence of such allowances in our estimation is mitigated by the fact that no attempt has been made to adjust for the capital needs on replacement account. Yet, there is need for more refined research work in this empirical area. Also, there is need for estimational work region-wise and plan-wise. It is quite probable the capital saving argument in favour of major irrigation is not valid for all regions and for all times.

Recurring Cost Advantage

Obtaining estimates of recurring costs for major and medium irrigation works is a comparatively simple task as the Comptroller and Auditor General of India compiles financial accounts of public irrigation works in one consolidated form. On the other hand, it entails considerable effort in estimational work for minor irrigation works, which are largely owned by individual farmers. We have attempted the exercise for the beginning of the eighties only. Needless to say, there is ample room for improving the estimational work.

Before presenting the estimates, it may be clarified that our estimation of recurring or operating costs are exclusive of interest and depreciation charges. Also, an attempt has been made to work out these in resource use terms. While we have tried to eliminate taxes and subsidies, no attempt has been made to shadow price the inputs. Thus, the cost of electricity used in wells equipped with electric pumpsets (now the most prevalent mode of groundwater irrigation in the country) is reckoned at the resource cost of supplying it to rural areas, and not at the highly-subsidised rates actually paid by Indian farmers.

Our estimates reveal that in the matter of operating costs major irrigation is possibly one-tenth less expensive than groundwater irrigation. For 1980-81, the unit cost for major and medium irrigation works averaged Rs 60/ha as compared to Rs 637-848/ha in the case of groundwater irrigation. That there is considerable room for improving upon these estimates becomes obvious as we review in the appendix note to this chapter the methods of our estimational work.

Concluding Remarks

It is imperative to grasp what is the key issue, especially in water short regions of the country. The issue is not of a choice between major and minor irrigation, nor between big canals and groundwater irrigation, and nor, for that matter, between wet and dry farming. These are essentially non-issues, partly for reasons of the interlinkages among them, and partly because of our particular conditions of greater scarcity of water than of land resource in large parts of the country. That is to say, we are not well endowed by nature in the matter of our water bounty. So except for water abundant regions like the east Gangetic plains (here groundwater may be a more cost - effective option), we have to tap all sources of water by all technologies if we wish to maximise irrigation cover for our agriculture. Presently, at the national level this cover extends to hardly one-third of our crop area. Even after full exploitation of our water resources through major and minor schemes, this coverage is not likely to go beyond the two-third mark. So, it is unwarranted to urge the planners to altogether abandon the Sardar Sarovar project and recommend instead the establishment of one lakh smallscale water holding schemes for the state of Gujarat,[1] which is a water-short state.

It is unfortunate that our irrigation planners have baulked at engaging in an open dialogue and discussion with their critics. As a result, more and more cross sections of the society have become very receptive to the criticism of big dams in the popular media. Maybe, a good deal of the criticism is either misplaced or not well founded in facts. But this does not warrant a policy of silence, both to the published critique and

1. This is the line mutely adopted by the Narmada Bachao Andolan, a Bombay-based group.

to requests from concerned scholars and men of public affairs for relevant information on controversial dams like Narmada Sagar and Sardar Sarovar. In the case of all highly controversial dams, the option of reducing their height needs to be seriously explored by the planners. This way we can accommodate substantially the genuine apprehensions of the critics in the realm of (1) resettlement of dam oustees, (2) loss of forest cover and (3) earthquake-related fears.

It is inappropriate to derive investment norms for irrigation, plan-wise and category-wise, from plan statistics on outlays and irrigation potential. Such norms for minor irrigation works are inherently underestimated. Their comparison with the corresponding norms for major and medium irrigation works give a misleading picture that minor irrigation is a less capital using option for the Indian economy. Not only the capital saving argument but also the recurring costs argument appears to be tilted against minor irrigation. Thus the case for according priority to minor irrigation development in Indian water planning on grounds of cost economy is not well founded in facts.

NOTE
COMPARATIVE OPERATIONAL COSTS OF IRRIGATION

The scope of this note is to indicate how the author worked out the estimates of operating costs for canal and well irrigation in this chapter. We first indicate our data sources.

The annual reports of the state irrigation departments are the principal source of information with regard to operational expenses of major irrigation works. The audited accounts of these reports are published by the Comptroller and Auditor General of India in its annual publication, entitled *Combined Finance and Revenue Accounts of the Union and State Government of India.* Account of major and medium irrigation works figure in two sets to tables, namely, (*a*) Account No. 101 for multipurpose river valley projects like Bhakra and Nagarjunasagar, and (*b*) Account No. 102 for irrigation, navigation, drainage and flood control projects. While the data in respect of irrigation is separately listed in Account No. 102 (and its sub-accounts), it is not so with the other account. Expenditure on two items, namely, maintenance and administration, is being deemed by us to be the operational cost of major irrigation works.

For getting at the operational costs of minor irrigation one has to carry out an estimational exercise. The task is not difficult because we have adequate data base for the purpose. First, we have the published records on electricity cost of supplying electricity consumed by the Indian agriculture sector, Since the resource cost of supplying electricity can be computed from the records of the State Electricity Boards, we can make a reasonable estimate of operational cost of well irrigation due to the use of electricity. Second, we have published records on the number of waterlifting devices by category of motive power, namely, electric pumpsets and diesel pumpsets. By adopting a suitable norm for petroleum oil consumption of diesel oil for well irrigation purpose, and this consumption can be valued at appropriate price of diesel oil. Third, repair and maintenance cost of pumpsets can be figured out by first adopting an investment norm per pumpset, and next applying the norm that repair and maintenace expenditure amounts to some 5 to 10 per cent of the cost of a pumpset. Fourth, operational costs for wells equipped with traditional waterlifts may be assessed with the help of estimates based on sample survey reports prepared by scholars/agencies who have studied the comparative economics of traditional and modern wells.

A word about the data source of on irrigated area is necessary. We are using the data on utilised irrigation potential given in Five Year Plan reports, and not from the land use statistics compiled by the state revenue departments and finally published by the central Ministry of Agriculture. The problem with the latter source, which is usually used by scholars of Indian agriculture, is that categorywise statistics of irrigated area are in 'net' terms and not gross terms. Without making assumptions about intensities of irrigation for major and medium irrigation works on the one hand and minor works on the other, it is not possible to convert net irrigated area into its corresponding gross irrigated area. Fortunately, the plan statistics of irrigation potential are on gross area basis.

The operational expenditure for the multipurpose river projects amounted to about Rs 279 million during 1980-81. In respect of major and medium irrigation projects the same totalled around Rs 1,083 million. Thus overall operational costs of canal irrigation may be reckoned at Rs 1,362 million, of which Rs 530 million was accounted by establishment cost alone. The maintenance and repair expenditure stood at about Rs 844 million, just about 15 per cent below the revenue income (Rs 986 million) from the canal system in 1980-81. Adopting a figure of 23 million hectare for area actually irrigated by major and medium works in 1980-81, one obtains an approximate estimate of Rs 60/ ha as operational cost for canal irrigation.

There were about 4 million electric pumpsets at the beginning of the financial year 1980-81. Indian agriculture reportedly absorbed in this year about 14,489 million KWHs. These statistics imply an annual consumption of about 3620 KWH per electric pumpset, which is about one-fifth higher than the norm of 3000 KWH per electric pumpset used by the Working Group on Energy Policy in its report of 1979. Assuming that some of the electricity was used for purposes other than pumping of groundwater, we are envisaging that about 13,000 million KWHs were used for groundwater pumping. Though farmers usually paid 15 to 20 paise per KWH, the resource cost of power generation and rural electrification in 1980-81 may be placed in the range 60 to 80 paise per KWH. For Uttar Pradesh. Rajadhyaksha Committee on Power (1980) found that resource cost of supplying electricity to rural areas during 1978-79 amouted to about 67 paise/KWH as against the average cost of 44 paise for all L.T. consumers. Thus, cost on account of electricity consumption may be placed in the range Rs 7,800-10,400 million.

Diesel oil used in agriculture, as per the national income accounts of 1980-81, amounted to about Rs 24,788 million at current prices. This was used by over 2.6 million diesel pumpsets, nearly 0.3 million tractors, an unknown number of harvest combines and threshers. The Working Group on Energy Policy (1979) adopted a norm of 0.8 tons per diesel pumpset. (We believe that this is on the high side, as it is derived on the principle of energy equivalence for 3000 KWH for an electric pumpset). If we follow this norm and assume a price of Rs 2200 per ton for diesel oil, the energy cost for diesel irrigation pumps maybe placed at Rs 4,576 million for 1980-81. But if we adopt a lower norm, say 0.6 tons per diesel pumpset, the cost for 2.6 million diesel pumpsets would be Rs 3,432 million. Thus we get a range estimate of Rs 3,432 - Rs 4,576 million for diesel consumption by diesel pumpsets for 1980-81.

Thus the expenditure on account of electricity and diesel oil fell in the range Rs 11,232 - 14,976 million, which, when divided by a groundwater irrigation potential of 23 million ha for 1980-81, gives rise to a range estimate of Rs 488-651 per ha. To this may be added a notional repair and preventive maintenance cost of Rs 49-98 per ha by making two assumptions, namely, (1) the investment cost per pumpset in 1980-81 was Rs 3,500 and (2) the repair and maintenance cost ranged between 5 and 10 per cent of the investment in pumpset. Therefore, the operational cost on account of pumpsets alone ranged between Rs 537 and Rs 749 per irrigated hectare. To this have to be added two more costs, namely, (1) cost of operating traditional wells and (2) repair and maintenance of dugwells and tubewell borings.

There were about 7.8 million dugwells and nearly 2.2 million tubewells in existence at the beginning of 1980-81. If 6.5 million pumpsets were used in 2.2 million tubewells and 4.3 million dugwells, 3.5 dugwells are presumed to be operated by traditional waterlifts. Since many of the dugwells fell into disuse as their owners acquired tubewells, we may say about 2.3 million dugwells were used with traditional waterlifts. We are adopting a figure of Rs 1000 per traditional waterlift. With this, the average operational cost per hectare for well irrigation stood somewhere between Rs 637 and Rs 849 during 1980-81.

Chapter 6

MEASUREMENT OF LINKAGES BETWEEN SURFACE AND GROUND WATER:
The Beneficial Role of Canal Seepage*

An unconventional view of economic development is one of converting adversities of Nature to mankind's advantage. From this standpoint the deleterious canal seepage from major irrigation works can now be looked upon benignly as it is a major source of artificial groundwater replenishment in groundwater short areas. In fact, the long-run sustainability of much-acclaimed groundwater-based agriculture in low rainfall regions of northern, western and southern India now hinges on the seeped-in waters from surface irrigation development works like canals and tanks.

A canal system is inherently very leaky, in the sense that a large part of the conveyed water is lost to groundwater table. In a completely unlined system serving farmers using conventional methods of water application to their fields, as much as 75 per cent of the canal water can be lost, mostly to the groundwater table. This cumulation of seeped-in canal waters, if unchecked, tends to raise the groundwater table, leading before long to problems of land waterlogging and soil salinity/alkalinity. No wonder, then, the fear of waterlogging from canal irrigation has been haunting irrigation engineers/administrators in India since the turn of the last century.

To contain the canal seepage via suitable canal lining and to prevent waterlogging-salinity through an extensive network of drains is a very costly proposition. Extra capital costs needed for canal lining and drainage are too high to be recouped from farmers practicing traditional, subsistence farming in which the economic value of irrigation is much less than that in modern, market-oriented farming based on intensive use of bio-chemical inputs. This is what made waterlogging

* Part of this already published as IJAE paper (Dhawan and Satya Sai, 1988).

in canal commands an inevitable consequence during the British rule in the Indian subcontinent. But this need not be so now because intensive irrigated agriculture today can yield enough extra output/farm income to cover the added costs of canal lining and drainage. The question is whether the drainage of seeped-in waters be achieved through conventional horizontal drains or via vertical drainage through establishment of wells within canal commands.

The recent thinking has been favouring vertical over horizontal drainage. This is for two powerful reasons. Firstly, the vertically-drained waters are put to good economic use by the farmers in a number of ways enumerated below. Secondly, it leads towards the development of conjunctive use of groundwater and surface water resources, an avowed objective of irrigation planning these days.

The value of groundwater to a canal farmer hinges on the type of canal. Evidently, it will be higher if the canal supplies are of a restrictive character. In a one-seasonal canal supplying water mostly for the main wet season cropping, the groundwater can be used to obtain an extra crop during the dry season when land lies fallow in much of our country. Even if a low yielding pulse crop is being grown in the dry season, the well water can enable a farmer to shift onto a more remunerative crop. Also, access to well water can also enable him to either advance the sowing of his wet season crop or prepare rice nurseries early enough in case canal releases are contingent on the onset of the monsoons.

Groundwater becomes a substantial source of augmenting the meagre canal supplies in northern India where the protective principle ensures that hardly one-third area of a farmer can be fully irrigated with canal supplies. As the canal system here is somewhat of a perennial nature, investment in groundwater irrigation strengthens irrigated agriculture in a major way. Farmers are able not only to complete their irrigation operations in time and on most of their land, but also go in for crops that cannot be easily matured on canal supplies alone. Thus private tubewells in Punjab and Haryana have enabled farmers to grow paddy which needs copious watering in a somewhat continuous manner —rotational irrigation system in vogue here is not conducive for paddy cultivation, except in lands prone to waterlogging. Likewise, in western Uttar Pradesh the canal irrigators' constraint of availability of summer supply, which hampers sugarcane cultivation, is removed by their installation of tubewells, leading to substantial expansion in cane production.

Even in a non-protective canal (loosely described as 'productive' canal) of the type existing in southern India, one's own well could be much more than a mere standby arrangement against canal deficiencies during drought. Here, the tail reaches are not well served because farmers in upper reaches appropriate more than their due share of canal supplies. In clear violation of the canal regulations these farmers grow more of heavily-irrigated crops like paddy and sugarcane. In such a circumstance, the tail-end farmer cannot practice intensive farming without the aid of well irrigation. Incidentally, this brings home an important truth: canal farmers are not going to invest in their own wells if they do not experience shortages of canal water. Then it is futile to plead for conjunctive irrigation in canals designed to meet full agronomical water needs of crops.

The key idea behind conjunctive irrigation is one of enhancing the magnitude of irrigational benefits from the given volume of water resources. In other words, the benefits attained under conjunctive irrigation are considered much more than the sum total of separate benefits to be realised from developing the two water bodies in isolation. In more rigorous terms, this may be stated as follows:

$$B_c > B_g + B_s$$

Where: B_c stands for the value of benefits to the society under conjunctive irrigation;

B_g stands for the value of benefits to the society from utilising its groundwater resources for irrigation purpose in total isolation from surface water irrigation;

B_s stands for the value of benefits to the society from utilising its surface water resources for irrigation in isolation from groundwater irrigation.

As the concept of conjunctive irrigation is not yet worked through for implementation purpose, some pertinent — and a bit uneasy —questions do arise. Will the extra resource cost of developing conjunctive system be justified by the extra benefits? In such a system, will every farmer be required to meet his water needs from both groundwater and surface water? When used conjunctively, does any positive interaction (in the sense of complementarity) between two water sources occur in the crop production activity?

Scope of Enquiry

Our focus here is not on conjunctive use of water resources, which is the watchword of the day among surface water planners who are mostly engineers. Neither this concept nor the above-mentioned questions are being investigated here. The scope of this chapter is confined to assessing the magnitude of beneficial effects of surface irrigation development on the groundwater-based farming of some groundwater short regions of India. It is hoped that this quantitative assessment would go a long way in sobering up the zealous proponents of groundwater irrigation, as also the crusaders against major irrigation works — both do not appreciate the harsh realities of irrigation in water scarce or low rainfall regions.

To begin with, we explore some issues of measurement. This is followed by empirical evidence for the following tracts/states:

1. Ahmednagar district and the Mula command in this disttrict of western Maharashtra;
2. Punjab State
3. Tamil Nadu State
4. Muzaffarnagar district of western U.P.

The Problem

The central problem is to assess how much of aggregate crop output of groundwater-based agriculture of a naturally groundwater-short area can be attributed to natural groundwater supply from rainfall infiltration, and how much to seeped-in waters from surface water-based irrigation works. Thus the crucial things to know are either of the following two sets of information:

(i) comparable survey data on crop activity of wells located within the commands of canals/tanks and of wells located outside these commands;

(ii) volume of groundwater used in crop activity and its composition by source of origin.

Admittedly, such information is not readily available. Whatever limited information is available has to used with care. Thus the straight forward information (*i*) has to be scrutinised for the comparability of two types of wells in respect of well dimensions, soil-climatic factors and ground geology. Even if the comparability aspect is free from doubt, one has to figure out how many additional wells can be developed from seeped-in waters from surface irrigation works. For, these waters not only improve water yield of a well but also enlarge the scope for sustaining more wells per unit square mile of arable land. In other words, we need additional information regarding the density of wells per square mile in and outside canal/tank command. In its absence, one may infer suitably from temporal data on the number of wells in existence prior to and after the construction of a major irrigation project.

The volumetric approach has its own hurdles. First of all, crop activity data by category of irrigation is seldom available. So, obtaining economy-wide estimates of aggregate crop output under groundwater irrigation is the first problem, which the author has fortunately resolved partially for some states of India in his last book. For the states of Punjab and Tamil Nadu, he had found that each net hectare of land area under groundwater irrigation generated crop output equivalent to about 6.5 tons of foodgrains. The second hurdle is to obtain the two components of groundwater recharge. The problem here is two-fold. On the one hand, the estimates of groundwater resource by volume are not yet firmly established in India. On the other hand, these are not being prepared according to the source of origin of groundwater. So, one has to use the available estimates with caution, and also make somehow the component-wise estimates of groundwater. This is a task in hydrological realm, where an economist has to be extremely wary in handling data generated by hydrogeologists.

ANALYSIS FOR WESTERN MAHARASHTRA TRACTS

Excluding Konkan area, western Maharashtra is a typical water short region of the Deccan plateau known for its drought proneness. Its normal rainfall of the order of 670 mm is both low and highly uncertain in precipitation within the specified monsoon period as well as from year to year. Though its underlying basaltic hard rocks keep the groundwater table high, their high impermeability and lack of porosity affect groundwater availability by volume. Because of the rocky geology, rainfall infiltration is impeded. In comparison to surface water flow, the annual groundwater recharge is poor, constituting hardly one-fourth of the total water resources. Thus natural availability of groundwater resource per unit of arable area here is one-third to one-half of that found in alluvial regions of comparable rainfall level.

Here, characteristics of the groundwater resource are not very conducive for private investments in well irrigation. There is much uncertainty about (1) the volumetric depth and (2) variations in water table from kharif to rabi and summer seasons on the one hand and from one year to the next on the other. Striking a good water bearing strata outside the canal/tank command areas, while digging a well, is a gamble, thereby constraining the rise of a thriving groundwater-based farming. Such thriving agriculture in the region is found in pockets where perennial wells happen to be located in fractured rocks or downstream of percolation tanks which are specifically constructed to improve groundwater availability. Western Maharashtra is known for its programme of percolation tanks, each typically costing about Rs 5 lakhs and sustaining about a dozen wells (each costing about Rs 25,000). In this context, the value of incidental canal seepage resulting from big irrigation works needs no commending. Let us, therefore, move on to its quantification in money terms.

Utillising Farm Management Survey (FMS) data and taluka-wise statistics for Ahmednagar district of western Maharashtra, this author had demonstrated (Dhawan, 1986 a) that the rate of return for dugwells in this low rainfall district (500-600 mm) averaged about 50 per cent for canal-irrigated talukas and just 13 percent for non-canal-irrigated talukas. This large differential is attributable to two factors. First, the net irrigated area per well in canal-irrigated talukas was 75 per cent more than that for wells outside the canal commands. Second, the crop pattern under wells in canal-irrigated talukas was heavily tilted in favour of more remunerative crops, especially sugarcane, which cannot be matured on seasonal wells that predominate in non-canal-irrigated talukas. (In the early seventies, to which the above exercise pertains, the farm business income from a hectare of sugarcane, according to the FMS data for Ahmednagar district, was almost ten times the average for all other seasonal crops taken together).

The aforesaid differential in rate of return is not a full measure of the external economy of canal seepage, because we have not reckoned with the extra number of wells that were sustained by the canal seepage. This deficiency is overcome in our study of the Mula project command. This is a canal with very high losses in transit. According to a WALMI (1984) study, only 22 per cent of the water released from the Mula reservoir reached farmers' fields. This low availability of canal supplies and restrictions on growing sugarcane has encouraged investments in well irrigation in the canal command. As per the record of the Director of Irrigation Research, Pune, the number of wells in the Mula Right Bank Canal command stood around 5900 at the time of its commissioning, rising to about 8600 a decade later. It is estimated that the number of wells in the Mula command rose by 50 per cent after its commissioning in 1971-72. Also, the area irrigated per well in 1982-83 stood 86 per cent over its level of 1.4 ha observed during the course of a soil mapping study of the command during 1966. Likewise, the new crop pattern under well irrigation stood radically altered in favour of sugarcane.

Aggregating all crops in terms of rice equivalents derived from crop prices recommended by the Costs and Agricultural Prices Commission, the crop activity based on groundwater rose from about 14 thousand tons in 1970-71 to about 117 thousand tons in 1982-83. This eightfold expansion in groundwater-based farming in the Mula command has to be credited to the seeped-in canal waters. It is to be pointed out that the expansion is overstated to the extent the following allegations are valid. That is to say, some of the reported sugarcane under well irrigation is actually raised through illegal appropriations of direct canal supplies -this is usually done with the connivance of the lower rung functionaries of the canal system.

If this added output of the order of 100,000 tons is considered as an indirect contribution of the public investment in canal irrigation, one would need to revise upwards the magnitude of production augmentation achieved by the establishment of the Mula project. According to the WALMI (1984) data, the overall crop yield of canal-irrigated lands in the Mula command averaged a little over two tons (in rice units) per net irrigated hectare during 1982-83 when about 31,000 net ha area was under canal irrigation. Thus, the true production from the Mula project was not 66,000 tons but nearly 170,000 tons(rice units), that is, about two and a half times the production realised from direct canal irrigation. Notwithstanding our earlier perception that the output based on canal seepage is overestimated, there is little doubt about the substantial importance of indirect output contribution vis-a-vis direct output contribution of Mula canal system.[1]

ANALYSIS FOR PUNJAB

Today, Punjab state is well endowed in groundwater. But this is not a natural occurrence. By nature, the state cannot be rated high in groundwater availability. Prior to the development of canal irrigation, good availability of groundwater was confined to narrow strips in the vicinity of its three perennial rivers. Elsewhere, groundwater was found deep below the land surface. In quantitative terms, it was not good because the total rainfall of the state is low. Even if one were to adopt the norms for rainfall infiltration for alluvial areas as per the Groundwater Estimation Committee (1984), the groundwater recharge amounts to somewhere betwee 12 and 15 cm per unit of land area. The gross inadequacy of this amount for providing irrigation in the state may be judged from the fact that for wheat crop during the rabi season one requires about 40 to 45

1. For more details about the Mula command, see Dhawan (1987a), and for production/productivity additions, see Dhawan and Satya Sai (1988).

cm of irrigation water (the recommended level by the Punjab Agricultural University is 45 cm). In fact, for the common paddy-wheat sequence the recommended irrigation applications would amount to 15 to 18 times the above level of groundwater availability.

But for canal seepage, much of the groundwater would be encountered far below the ground surface as the sandy soils of the state fail to impede the downward pull of gravity on the infiltrated water. No wonder, then, that much of the groundwater-based farming in the state in the pre-canal era was confined predominantly to tracts adjoining perennial rivers of the state which kept the groundwater table high enough for animal-operated persian wheels that could not cope with water table deeper than 35 feet below the ground surface. In such a groundwater regime, the establishment of a state-wide network of canals is akin to perennial rivers keeping the groundwater table high all over the state. Despite over-exploitation of groundwater due to rainfall deficiency in recent years, notably since the drought of 1979-80 and the resultant lowering of water table, the lowered water table is still far above the pre-canal level of 50 to 100 feet observed during the Mughal days.

It is not possible to adopt a la Mula command the approach of comparing the performance of tubewells located within and outside the canal commands. For one, all the districts are covered by canal commands. For another, in alluvial formations the seeped-in canal waters can easily move out of the canal to non-canal irrigated tracts in their vicinity. The situation here demands that we resolve the problem at hand via the other route, namely, by working out the composition of groundwater used in groundwater-based output of the state.

The land productivity under wells during the mid-eighties stood around 6.5 tons per net hectare in terms of foodgrain equivalent units. It is a projected estimate based on the following past benchmark estimates: 1.75 tons for 1950-51, 3.06 tons for the mid-sixties, and 5.46 tons for the late seventies. Its multiplication with the reported area of 2.21 million hectares under well irrigation in 1984-85 gives rise to an output figure of about 14 million tons. The corresponding estimate for output originating from nearly 1.4 million ha of canal-irrigated area may be placed at 4.9 million tons.

This volume of output is from nearly at 0.7 million private tubewells. It is almost a situation of full utilisation of the state's groundwater resources. According to the Task Force Group of the Planning Commission (Government of India, 1972), Punjab's groundwater resources could sustain the establishment of 0.6 million shallow tubewells in the state. This is suggestive of overdevelopment of groundwater in the state by about one-sixth. But according to Sangal (1987), there was almost one-sixth underdevelopment, as the groundwater withdrawals in the state amounted to 1.55 million hectare-metres out of a net groundwater potential of the order of 1.82 million hectare-metres (assessment as of mid-1986). It is safe to proceed on the assumption that the groundwater resources of the state are fully utilised for the production of aggregate crop output of the order of 14 million tons of foodgrain equivalents.

The issue to be sorted out now is: what is the proportion of the groundwater resources that can be ascribed to the seeped-in waters of canal origin? In a small note to this chapter, this issue is discussed in detail, and we believe that somewhere between 50 to 70 per cent of the agricultural output based on groundwater irrigation in Punjab state may be traced to canal seepage. Thus anywhere between 7 and 10 million tons (foodgrain equivalents) in the mid-eighties in the state were raised with the help of percolated water from the main and minor canals, from water courses below the final outlet (turnout), and from canal-irrigated fields. When this is reckoned alongwith the direct output from the canal-irrigated fields, the total output augmentation from the establishment of major surface irrigation works in the state becomes much more impressive. For, in the mid-eighties the net canal-irrigated area of the state is estimated to have yielded about 5 million tons in foodgrain equivalents. Thus, the ultimate contribution of canals is 2.4-3.0 times the directly reported output from canal irrigation.

ANALYSIS FOR TAMIL NADU

The natural availability of groundwater in Tamil Nadu is modestly good, except in the low rainfall districts like Coimbatore and Dharmapuri. For one, it is a state with medium rainfall conditions. Secondly, its normal rainfall of the order of 1000 mm is rather well distributed over both the south-west and the north-east monsoon periods of the year, thereby enhancing scope for groundwater replenishment through a greater fraction of rainfall infiltration into the ground. Thirdly, though much of the state is underlain with rocky geology, the rocks here are not that impervious as of the basaltic areas of Karnataka and Maharashtra in the Deccan plateau. Their lack of compactness and crystalline character at places provides more porous space for water storage underneath the ground.

The groundwater regime of the state has further improved because of extensive development of surface irrigation works. The state is well known for its long recorded history of both smallscale and largescale irrigation works based on surface water flows. Half the state area is presently under irrigation. Now, further development of irrigated agriculture is getting hampered because the irrigation potential of the state is now almost fully exploited. Eversince the full development of surface irrigation potential was attained towards the beginning of the Fourth Five Year Plan, more and more attention got focussed on groundwater development.

In terms of number of wells/pumpsets per unit area, the state ranks at the top among the Indian states. But for the seepage from canals and tanks, the level of development of well irrigation in the lower rainfall tracts of the state would have been seriously impeded. The portion of field percolation in total canal/tank seepage here is relatively high because of the mono culture of paddy under surface irrigation works in the state. Anyway, now well irrigation is the single most important source of irrigation. It is estimated that gross cropped area under state's wells during 1978-79 was about 1.7 million ha as compared to about 1.2 million ha under canal irrigation and about 0.9 million ha under tank irrigation. When one reckons with the higher land productivity under well irrigation, nearly two-thirds of the state agricultural output turns out to be from groundwater-irrigated lands.

Towards the end of seventies, each net hectare area under well irrigation produced about 6.50 tons in foodgrain equivalent units. Thus, the total production from lands under well irrigation amounted to about 6.95 million tons. Somewhere between one-fourth and two-fifths of this production may be attributed to the seeped-in canal and tank waters. For, the contribution of rainfall infiltration to total groundwater recharge is anywhere between 59 and 74 per cent, as shown in the appendix note to this chapter.

A rough idea about the indirect contribution of both canal and tank irrigation can also be formed from the available data with us. It is gathered that canals of the state carry annually 800 TMC of water, about four times the volume of water delivered through state tanks, of which some receive replenishment from canals over and above the run-off from their own catchments. These waters directly produced about 4.4 million tons in foodgrain units in the late seventies. Their indirect production contribution (via wells) is found to be in the range 1.8-2.9 million tons. Thus, the indirect contribution of the state surface irrigation works amounts to anywhere in the range two-fifths to two-thirds of their direct output. For canals alone, the relative role of indirect contribution was greater than that for tanks, as revealed by the following statistics:

	canals	tanks
	(tons/crop ha)	
Direct crop yield	2.00	2.10
Indirect crop yield	1.21-1.91	0.38-0.60

ANALYSIS FOR MUZAFFARNAGAR DISTRICT (WEST U.P.)

The water endowment of western U.P. is comparable to that of Punjab. In fact, the natural groundwater regime here is similar to that state. That is to say, groundwater is naturally quite scarce here. Thanks to the development of an extensive canal network based on the diversions of the Ganga and Yamuna waters for over a century and a half, there is a sea-change in groundwater availability in the region. It is said that 50 per cent of the waters released in the Ganges Canal system end up in groundwater table. But for these seeped-in waters, the explosive growth in tubewell irrigation witnessed in the region since the onset of the green revolution era would have been hampered.

Unfortunately, it has not been posible for this author to work out the estimates of land productivity of western U.P. region by irrigation status. It is with the aid of a recent micro study by NABARD (1987) that he proposes to bring out the vital role of canal seepage in sustaining the much-acclaimed shallow tubewell irrigation that has developed under private aegis in this region. The study area is situated in Muzaffarnagar district, a prosperous highly irrigated tract in the upper Ganga basin. Because of the protective nature of the canal supplies from the two canals of the Ganga and the Yamuna rivers, the farmers here can neither grow as much sugarcane as they want nor irrigate adequately their principal crops of wheat, paddy and sugarcane. To overcome these constraints, as also the irregular canal supplies, they have installed their own shallow tubewells. A sample survey of 87 shallow tubewell owners by the NABARD, which had promoted their installation under a land development proposal of the U.P. Land Development Bank, brought out that the incremental production per tubewell averaged 6 tons in foodgrain units during 1981-82 (see next chapter).

According to the NABARD (1987), a tubewell in the sample area lifted about 240 acre-inches (about 2.4 hectare-metres) of water in a year. This is an excessive withdrawal, in the sense that natural groundwater recharge from rainfall and river floods for a land area of about 3.4 ha served by a sample tubewell is much less. From a rainfall of the order of

750mm the groundwater recharge would be at most 200 mm. Thus for 3.4 ha of land area the rainfall infiltration to the groundwater table is about 0.68 ha-metres, which is hardly one-third of groundwater pumped by a tubewell. Even if we reckon with the groundwater recharge from the two nearby rivers Ganga and Yamuna, it is safe to conclude that at least half the groundwater draft of a tubewell would be from seeped-in canal waters under conditions of full exploitation of groundwater resources of western U.P. (While condition of full utilisation of groundwater resource is not yet reached in Muzaffarnagar district, districts like Meerut, Bulandshahr, Aligarh and Ghaziabad are almost at the threshold of full utilisation).

Summary of Findings

Hydrologists invariably emphasise hydrological linkages of water bodies, but without a precise quantification of their economic implications. Our limited attempt to quantify these reveals interesting results with regard to the beneficial role of canal waters in improving groundwater regime and groundwater-based agriculture in water-short regions. These seeped-in waters are found to quadruple the rate of return on investment in well irrigation in Ahmedanagar district of western Maharashtra. In a specific case of the Mula canal in this very district, these waters have boosted the groundwater based farming both in terms of number of sustainable wells and crop output per well. The eight-fold increase in output from wells is an indirect output contribution of the Mula project, and is no less than the direct output resulting from the canal-irrigated acreage of this project. No less striking are the empirical results for the Punjab. Here, at least half of the state output from private tubewell irrigation can be confidently attributed to groundwater that is of canal origin. A similar result is true for private tubewells in Muzaffarnagar district of western U.P.

In Tamil Nadu state, both canals and tanks together make a substantial augmentation to its natural groundwater availability. Somewhere between one-fourth and two-fifths of the total output of the order of 7 million tons from wells established in the state may be traced to seeped-in waters of canal/tank origin. Whatever be this fraction, bulk of the seepage into groundwater table is from the state canal network. These findings should set at rest the controversy about surface versus groundwater irrigation in low and medium rainfall regions.

NOTE

Share of Seeped-in Waters of Surface Irrigation Origin in Total Groundwater Potential in Punjab and Tamil Nadu.

Punjab

There is considerable uncertainty about the very volume of groundwater available for irrigation and for meeting other non-agricultural needs like drinking water requirements. The estimate ranges between 1.3 and 1.8 million ha-metres. The lower estimate is from a recent document of the Central Water Commission (CWC) (Government of India, 1987), whereas the higher one is from Sangal (1987). Both are rather authentic estimates. The CWC bases itself on the estimational work of the Central Groundwater Board (CGWB), and Sangal bases himself on the estimational work done by the Groundwater Investigation Directorate of the state of Punjab. Since Sangal is a technical expert - as the General Manager of NABARD he monitors and evaluates groundwater development programmes -, I am more inclined to accepting his estimates of groundwater potential and utilisation in the state of Punjab.

That a shallow tubewell in Punjab makes an intensive use of groundwater is revealed by Gurcharan Singh's careful measurements of a sample of 42 electric shallow tubewells from the four districts of Amritsar, Jullundur, Hoshiarpur and Gurdaspur. According to his work (Singh, 1987), a tubewell withdraws about 2.16 ha-metres of groundwater in a year, six-tenths in the kharif season during which heavily-watered paddy crop is grown. Note that this draft compares well with the estimated draft of 2.40 ha-metres per sample tubewell in Muzaffarnagar district where sugarcane is the dominant kharif crop. Evidently, this rate of withdrawal of groundwater is not sustainable without massive recharge of groundwater table from the canal waters. Assuming that one-fourth of rainfall infiltrates into the groundwater table, the natural recharge over a 5 million hectare of geographical area would amount to about 0.75 million ha-metres. Collating it with the total recharge of 1.81 million hs-metres, we find that the seeped-in canal waters could account for nearly sixty per cent of the total groundwater resource of this state.

Had we assumed that only one-fifth of the rainfall becomes groundwater, the share of canal seepage in total groundwater recharge of 1.81 million ha-metres would rise to 67 per cent. Likewise, had we adopted the CWC estimate of 1.3 million ha-metres, the assumption of one-fifth of rainfall infiltration would bring out a lower percentage share of 54 per cent for the seeped-in canal waters. These exercises should convince a discerning reader that we are justified to adopt a range estimate of 50 to 70 per cent for the share of canal seepage in total groundwater.

Tamil Nadu

In the case of Tamil Nadu, our data sources for the groundwater potential are the same as for Punjab. But now the estimate based on the work of the state Groundwater Investigation Directorate is somewhat lower than that by the CGWB. Whereas the former organisation places the estimate at 2.14 million ha-metres, the latter puts it at 2.69 million ha-metres. If we place the recharge from rainfall at 1.59 million ha-metres, the share of the waters from canals and tanks is found to lie somewhere between 26 and 41 per cent of the total groundwater recharge.[1]

There is considerable difference of opinion as to the extent of groundwater exploitation. According to Sangal (1987), 57 per cent of the potential of 2.14 million ha-metres was tapped by mid 1986. This very percentage is reckoned at 37 per cent in the CWC report (Government of India, 1987). If area statistics of the Planning Commission are brought into the reckoning, nearly 82 per cent of the groundwater potential of the order 1.5 m ha had been tapped by the mid-eighties (Government of India, 1984). This appears to be nearer the ground reality than the position conveyed through the volumetric approach.

1. Of this range estimate, this author is inclined to the upper end of the range.

Chapter 7

RISE OF PRIVATE TUBEWELL IRRIGATION IN CANAL COMMANDS*

INTRODUCTORY REMARKS

For long, the north-western parts of the Indian sub-continent have been known for their extensive network of public canals. These protective canals are certainly not designed to promote intensive farming. Yet, this very region acquired world-wide fame for 'green revolution' based on high-yielding varieties of wheat and paddy. This paradoxical development is usually resolved by drawing attention to the fact that the tubewell explosion of the Indian sub-continent occurred mainly in this region. These tubewells were set up both within and outside the canal commands, partly supplementing canal irrigation and partly displacing dugwell irrigation.

Two features of these tubewells need mentioning here. First, their level of development diminishes in force as one moves eastwards in the vast Indo-Gangetic plains (Dhawan, 1982). Among the numerous factors that have brought about such a spatial pattern in Indian tubewell irrigation is the prior development of canal irrigation, a factor that has not received due consideration from scholars of Indian agriculture. Instead of making a positive reference to the factor, it is alluded to in a somewhat negative manner, namely, farmers had to instal tubewells because the protective canals were inadequate for supporting intensive farming with HYV seeds. Second, over 80 per cent of the Indian tubewells are individually owned by the farmers. The rest of the private tubewells were mostly held in joint, and not cooperative, ownership (NSS, 1984, and 1985). Innumerable scholars have drawn pointed attention to the marked superiority of private tubewells over other means of irrigation,

* The paper was presented at the National Seminar on New Perspectives in Water Management held at Indore during 15 to 17 April 1989 under the joint auspicies of the Indian National Academy of Engineers and the Central Water Commission.

namely, canals, traditional dugwells, tanks and government tubewells. How prior development of canal irrigation in north-western India has facilitated the rise of private tubewells needs due recognition. Here, two aspects are noteworthy. On the one hand, there occurs improvement in the availability of groundwater through the seeped-in canal waters. In low rainfall regions not underlain with brackish waters, the improvement in groundwater regime has two beneficial consequences. One is the reduction in waterlifting cost because of the rise in groundwater table from its very deep level of the pre-canal days. The other advantage of canal seepage is that of added scope for sustaining many more tubewells than are feasible simply on the basis of natural groundwater recharge (Dhawan and Satya Sai, 1988). But for canal seepage (including field percolation) the introduction of tubewell technology in this region would have surely led to a serious permanent lowering of water table. In other words, canals act as a powerful check on groundwater depletion that is otherwise inherent in introducing tubewell technology in low rainfall tracts. It is time we appreciate that the sustainability of tubewell-irrigated agriculture in low rainfall areas hinges far more on canal seepage than on enactments on highly impracticable groundwater regulation recommended by hydrogeologists in India.

On the other hand, the prior experience with canal irrigation has proved helpful to farmers going in for their own tubewell investment. Canal irrigation leads to accumulation of savings which come handy in meeting the enhanced working capital needs of intensified farming under private tubewell irrigation. Otherwise, the constraint of working capital can reduce returns from investment in a tubewell, an important factor behind lower returns from private wells realised by farmers in purely rainfed tracts of this country.

We must not forget some larger perspectives while singing praises of private tubewells *a la* B.B. Vohra. But for the canals the returns from private tubewell irrigation would not be all that high - this also holds good for dugwells (Dhawan, 1986a). From a macro angle, it is doubtful if private tubewell irrigation is truly less costly than canals. For one, substantial investment on public account in power generation and its transmission to rural pumps is needed (almost about Rs 20,000 per pump energised). And the low operational cost of an electric tubewell is largely due to the government policy of subsidising rural electric power. In view of (*a*) interlinkages between groundwater and canal irrigation and (*b*) the subsidy in electricity, one has to be wary of policy prescriptions made in favour of well irrigation — and against major irrigation works — by comparing costs/returns lacking comprehensive perspective.

To promote conjunctive irrigation of groundwater and surface water within the commands of public canals and tanks is an important goal of Indian irrigation planning. Such groundwater development is expected to improve the productivity and long-run sustainability of surface irrigation works. In the case of canals designed for meeting full water needs of the crops, the productivity gains from groundwater development are likely to be lower, except in (1) poorly served tail reaches of the canal network and (2) in seasonal canals. But in the case of canals providing protective irrigation, the productivity (as well as the stability) gains can be substantial following the development of private groundwater irrigation. In fact, the farmers' own urge for such development is more intense when their canal supplies are inadequate for making a transition from traditional to modern agriculture.

The history of irrigated farming points to some evolutionary stages. There is greater concern with cost reducing techniques of irrigation when the mode of agriculture is traditional. Once agriculture has become modern in character, the irrigators are more preoccupied with realising income gains through enhanced productivity of limited resources of land and water.

SCOPE OF PAPER

The paper is focussed on the following questions. What impels canal farmers to invest in their own means of irrigation? How does private tubewell irrigation compare with public canal irrigation in the matter of costs? Are the production and income gains commensurate with the added investments? How much indirect or incidental benefits arise from a tubewell investment? What is the differential in production/income impact between an electric and a diesel tubewell? In what follows these questions are explored for both small and large farmers separately. Also, an attempt is made to assess the government subsidy in rural electrification per electric tubewell.

The paper is a case analysis, based on a re-analysis of the data/results of an evaluation report prepared by the apex credit institution, National Bank for Agricultural and Rural Development (NABARD), Bombay. The analysis rests on a bit old data, namely, for 1981-82, though the report (NABARD, 1987) became public about two years back. In view of the farmers' agitation, the author has critically scrutinised the data as well as the estimates of this report. He has found these firm and reliable in respect of additional income/output from crop enterprise of the tubewell owners. However, the magnitude of indirect or incidental benefits is found to be on the high side, requiring some downward revision — this is discussed in Note I. In the second Note to this paper the amount of electricity subsidy per tubewell and the capital cost not borne by a farmer are broadly assessed.

THE STUDY AREA

The NABARD study area is in Mazaffarnagar district, a prosperous, highly irrigated (86 percent) tract of the upper Ganga basin. Prior to the establishment of the Upper Ganges Canal and the Eastern Yamuna Canal (the two main canals of western U.P.) in the mid-nineteenth century, open wells were the principal means of irrigation. In the beginning, the advent of canal irrigation led to abandonment of wells by farmers, partly because of their higher cost and partly because of the crumbling of 'Kutcha' wells due to canal seepage. But after 25 years or so, well irrigation revived as the protective nature of the canal supplies began constraining the canal farmers. This time, they constructed masonry wells to cope with the seeped-in canal waters (Stone, 1984). The extra funds for investment in masonry wells partly came from farmers' own cumulations from enhanced income due to canal irrigation.

Agro-climatically, the district is good from the soil fertility angle but not rainfallwise. Being in the 'doab' of the Ganga and Yamuna rivers, the soils are alluvial and fertile. But the rainfall conditions are far from favourable. For realising good crop yields, irrigation is necessary, especially for the annual sugarcane crop which presently dominates the farm economy of the area. Though the district is criss-crossed by a network of canals, private tubewells are now a major source of irrigation in the district.

TUBEWELLS AS AN ALTERNATIVE TO CANAL

The analysis is based on a sample of 87 tubewell-owning farmers. These sample farmers are selected from over 2,900 farmers who established their own tubewells during 1976-78 when the U.P. Land Development Bank (UPLDB) executed a scheme for minor irrigation development in the district. Under the scheme, a variety of works were envisaged, including construction of pucca field channels and new open wells. But the farmers opted only for setting up shallow tubewells. They installed the tubewells for irrigating lands which were already irrigated by canal waters. But they decided not use them as a supplementary source of irrigation, (they took their tubewell-watered fields off the canal roster). As this is contrary to the general impression formed on the studies of other investigators (e.g. Chawla et. al. 1989, and Central Bank of India, 1983), it necessitates some probing.

These farmers certainly saved the canal charges by disconnecting themselves from the public canal system. The released share of the canal supplies most probably improved the quantum of canal water application elsewhere. It is improbable that the water so released was used by the state irrigation department for extending canal-irrigated area elsewhere in the Ganga-Yamuna canal system. In a protective canal, the most likely outcome is one of an outright reduction in canal-irrigated area. In fact, one discerns a perceptible downtrend in the official statistics of canal area for the five districts of Muzaffarnagar, Meerut, Ghaziabad, Bulandshahr and Saharanpur of western U.P., which have canal irrigation since long but have also witnessed rapid development of private tubewell irrigation. In some villages, the displacement of canal irrigation is very heavy. For instance, in Walidpur village in Meerut district, the area under canal irrigation diminished from 425 acres in 1963-64 to 100 acres in 1983-84, while the area under private tubewells shot up from 50 to 575 acres in the same 20 year period (Tyagi, 1988).

In gross area terms, each tubewell benefited about 4 hectare of crop area during the survey year of 1981-82. When we deduct the canal-irrigated area of the period prior to the installation of tubewells, the net addition to total irrigated area works out to barely half an hectare per tubewell — the installation of private tubewells in Rohtas district of Bihar by the canal farmers also resulted in an addition of only 0.4 ha in irrigated area per tubewell (Central Bank of India, 1983). This signifies that irrigation potential created through minor irrigation works in canal commands does not result in same order of expansion in total irrigated area of the economy. This non-additivity aspect of irrigation development is not appropriately reckoned with by our irrigation planners.

The main driving force behind tubewell installation by the sample farmers was not one for enlarging the irrigation coverage of their landholdings but of strengthening the quality of irrigation, both in terms of quantum and timeliness. The NABARD investigators tried to ascertain the reasons for installing tubewells. In this context, the following NABARD observations may be noted:

''Due to untimely and insufficient number of irrigations available from canal, as also high cost of canal water, the farmers had gone in for the tubewell investment.'' (para 12, p. 13).

"....the decision of farmers to go in for the investment in a tubewell was influenced by factors like untimely and lesser number of irrigations available from canal, ready availability of electric connection and low cost of operation and maintenance of electric tubewell". (para 4.6, pp. 22-23).

It is quite a task to unearth factors and forces that motivate human beings to a particular course of action, as socio-psychic considerations (e.g. the prestige value of a tubewell, or the discomfort of canal watering at night in wintry season) are no less weighty than sheer pecuniary aspects. Whatever be the motivations in establishing tubewells, it is noteworthy that, besides the already known fact of canal supplies being insufficient and undependable, the farmers perceive the subsidised canal irrigation being costly as compared to irrigation by electric tubewells of their own. Is this a valid perception? This brings us to comparative costs of irrigation in our sample.

COMPARATIVE COSTS

In the absence of information on canal water either by volume or by number of waterings per unit of irrigated area, the cost comparison between tubewells and canal irrigation has to be conducted per force on area basis. The reported canal charges (about Rs. 100/- acre) turn out to be markedly less than the corresponding costs mentioned in the NABARD report for diesel tubewells, namely, Rs 495/ acre for small farmers and Rs 432/ acre for other category of farmers. But the reported hiatus is narrow in the case of electric tubewells vis-a-vis canals. More specifically, the cost per acre for electric tubewells is placed in the NABARD report at Rs 126 for medium and large farmers, and Rs 174 for small farmers. Before saying more on the cost differentials, the following four points need mentioning:

(1) The true cost of canal irrigation becomes more than the canal charges as we reckon with the following incidental costs of canal irrigation:
   (i) illegal exactions extracted by the lower rung canal functionaries from farmers;
   (ii) the onerous task of watering the fields at night during cold winter season; and
   (iii) the cost of labour time spent in mending channels connecting the fields to the canal outlet point.

(2) The aforesaid costs of tubewell irrigation are exclusive of interest and depreciation charges on tubewell investment.

(3) The NABARD computations of costs are on net cropped area basis.
(4) The costs are from the personal angle of the farmers, without reckoning with either subsidies (in canal and electricity) or taxes (in diesel oil).

Reckoning with the incidence of interest and depreciation charges, the picture of comparative costs of irrigation per net acre for the two categories of farmers would become as shown in Table 1. The cost differential is somewhat more than the one reported by Sidhu et.al. for Punjab canals and tubewells.

Table 1

Comparative Irrigation Costs in 1981-82 for Electric and Diesel Tubewells vis-a-vis Canal

Farmer Category	*Electric TW*	*Diesel TW*	*Canal*
	(.......Rs per net irrigated acre.......)		
Small	336	678	99
Others	267	559	97

Diesel tubewell irrigation is decisively much more costly than canal irrigation. Even electric tubewell irrigation is more costly than canal irrigation so long as the incidental costs of canal irrigation for a farmer are low. Thus, despite the hidden subsidy in the electricity bill, electric tubewell irrigation, acre for acre, does not turn out to be cheaper than canal irrigation for most farmers. The cost advantage, if any, may be in terms of cost per unit volume of water. But one should not harbour any doubt that the above cost comparison is faulty because it is not worked per unit of gross cropped area. For, there is no evidence that the intensity of multiple cropping on sample tubewell-irrigated land is more than that on canal-irrigated land. In fact, this intensity in the NABARD sample was 138 per cent on tubewell-irrigated lands, about 5 points lower than the corresponding intensity on canal-irrigated lands during 1981-82. On the basis of a more recent survey, Chawla et. al. (1989) report cropping intensity of 145 per cent for private tubewells in the neighbouring districts of Saharanpur and Meerut. I must hasten to add that these are the conventional measures of intensity of cropping, without any upward adjustment for sugarcane being a long duration crop — the claim of a rise in intensity of cropping in the wake of tubewell installation in the NABARD report is based on such an adjusted measure of intensity in which sugarcane is counted equal to three seasonal crops of wheat, paddy, gram etc.

PRODUCTION EFFECTS

The sample farmers achieved adequate irrigation with the help of tubewells. The two principal crops of sugarcane and wheat were irrigated upto the recommended extent of 12 waterings for sugarcane and 6 for wheat. No less importantly, they enlarged the acreage under sugarcane, the most remunerative crop. In the pre-tubewell period the relative share of sugarcane in total crop area was about 16 per cent in the case of small farmers, and 35 per cent for other farmers. Following tubewell irrigation these percentages rose to 40 and 46, respectively. Tubewells, thus, loosened the water constraint far more for small than for large farmers.

Some increase in crop yields occurred mainly because of better crop fertilisation in the presence of requisite irrigation assured by one's own tubewell. The increments to yield, as measured by the difference in canal and tubewell-irrigated yields, were 8 quintals/ha for wheat, 135 quintals/ha for sugarcane, and 5.5 quintals/ha for paddy. No marked yield rise was observed in the case of gram and coarse grains whose irrigation requirements, unlike those of wheat, paddy and sugarcane, are indeed lower and truly much less exacting in time of application. In relative terms, the increase in crop yields varied as follows: two-fifths for wheat, one-third for sugarcane and one-fifth for paddy.

For the entire scheme of over 2,900 tubewells, installed at a cost of Rs 27 millions, the value of the increased crop output for the year 1981-82 is placed in the NABARD report at about Rs 30 millions. Given the tremendous expansion in area under sugarcane following tubewell installation, sugarcane looms large in the additional output, so much so that the value of additional cane output alone equals the total value of additional output of all crops taken together. Among the other changes in the composition of aggregate crop output is the increased production of paddy as well as potatoes. But the production of maize and pulses contracted — slight contraction is noticeable in wheat and jowar/bajra output also. On the whole, the tubewell scheme led to a 10 per cent reduction in foodgrains output. This adverse impact on grain supplies has to be weighed against the enlarged availability of sugar/gur (from sugarcane) and potatoes. In quantitative terms, the pluses and minuses of the UPLDB tubewell scheme compare as follows:

1. As a result of 10 per cent decline in the output of foodgrains	(–) 1,800 tons
2. As a result of almost doubling of sugar-cane output	(+) 1,42,000 tons of cane or (+) 14,200 tons of sugar
3. As a result of tubewells enabling farmers to raise potatoes	(+) 3,700 tons

In terms of sheer food energy (whereby one ton of sugarcane = 0.11 tons of foodgrains, and one ton of potatoes = 0.25 tons of foodgrains), the tubewell scheme increased farm output by a little under 15,000 tons of foodgrains energy equivalents (FEES), that is, about 5 tons per tubewell (see Dhawan 1988a for a rationale of the unit of measurement FEES). As the net irrigated area per sample tubewell is 2.84 ha, the incremental output from each net hectare brought under tubewell irrigation is of the order of 1.8 tons (FEES) - 1.3 tons if computed per gross irrigated hectare. These estimates need to be raised by about one-fifth if we wish to somehow take into account the added output of neighbouring farmers to whom the sample tubewell owners sold surplus water. Thus, we may adopt the following impact values from the economy-wide angle:

Incremental output per tubewell	6 tons
Incremental output per net ha under tubewell irrigation	2.1 tons
Incremental output per crop ha under tubewell irrigation	1.5 tons

INCOME BENEFITS

The income benefits to a tubewell owner accrue in both direct and indirect manners. The direct benefits arise from the use of tubewell water on the owner's own fields, whereas the indirect or incidental benefits can arise either from sale of surplus tubewell water to fellow farmers, or from use of tubewell motor/engine for doing one's wheat threshing, cane crushing and fodder cutting. Evidently, the indirect benefits are likely to shrink as the landholding rises to irrigation capacity level of a tubewell. According to the NABARD report, a sample tubewell with a rated discharge of 10,000 gallons per hour (12.60 litres per second) could command 20 acre holding during the main rabi season (60 per cent under sugarcane and 40 per cent under wheat). In the sample, however, the average size of landholding is 9.3 acres, of which about 7 acres benefited from tubewell water. Thus, the sample tubewell owners had ample scope for realising incidental benefits from their tubewell investment.

The annual value of incremental net output (net of cost of cultivation) was of the order of Rs 3,900 per tubewell, 85 per cent more than the level prevailing in 1981-82 under pure canal irrigation. The small farmers gained much less even if we do not reckon with the imputed cost of their family labour. As expected, the owners of electric tubewells gained much more than the diesel tubewell owners. These income gains from crop enterprise were more than farmers' own funds used in installing the tubewells. The investment costs and direct income gains per electric/diesel tubewell are listed in Table 2.

Table 2

Incremental On-Farm Income and Farmers' Own Investment in a Tubewell

S.No.	*Item*	*Electric TW*	*Diesel TW*
1.	Actual investment per tubewell	Rs. 11,823	Rs. 7,452
2.	Proportion of institutional financing of TW investment	0.65	0.92 (0.73)
3.	Amount of self-finance per tubewell	Rs. 3,949	Rs 596 (2,012)
4.	Annual addition in on-farm income per tubewell	Rs. 4,971	Rs. 2,835

Note: Figures in parentheses are computed by excluding cases of "overfinance", that is, where loan amount turned out to be more than 75 per cent of the investment-this happened somewhat inadvertently as the diesel tubewell owners did not construct the pump house that would have costed nearly Rs 3,000

NABARD's estimates of incidental benefits of investment in a private tubewell are placed as follows:

(*i*) About Rs 378 per annum are from the sale of surplus tubewell water. This is an average value for the entire sample of 87 tubewell owners of whom 60 per cent were engaged in this agri-business of selling water for about 128 hours in a year — the water rate during 1981-82 was Rs 4 per hour for electric tubewells and Rs 8 per hour for diesel tubewells.

(*ii*) Some of the electric tubewell owners were engaged in gur-making, a major agricultural processing activity of Muzaffarnagar district. They could thus use their electric motors for cane crushing also. Though the number of hours devoted to this processing work is considerably less than the corresponding hours utilised in water selling activity, NABARD's estimate of benefits on this account is rather high: Rs 2,755 per electric tubewell in the sample, or Rs 1,330 per tubewell for the entire sample of 87.

(*iii*) Some tubewell owners, mainly those having electric tubewells, permitted the use of their engines/motors for wheat threshing by other farmers. This custom hiring work netted in Rs 574 per sample tubewell owner (Rs 1,008 per electric tubewell owner), which is more than the income from sale of water.

Were one to go by the NABARD evaluation, returns from investment in a private tubewell, especially an electric one, are truly tremendous. For, with an investment of Rs 11,000 in an electric tubewell the additional income benefit to the owner in a single year turns out to be of order of Rs 10,000 - such high level of returns is not aptly conveyed by the NABARD assessment that the internal rate of return on electric tubewell investment is more than 50 per cent. In view of such high returns, how can one sympathise with the militancy of the farmers of this region in resisting so vigorously some upward revision in electricity charges by the state government of Uttar Pradesh? (Mr. Tikait, the militant farmer spearheading the farmers' recent agitation, is from Muzaffarnagar district).

Before presenting a revised picture of returns from tubewell investment, it will be useful to look into two aspects, one pertaining to the issue of indivisible nature of the tubewell investment and the other about the effects of tubewell development on groundwater regime in the canal commands.

LIMITS TO FARM SIZE

It is widely felt among economists that investment in a tubewell, being lumpy or indivisible, is more suited to large than small and marginal farmers. In this connection, NABARD's effort to measure the minimum farm size for a tubewell is worth taking note of. The minimum farm size for a tubewell, costing Rs 15,000 at 1981-82 prices and carrying a water discharge rating of 12.6 litres/second, is defined as the one for which incremental income amounts to 17 per cent of the investment cost - 5 per cent more than the interest payable to banks.

It appears that a small farmer having a landholding of 2.37 acres only (0.96 ha) can break even in installing a tubewell of his own provided (1) he has no prior irrigation from any source, (2) the state invests in power sector so as to enable him to go in for the more economical electric tubewell and (3) the opportunity cost of his family labour is nil. But if the family labour for him has as much opportunity cost as for hired labour, the minimum farm size would become 3.19 acres (1.29 ha). In case he is switching from less dependable canal irrigation, the minimum size is still higher, namely, 3.76 acres (1.51 ha) - 4.66 acres (1.81 ha) if he costs the family labour fully. In the absence of rural electrification, he would have to use the diesel engine for powering his pumpset, thereby resulting in a further rise in the minimum farm size by one to 3 acres. The size becomes 7.61 acres (about 3 ha) in the most unfavourable conditions.

An implicit assumption in the above assessments is one of landholding being consolidated in one compact field. Otherwise, the estimates for minimum farm size would become still higher, the new values varying with the degree and nature of land fragmentation. In the absence of land consolidation, extra investment (over and above Rs 15,000 in tubewell proper) in buried pipes would be needed to carry tubewell water to all the fragmented plots of his holding. In the event of land fragmentation, however, there is likely to be some additional income from the agri-business of water selling to other farmers. This may substantially counter-balance the twin disability of land size and land fragmentation for a tubewell owning farmer. It appears that small and marginal farmers in canal commands would have to depend mainly on the rise of a private market in groundwater in order to augment their irrigation capability. The question is: will this market function fairly?

NO GROUNDWATER DEPLETION

A question of social relevance is to satisfy ourselves that the private and macro gains from the development of tubewell irrigation have not given rise to some environmental problem such as groundwater depletion. This requires looking into any evidence of decline in water table in the region.

According the NABARD calculations, a sample tubewell lifted about 240 acre-inches of groundwater per year. Of course, owners of smaller landholdings extracted less groundwater than did those with larger landholdings. On the average, the withdrawals for small farmers amounted to 180 acre-inches, about 40 per cent less than the corresponding magnitude for the other farmers. These rates of groundwater utilisation are rather excessive when adjudged in relation to the natural rate of groundwater replenishment in western U.P. region where about 20 to 22 per cent of the rainfall infiltrates into the groundwater table. For Muzaffarnagar district, such annual recharge may be deemed to be of the order of 7 to 8 acre-inches per acre of land area. To this may be added the natural recharge from the rivers of the district whenever these are in spate during the monsoon period when the level of river surface is above the level of the surrounding groundwater table.

The sample tubewells benefited about 7 acres of land of the owners plus some land of the neighbouring farmers who purchased the surplus water from these owners. In terms of the annual working, each tubewell in the sample had total running hours average of about 800, of which 675 hours were devoted to irrigating their own land of 7 acres. Thus, about 200 acre-inches, constituting 84 per cent of total draft, were applied to 7 acres of net cropped area. This means an irrigation depth of nearly 29 inches per acre per year, which is possibly three times the natural rate of groundwater recharge. This could potentially lower groundwater table in the region, but it does not. There are the following favourable circumstances that have prevented groundwater depletion in the region.

The district of Muzaffarnagar has an extensive network of canal irrigation, most of it unlined. The seepage from these canals, their distributories, minors and field channels, along with field percolation from canal-irrigated fields, constitutes a major source of groundwater supply of the district. The total recharge from all sources is placed at about 1185 million cubic metres by the Groundwater Directorate of U.P. As on April 1, 1981, hardly half of this groundwater had been exploited. There were actually 45,000 private tubewells in operation in the district during 1981-82, and NABARD report mentions half as many more tubewells could be set up without disturbing the groundwater balance of the district. Anyway, one may say that the unutilised portion of the groundwater potential is one of canal origin. Thus, canal irrigation both raises the number of sustainable tubewells and also prevents a permanent lowering of the water table in the area. Finally, the tubewell investors have done social good by doing vertical drainage in the canal command — the value of this social benefit is equal to the averted cost of horizontal drainage (Chawla and Sharma, 1984) have shown that the cost of preventing the seepage through canal lining is a less cost-effective option than through draining with tubewells). These facts would justify subsidies in the development of groundwater irrigation within canal commands.

REVISED PICTURE OF RETURNS

The altered picture of returns from tubewell investment is shown in Table 3. These estimates are worked out on the assumption that the cost of family labour is as much as that of hired labour. This being an unrealistic assumption in the case of small farmers, I have mentioned

Table 3

Revised Estimates of Income Benefits from a Tubewell, 1981-82

Tubewell/Farmer Category	*On-farm Benefits*	*Incidental Benefits*	*Total Benefits*
	(..............	*Rupees per tubewell*	...............)
I. ELECTRIC TWs			
1. Small farmers	1908	2422	4330
	(3030)		(5452)
2. Other farmers	7055	2057	9112
3. All farmers	4971	2219	7190
II. DIESEL TWs			
1. Small farmers	1659	623	2282
	(2553)		(3176)
2. Other farmers	4302	290	4592
3. All farmers	2835	470	3305
III. AGGREGATE	3866	1314	5180

in parentheses the estimates based on the extreme assumption that the opportunity cost of family labour is nil for such farmers. Thus, for small farmers the annual returns are in the approximate range of Rs 4300-5500 when they go in for electric tubewells, each costing about Rs 15,000 at 1981-82 prices. In the absence of rural electrification they have to opt for diesel-driven tubewells, each costing about Rs 10,000 at 1981-82 prices—NABARD has erred in presuming that each diesel tubewell in the sample, installed at historical cost of Rs 7452, would cost Rs 15,000 at 1981-82 prices. Such a tubewell is likely to augment a small farmer's income by about Rs 2300–3200 annually.

Without reckoning with depreciation charge, gross rate of return on the tubewell investment, the increased income constitutes 23 to 32 per cent of the private investment in a diesel tubewell by a small farmer, about 5 to 6 percentage points below the corresponding gross rate of return on an electric tubewell. This differential in rate of return in the case of a large farmer is much higher, 61 per cent for diesel tubewell option.

The rates of return in respect of electric tubewells contract sharply when the hidden subsidy in electricity is deducted from the income benefits. With this deduction, the gross rate of return shrinks to 12 per cent for small farmers and 42 per cent for the other farmers. Since the depreciation charge averages about 6 per cent of the investment cost of an electric tubewell, the net rate of return for small farmers (net of depreciation cost and electricity subsidy) becomes well below the institutional rate of interest on long term loans for farmers. Thus the viability of a private investment in an electric tubewell for a small farmer hinges vitally on the subsidy in rural power for pump irrigation. Only medium and large farmers can earn a net rate of return that is above the rate of interest on institutional loans. In fact, they can earn, on the average, about 22 per cent rate of return from tubewell investment even when they do not derive any incidental benefits from their electric tubewells. This shows that a private tubewell, in the ultimate analysis, is not all that high rate of return investment option from the viewpoint of the economy as a whole — this was so in the initial stages of 'green revolution' when tubewell owners minted money by selling wheat in the HYV seed market. Nor is it a low cost option from the macro angle, a point that is not fully grasped by the champions of groundwater irrigation cause.

Concluding Remarks

For a variety of reasons, the Indian water planners are keen to promote groundwater development within canal commands — what a contrast to the pre-Independence days when well irrigation within the canal areas was positively discouraged by the then canal administrators. To begin with, such well irrigation provides the much-needed drainage to the canal system, thereby minimising investments in horizontal drainage to keep waterlogging-salinity problems at bay. Second, the seeped-in canal waters are put to good economic use by well owners. Third, the wells and tubewells enable canal farmers to better cope with the inadequacies of a large canal network, thereby improving productivity of canal irrigation.

It is now being increasingly realised that canal irrigators are not likely to invest in well irrigation if they do not experience acute scarcity of water, a condition that is admirably fulfilled in a protective canal. In non-protective canals (loosely called productive canals), the possibility of groundwater development under private aegis is minimal. Here, two exigencies can give rise to groundwater development. One is that of farmers in the tail reaches failing to get their due share of canal water, and thus deciding to go in for well irrigation. The second one stems from restrictive practices of a canal e.g., declaring dry and wet crop zones;

crop zoning for annual crops like sugarcane; restricting canal flows to one or two seasons in a year; etc.

Irrespective of how water scarcity comes to arise, one problem area is the small and marginal farmers. Such farmers may find it uneconomic to invest in their own wells. In this context, we need to study the rise of market in groundwater.

NOTE 1

INDIRECT INCOME BENEFITS FROM A TUBEWELL

The purpose of this note is two-fold: (*i*) to appraise the firmness of the NABARD data and methodology in respect of indirect or incidental benefits from a tubewell investment and (*ii*) to offer more firm estimates in this regard. In what follows, we first review the estimates with regard to the incidental benefits from cane crushing. Next we take up the value of benefits from wheat threshing and sale of surplus tubewell water.

CANE CRUSHING

Only some owners of electric tubewells (13 out of 42) used their electric motors to crush cane for gur-making purpose. The annual use of motor for this purpose averaged 400 hours in respect of the seven small farmers and about 600 hours for the six large farmers. Such incidental use is valued in the NABARD report at Rs 9,500 per small farmer and Rs 8,200 per large farmer. One is intrigued why the value of the benefit is higher for smaller farmers who used the motor for shorter duration for crushing purpose. This calls for an examination of the methods used in the report in putting a monetary value on the use of tubewell motor for cane crushing activity.

In the Annexure III of NABARD report are spelt out the details about the economics of a small-scale gur-making unit producing 800 quintals of gur in a single working season of 200 days and daily working of 12 hours. The unit uses both electric and diesel power for crushing purpose — 1400 hours of diesel engine and 1000 hours of electric motor. It is not mentioned why twin energy drive is needed for the cane crusher. Most probably, the intermittent power supply in the U.P. countryside supply necessitates the use of a diesel engine whenever there is an electric shutdown, so as to maintain continuity in the processing work. Normally, a farmer-enterpreneur would maximise use of electric motor and minimise the use of diesel engine because his electricity charges, thanks to flat power tariff, are invariant with the quantum of electricity use, whereas his diesel oil bill is almost proportional to the running hours of the diesel engine (about Rs 7.75 per running hour). In this optimisation, he is, however, hampered by two constraints, one external and the other quite internal to him.

The irregular and insufficient position of electricity supply during peak agricultural season is an external constraint which can disrupt the seasonal gur-making activity. If the same motor is to help in on-farm irrigation also, its use for gur processing is further constrained, as the farmer has to resolve, now and then a basic conflict in his two demands. The processing season for gur (October-May), a dry season of the agricultural year, coincides with his irrigation needs for wheat and sugarcane. He is bound to give precedence to waterlifting over cane crushing. No wonder, then, the sample tubewell owners could use 400 to 600 hours of motor time in cane crushing, even though power supply was probably available to them for over 1000 hours during the gur-making period. In such a situation, either they could curtail their working season of gur-making from 2400 to 1800-2000 hours, or use their diesel sets for 1800-2000 hours instead of 1400 hours so as to maintain their gur-making activity. In either case, their profits from gur-making are adversely affected. Which of the two options is more economical? It is argued in what follows that the use of diesel is a better option.

Based on the data given in the NABARD report one can compute the additional costs of using diesel set for 400 and 600 hours, respectively. These are about Rs 3100 and Rs 4650, respectively. On the other hand, not working the gur unit for these durations implies lesser gur production by 133 quintals and 200 quintals, respectively. These foregone outputs carry values of Rs 23,300 and Rs 35,000 respectively. Reckoning with corresponding savings in avoidable costs on account of sugarcane cost (Rs 13,340 and Rs 20,000, respectively) and labour charges (wages are paid on a piece rate system, i.e. Rs 15 per quintal of gur), the values of reduction in profits are Rs 8,000 and Rs 12,000 respectively. These being more than the corresponding additional costs of diesel engine use, the tubewell owners are likely to opt for extra running of diesel engine instead of curtailing gur output. In that case, the value of using electric motor of the tubewell for cane crushing is equal to the averted cost of using diesel engine for the same period. On this logic, the incidental benefit amounts to Rs 3100 for 400 hours of running of electric motor by a small farmer, and Rs 4650 for 600 running hours of motor by the category of other farmers. Thus, NABARD has over-estimated these benefits by 206 per cent (by Rs 6,400) for small farmers, and by 76 per cent (by Rs 3,500) for other farmers. Therefore, its estimates of benefits from cane crushing need revision as follows:

		NABARD estimate	*Revised estimate*
1.	Average for 17 sample small farmers owning electric TWs	Rs. 3,913	Rs 1,276
2.	Average for 25 sample other farmers owning electric TWs	Rs 1,967	Rs 1,116
3.	Average for 42 sample electric TWs	Rs 2,755	Rs 1,181
4.	Average for all 87 sample TWs	Rs 1,355	Rs 570

Our appraisal shows that the NABARD assessment of incidental benefits of investment in an electric tubewell is *ceteris paribus* overdone by about Rs 2600 in the case of small farmers, Rs 850 in the case of other farmers, and Rs 1575 in the case of all electric tubewell owners. The main reason behind this over-assessment is the faulty approach, whereby profits from gur-making are allocated to tubewell in proportion to the share of its motor in the total working duration of a gur unit. As a result, the returns from investments in gur-making enterprise are partly credited to the tubewell investment.

THRESHING AND WATER SELLING

We first look into the threshing aspect. To the extent threshing of one's farm produce is concerned, the benefit on this account is already taken care of while computing on-farm net output benefits of tubewell irrigation. The problem here is to put a monetary value on the motor/engine hours used for custom service. For this purpose, NABARD looked into the economics of custom service in threshing in the survey area. Hiring rate for a wheat thresher in 1981-82 was Rs 9 per quintal of threshed wheat (3 quintals of wheat were threshed in one hour). Assuming (*i*) zero cost for the use of electric motor and Rs 7.75 per hour for diesel engine and (*ii*) labour charges at Rs 2.50/hour, NABARD values the hours used in wheat threshing at the rate of Rs 24.50 per hour for electric tubewell owners and Rs 16.75 per hour for diesel tubewell owners. Hence, its following estimates of incidental benefits (implied number of hours per tubewell are shown in brackets).

Diesel Tubewells	
1. small farmers	Rs 193 (11 hours)
2. other farmers	Rs 139 (8 hours)
3. all farmers	Rs 169 (10 hours)
Electric Tubewells	
4. small farmers	Rs 942 (38 hours)
5. other farmers	Rs 1053 (43 hours)
6. all farmers	Rs 1008 (41 hours)
All Tubewells	Rs 574 (25 hours)

While the benefits for diesel tubewell owners are of marginal significance, these are of considerable importance for the electric tubewell owners. But these are somewhat overassessed as no attempt has been made to separate these into two portions: (1) those from the investment in the threshing machine and (2) the ones from the investment in the tubewell. If these joint benefits, being incidental to the investment in both the thresher and the electric motor/engine, are separated in proportion to the investments in thresher and electric motor/engine, one can apportion them in two parts. On this reckoning, let us compare the two investments.

According to the NABARD report, the sample farmers acquired 28 more threshers after the tubewell installation, which at 1981-82 prices were worth of Rs 86,000. When the average price of a thresher is of the order of Rs 3100, the corresponding sample prices for an electric motor (Rs 2737) and a diesel engine (Rs 3573) are of comparable magnitude. It is thus fair to apportion the income from joint investment in a thresher-cum-prime mover into two equal parts. By this procedure, the income benefit from threshing for all electric tubewell owners appears over-assessed by about Rs 500 per farmer—the corresponding over-assessment for diesel tubewell owners is about Rs 85.

As for the realised benefits from water selling business, the NABARD evaluation in the case of electric tubewell owners has erred on the lower side. This undervaluation has arisen because the net price for sold water, namely, Rs 2,51 per running hour, is lower than that for owners of diesel tubewells, namely, Rs 3.51 per running hour. This calls for a probe, more so when the actual water discharging capacity of the two categories of the sample tubewells is the same. The selling rate was Rs 4.00 per hour for electric tubewells as compared to Rs 8.00 for diesel tubewells. In netting the rate for the operational cost, NABARD has erred in using the average instead of the marginal cost of operation of a tubewell. While the marginal and the average cost are almost the same for diesel tubewells, it is not so for electric tubewells whenever their owners pay the electricity bill on the basis of flat, fixed tariff linked to horse power of the tubewell motor only. In this situation, the marginal cost is almost nil — at most, it can be placed at 18 paise per hour of tubewell operation if we consider the non-energy portion of the operational cost to be of perfectly variable nature. Thus, the correct net price for electric tubewell water is anywhere between Rs 3.82 anf Rs 4.00 per hour, perceptibly more than the corresponding net price of Rs 3.35/hour for diesel tubewells.

It appears that the correct net price for electric tubewells is at least 50 per cent higher than the one used in the NABARD study. The underestimation in this case, however, is less than the corresponding overestimation in benefits from threshing activity. On the whole, incidental benefits from tubewell investment are overassessed in the NABARD report. The revised values, alongwith the NABARD estimates in parentheses, are given in Table 4. Whereas the over-assessment is of a marginal nature in the case of owners of diesel tubewells, it is quite substantial in the case of electric tubewell owners, more so for small farmers.

Table 4

Revised and NABARD's Estimates of Incidental Benefits from Tubewell

Tubewell/farmer category	*Cane crushing Rs*	*Threshing Rs*	*Sale of water Rs*	*Total Rs*
Electric TWs				
1. small farmers	1276 (3913)	471 (942)	675 (450)	2422 (5325)
2. other farmers	1116 (1967)	527 (1053)	414 (276)	2057 (3296)
3. all farmers	1181 (2755)	504 (1008)	534 (356)	2219 (4119)
Diesel TWs				
1. small farmers	–	97 (193)	526	623 (719)
2. other farmers	–	70 (139)	220	290 (359)
3. all farmers	–	85 (169)	385	470 (554)
All TWs	570 (1355)	287 (574)	457 (378)	1314 (2307)

Note: Figures in brackets pertain to NABARD's estimates.

NOTE II

ESTIMATES OF ELECTRICITY SUBSIDY AND COST OF RURAL ELECTRIFICATION PER TUBEWELL.

At the outset, it is necessary to point out that estimates in this note lack firmness. At best, these have some indicative value, so as to underline the harsh fact that the true resource cost, both in capital cost and operational cost terms, of electric pumpsets used in groundwater irrigation in India is far more than reported in survey data on electric pumpsets/tubewells.

ELECTRICITY SUBSIDY

In the NABARD sample, the annual recurring cost on account of electricity charges for an electric tubewell amounts to Rs 1,355. Though it is about 10 per cent lower for small farmers vis-a-vis other farmers, it bears no definite relation with the quantum of electricity consumption or annual working duration of tubewell - in the sample, the annual running hours for an electric tubewell averaged one-third more for other farmers than for small farmers. This fixity as well as unavoidability in the variable cost is due to the prevalence of fixed flat tariff of Rs 15 per horse power (hp) per month: Rs 1,020 for 5 hp motor, Rs 1,470 for 7.5 hp motor, Rs 1,560 for 8 hp motor and Rs 1,920 for 10 hp motor. The informed opinion is that the resource cost of supplying rural electric power for agricultural pumps is three to four times the price paid by the farmers. If we place it at three times in the present case, the subsidy would amount to about Rs 2,500 for a small farmer and Rs 2,800 for a large farmer per year.

It is worth noting here that these amounts of subsidy are somewhat higher than the corresponding extra energy cost of diesel tubewell owners (Rs 1,600 in the case of small farmers and Rs 2,400 in the case of large farmers). Anyway, the subsidy in the case of the small farmers accounts for a lion's share of his on-farm income benefits from tubewell irrigation (about Rs 3,000 per annum when imputed cost of family labour is excluded from the reckoning). In the case of large farmers, the subsidy amount is substantial in relation to on-farm income benefits of the order of Rs 7,000 per annum.

CAPITAL COST OF ELECTRIFICATION

The capital cost of pumpset energisation is not included in the installation cost of an electric tubewell. For the sample electric tubewells, the average horse power of the motor works out to 6.8, much higher than the needed/recommended one. To meet electricity needs of such a motor, a power generating capacity of a little over 5 KW is to be established in the power system by the State Electricity Board. Assuming a capital outlay of Rs. 3,000 per KW of generation capacity, the capital cost on public account comes to Rs 15,000 per tubewell, to which has to be added capital sum on account of transmission and distribution cost for delivering the power to the rural areas.

The whole of this capital cost cannot be attributed to tubewell irrigation. The sample average of running hours comes to a little over 1150 hours per electric tubewell. Assuming 45 per cent plant factor (that is, each KW of generating capacity is used for 3,942 hours out of 8,760 hours in a calendar year), one may say at least about Rs 4,000 plus a major part of the capital cost of transmission and distribution (presently reckoned somewhere between Rs 5,000 and Rs 10,000 per tubewell) have to be reckoned as the capital cost on public account. Thus, the capital outlays required for a single electric tubewell coming up the private sector are probably about twice the reported investment figure for a private tubewell on private account.

Chapter 8

IRRIGATION'S IMPACT ON FARM ECONOMY IN HIGH RAINFALL AREAS*

Introduction

There is spatial unevenness in irrigation development in India. A noteworthy aspect of this unevenness is one of negative association between irrigation and rainfall of a region. Thus districts with high rainfall have low level of irrigation ratio which averages about 30 per cent for the country as a whole. Historically, areas of low rainfall of the country have kept ahead of other areas in the rise of irrigated agriculture. This was especially so during the era of British colonial rule when public investment in major irrigation works went largely to tracts of low and medium rainfall conditions in the Indian sub-continent.

In the post-Independence period, public irrigation works have been constructed in all parts of the country. However, in the same period irrigation development under private aegis in low and medium rainfall regions occurred at a much higher pace. To some extent, this regional differential in irrigation development on farmers' own account may be ascribed to the difference in state and institutional support provided to the farmers for establishing their own wells and tubewells. Thus state plans for rural electrification and programmes for subsidised financing of wells, tubewells, pumpsets etc installed by small and marginal farmers made a difference to the rise of private groundwater irrigation in different states of India.

The question is: why have the State Governments (as well as Central institutions, like NABARD and commercial banks) in high rainfall regions been much less zestful in aiding the rise of private well irrigation? Did they perceive that investment in a private well is not an attractive

* The paper is already published in EPW, Review of Agriculture, Dec. 1988.

proposition in high rainfall regions? Is the perception linked to the feeling that demand for irrigation is bound to be low when rainfall is high? Or, is there a perception that, land holdings being small and fragmented in space, few farmers can overcome the problem of indivisible investments in a well/tubewell? Whatever be the reasons, a lingering feeling exists in the concerned circles (of agricultural economists, irrigation engineers and administrators) that returns to irrigation investment, both in the public and the private sector, are rather low. Because of paucity of expost evaluation studies it is not possible to say if this feeling is duly substantiated by facts. Yet, the three noteworthy factors behind the feeling are as follows:

1. As irrigation water is actually a close substitute for natural rain water, the need for its use in high rainfall regions is *ceteris paribus* much less than in low rainfall regions.
2. As the level of crop yield is already high (in comparison to low rainfall regions), the yield-raising impact of irrigation in high rainfall regions, other things being equal, is bound to be lower.
3. Income and production gains via the pure crop pattern effect, though so substantial in low rainfall regions, are likely to be restricted in high rainfall areas where paddy continues to dominate the crop pattern both before and after the introduction of irrigation.

Thus in the conventional paradigm for high rainfall areas the main impact of irrigation would come via the intensity of cropping effect, and far less from the yield and crop pattern effects. To the extent it is true that the capital cost of establishing irrigation works in high rainfall tracts are more, the force of the conventional argument about the non-viability of irrigation in high rainfall areas begins to strike us in a rather appealing manner. This appeal is reinforced whenever one comes across evidence of (1) gross underutilisation of irrigation capacity in a project located in a high rainfall area, and (2) the difference between irrigated and unirrigated yield of paddy in these areas being modest, if not marginal.

Scope of the Paper

The focus is on the impact of the Kal irrigation project on the crop economy of the Konkan area. The main parameters of this economy under evaluation are aggregate crop output, national income generation, income from crop enterprise, and labour employment. While doing so, the impact has been measured per crop hectare area of the sample households actually brought under irrigation during 1984-85. In this, the author has departed from S.G. Borude and Shobha R. Pawar's analysis in their study, entitled *Socio-Economic Impact Survey in the Command Area of Kal Irrigation Project*, as they evaluate the impact per household as well as on per capita basis. To that extent, the results presented here are of a supplementary nature to their work. Yet, two following observations are worth making here.

First, while they have not evaluated altogether the aspect of national income generation from the project, their analysis of the aggregate crop output impact is very meagre. Second, their impact magnitudes are seriously overstated because they fail to make due correction for the problem of beneficiary farmers' land endowment being about one-third higher than that of the non beneficiary farmers. This aspect of their evaluation is commented upon in a later section of this paper.

The author has refrained from utilising the impact results of a single project to conclude anything about the conventional wisdom about irrigation of high rainfall areas. For one reason, doubts about the viability of irrigation in such areas cannot be resolved with the aid of results for a single project. For another, he does not have access to the requisite data for carrying out the standard benefit-cost analysis. In fact, even Borude and Pawar do not attempt any BC analysis for the Kal project.[1]

Kal Irrigation Project

The Kal project is one among the few attempts to harness for irrigation purpose the huge waters of the west-coast rivers of the Konkan-Malabar region. It taps the waters of the Kunalika for the benefit of Mangaon and Roha talukas of Raigadh district of Konkan Maharashtra. Constructed at a cost of Rs. 78 million (revised figure of 1985-86), it was completed in the late seventies. Its live storage of 1.83 million m^3 (about 18,300 ha-meters) is designed for irrigating crop area of the order of 8,000 ha. Rainfall in the command area being very high (3 to 4000 mm per year), paddy is the principal crop of the area both under rainfed and irrigated conditions. The project planners did provide for some crop diversification by visualising 2 to 3 per cent of the irrigation protential absorbed in each of the following crops:

1. sugarcane
2. rabi groundnut

1. In passing, they mention on p.22 a BC ratio of 1.53 for the project. Most likely, this is an *exante* value that normally figures in project reports.

3. fruits
4. kharif vegetables
5. summer vegetables
6. rabi fodder

Yet, these crops were hardly to account for one-fifth of the total irrigated area, thereby assuring the continuation of the pre-eminent position of paddy cultivation in the area.

Measurement of Irrigation Impact

The measurement of the irrigation impact is usually achieved through a comparison between farmers with irrigation and those without it. To operationalise this approach to the problem, scholars gather survey data about these two categories of farmers. This is what Borude and Pawar do for the Kal irrigation project. To begin with, two categories of villages are selected, one benefiting from the project and the other non-benefiting. The sample of benefited villages in the present study is 14, constituting one-tenth of the benefited villages in the Kal command. The unbenefited villages are chosen from the peripheral region around the Kal command. These number 10 in all. Borude and Pawar choose 20 village households randomly from each of the selected village. Thus, the main sample comprises 280 households while the 'control' sample consists of 200 households. Details about the farming and non-farming activities of these sample 480 households were obtained for the agricultural year 1984-85.

A crucial assumption in the above evaluation approach is that the state of the households in the control sample serves as the proximate but hypothetical state of the command households for the survey period had they not benefited from the establishment of the project in question. In practice, this assumption is not so easy to fulfil, whereby biases in impact assessment do arise. *A priori* it is difficult to specify the direction of such bias in evaluation. A major source of the biases is the difference in land endowment in the two samples. Land being such a primary source of crop output — which in turn determines income and the level of use of farm inputs (including labour) — any noteworthy difference in this regard between the two samples affects the magnitude of the impact findings. To a large extent, however, the bias can be overcome through appropriate analysis. In fact, a simple (i.e., pro-rata) correction for area difference, as shown here in this paper, can substantially rectify the bias.

In the present case, the land endowment of the sample households from the command villages is considerably more than that of the control sample. This is evident from the following land statistics:

	Area per sample household		*% difference*
	Command	*Control*	
1. land ownership	0.74 ha	0.55 ha	(+) 35
2. operated land area	0.69 ha	0.52 ha	(+) 33
3. cultivated area (other than fallow and grazing land)	0.53 ha	0.43 ha	(+) 23

One main reason why the land endowment turns out to be higher for the households in the command area sample is the larger proportion of cultivator households, they constituted 73 per cent in the command sample as compared to 56 per cent in the control sample. Another factor is that comparatively more small and marginal farmers are found in the control than in the main sample of households. Whatever be the reasons, these differences in land are not project-related but the outcome of the very sampling process under which choosing a control sample as a perfect foil to the main sample from the benefited villages is inherently problematic. For, achieving comparability in land endowment and its distribution is just one aspect of the problem of setting up a control sample. Yet, one is likely to be much more near the mark in evaluation of irrigation impact in respect of income/output from crop enterprise if the measurement is per unit of land area than per household, or per capita. In particular, the measurement per unit of irrigated crop area is helpful in later estimating the total project impact in the principal parameters of the crop economy.

CROP OUTPUT IMPACT

Borude and Pawar's analysis is suggestive of a boost in aggregate crop output in the Kal command area as a consequence of the establishment of the irrigation project. In value terms, the aggregate output per sample household rose by nearly 183 per cent (vide Table 11.46, p. 227). In this rise, the output of the principal crop of the area, namely, paddy, rose even faster (207 per cent). However, these magnitudes of the project impact need downward revision for reasons of land endowment difference between the command and the control sample households.

If the adjustment is carried out with reference to the differential in operated area, we have to first inflate the without-canal figure of aggregate output/paddy output by a factor of 1.33 (or deflate the with-canal figure of output by a multiple of 0.75) and then work out the per cent changes. With this procedure, the revised magnitudes of the Kal project turn out to be about 113 per cent for aggregate crop output impact, and 130 per cent for paddy output impact. But if the adjustment is effected with reference to the lower differential of the cultivated area per household, the revised magnitude of the aggregate output impact becomes 130 per cent, and that for paddy crop output 149 per cent.

As a result of the above adjustments, one may place the aggregate output impact of the Kal project in the range 113-130 per cent. Though this is well below the unadjusted impact figure of 183 per cent, there is no doubt about the substantial step-up in crop output, primarily in the shape of paddy grain, in the wake of the project. A more than doubling of the output is all the more significant as it pertains to a region of high rainfall.

The entire addition to grain supplies is of HYV rice, mainly Jaya and Ratna varieties. Though consumer preference for local rice does exist, yet the additional rice did not give rise to any consumption or disposal problem to the beneficiary households in the main sample. One reason behind the smooth adjustment to HYV rice could be the largescale adoption of HYV paddy seeds by the non-beneficiary households as well—they allocated only 7 per cent area to local paddy in 1984-85. The price premium for local over HYV paddy of the order of 10 per cent proved unattractive to these subsistence farmers in comparison to the yield advantage of HYV paddy over local paddy: 32 per cent in the yield of clean rice and 17 per cent in the yield of paddy straw. In overall terms, the gross value of production, acre for acre, for HYV paddy turns out to be about one-fifth more than that of local paddy.

If we assess the aggregate output impact of irrigation projects with reference to one irrigated hectare instead of one farm household, we can easily work out the total output addition due to a given irrigation project, as also analyse a la Minhas-Vaidyanathan the three components of this output change, viz, the pure area effect, the pure yield effect, and the pure crop pattern effect of irrigation. With this departure from Borude and Pawar's analysis, let us proceed to assess first the output contribution of each crop ha actually brought under irrigation during 1984-85 by the Kal irrigation project.

In view of the fact that without canal output of the control farmers consists of paddy, 'nagli' (ragi) and some vegetables, the overall output per force gets assessed usually in monetary terms. This procedure of crop aggregation is quite suited for taking due note of changes in crop by-products as well. But since the true purchasing power of the rupee in India, thanks to the price inflation, is dated in time, one can abstract away from the problem of datedness of the monetary unit by the simple device of converting all diverse crop outputs into their equivalent outputs in terms of a single crop (jowar, wheat, rice, etc.). In this paper, we are using the rice equivalents. These rice equivalents are compared for the entire crop output, inclusive of the by-products, as also for the main products separately. However, for working out the yield impact of irrigation, the yield of by-products should better be left out lest confusion may arise. The sample areas and their crop yields are listed in Table 1.

Table 1

Kal Sample Area and Crop Yields for 1984-85

S No.	*Item*		*Main sample*	*Control sample*	
	Crop area:				
1.	Kharif HYV paddy		147.76 ha		70.48 ha
2.	Kharif local paddy		Nil		5.00 ha
3.	Kharif 'nagli' crop		Nil		10.59 ha
4.	Rabi HYV paddy*		132.52 ha		Nil
5.	Total		280.28		86.07 ha
	Crop yield (quintals/ha):				
6.	Kh. HYV paddy:	paddy	30.53	paddy	30.46
		straw	26.54	straw	24.90
7.	Kh. local paddy		–	paddy	23.00
				straw	25.14
8.	Kh. 'nagli'		–	grain	11.33
				byproduct	5.00
9.	Rabi HYV paddy*:	paddy	38.95		–
		straw	36.05		

* irrigated

Borude and Pawar give an estimate of about 9,714 quintals of paddy output by the 280 households in the main sample, consisting of 4,552 quintals from the kharif season and about 5,162 quintals from the rabi season of the reference year 1984-85. Rainfed rabi paddy being not reported at all by any household in either of the two samples, one may conclude that it is not a feasible proposition in the absence of irrigation — the source of irrigation must be copious and dependable as the water needs of paddy in dry season are both heavy and exacting. Given this perception, one is justified in presuming that the Kal project enhanced crop output by *at least* 5,162 quintals of paddy (nearly 3407 quintals of rice) which is the rabi season's output of the sample households in the 14 command villages. Their total irrigated acreage being about 133 ha, the output addition per canal-irrigated ha is about 2.6 tons of clean rice (3.1 tons of rice equivalents if the byproduct yield of paddy straw were taken into account). Even though it is truly a substantial number in foodgrains augmentation with canal irrigation, it requires some upward adjustment for the 'cross effect' of rabi irrigation on kharif output for the reasons given below.

The pattern of kharif season cropping in the command villages is superior to that in the non-command villages. Though this difference is not directly linked to irrigation factor (both being totally under rainfed situations), yet an indirect connection may indeed prevail in the present case. To begin with, the Kal project, by generating additional income from rabi cropping, improves the resource position of the beneficiary households. As a result, their capacity to raise more resource-using HYV paddy in lieu of local paddy and 'nagli' grain rises, not to mention their better capacity to withstand the higher risk of mono cropping of HYV cultivation in comparison to lower risk of a diverse crop pattern under rainfed conditions. Secondly, there exists the extreme risk of severe crop failure due to a prolonged break in the monsoon even in an area of high or assured rainfall. The existence of the Kal reservoir lowers this risk as farmers in the command know full well that the canal system is designed both for kharif and rabi seasons, notwithstanding their decision to do kharif farming under unirrigated conditions only.

The rainfed kharif yield, expressed in rice equivalents, is 20.15 quintals per ha for the command sample, about one quintal more than the corresponding yield for the control sample (19.21 quintals). Thus, each hectare of canal-irrigated area of the Kal command added about 2.7 tons of rice production, about 2.6 tons directly from rabi irrigation and about 0.1 tons indirectly from cross effect on kharif farming. By any yardstick, it is a noteworthy contribution of the Kal project. For one reason, it is over and above 1.9 tons of rice equivalents from the same piece of land under rainfed conditions. Secondly, it is somewhat higher than that of the Punjab canals. The total output addition from the Kal project during the single year 1984-85 appears to be of the order of 12,000 tons, carrying a value of nearly Rs. 29 million (without counting the addition to straw output). This estimate rests on the following two premises:

1. Each canal-irrigated ha raises output by 2.7 tons.
2. Total irrigated area of the Kal project in 1984-85 was 4,600 ha[1] (42 per cent below the created potential), the whole of it being used in the rabi season.

Rabi paddy under rainfed conditions being infeasible in the Kal command, one must be careful in analysing the yield consequences of the Kal project. More specifically, one must distinguish between the apparent and the effective yield impact on the one hand, and bear in mind the distinction between pure crop yield improvement and rise in overall land productivity. For paddy crop the apparent yield impact of the Kal, as would be conventionally computed by differencing the reported average yields for irrigated and unirrigated paddy, turns out to be modest. Excluding straw yield from the reckoning, the irrigated yield for paddy was 38.95 quintals/ha during the rabi season of 1984-85. This is 69 per cent higher than the unirrigated yield for kharif local paddy in the same year. But this percentage is only 28 per cent when the differencing is done for HYV paddy of the kharif season. Given the high weightage of HYV vis-a-vis local paddy under unirrigated conditions, the apparent yield differential due to the Kal irrigation is of the order of 9 quintals/ha, about 30 per cent above the overall unirrigated yield level of the order of 30 quintals/ha. This pure yield differential for paddy crop is way below the effective yield impact of the Kal project, reckoned equal to nearly 39 quintals of paddy.

Reckoning with both main products and byproducts, the land productivity per ha of sown area is about Rs. 4800 (Rs. 3950 per ha of operated area) in the absence of canal irrigation, but rises to Rs. 11,050 under canal irrigation (Rs. 8440 per ha of operated area). Thus, Kal project boosts land productivity by 113-130 per cent, the lower estimate being for the measurement on operated area basis. This more than a doubling in the productivity of land resource gets reflected in a rise in land prices. According to Borude and Pawar, the price for paddy land without access to irrigaiton was nearly Rs. 22,000 per ha, whereas the same for canal-

1. Borude and Pawar do not report any such number. This is worked out by the author by blowing up the irrigated acreage of the selected command villages, namely, 464 ha, reported by them in Table 4.1 (p. 24), by using a factor of 10. The basis for this factor is the fact that the sample command villages constitute 10 per cent of all the 138 villages served by the Kal project.

irrigated paddy land was Rs. 30,500. Of course, the price differential is incommensurate with the differential in land productivity. Why? Because of notional nature of land prices owing to few transactions in land? Or, reported land values, though based on actual transactions, are distorted by land buyers with a view to save on registration fees?

Distribution of Output Gains

An idea about the relative contribution of different categories of farmers to additional production of the order of 12,000 tons of rice per annum by the Kal project can be formed by analysing these farmers' relative shares in total rabi rice output of the sample beneficiaries, which amounts to 5,162 quintals of paddy (vide Table 8.12). There being no farm household with big landholding in the sample, the three categories of cultivating households, namely, marginal farmers (upto one ha), small farmers (one to two ha)and medium farmers (4 to 10 ha) together account for nine-tenths of the above output — the rest of the one-tenth is mostly from small plots held by agricultural labourers, artisans, traders, service men etc in the sample command villages. Marginal cultivators, each operating half a hectare of canal-irrigated field but being otherwise very numerous in the sample, account for almost six-tenths of the total rabi output. Since small and marginal cultivators account for nearly seventy one per cent of the total output benefit, Kal project may be rated high on the equity scale.

Marketed Surplus

How much of the additional grain output due to the introduction of the Kal canal irrigation did reach the grain market? At first thought it appears as if the whole of it became marketed surplus. This is suggested by the empirical finding of Borude and Pawar that paddy sold by the beneficiary farmers during 1984-85, namely, 5, 276 quintals, was a shade more than the rabi paddy output. The same is true for the marginal as well as small farmers. However, the marketed surplus may become considerably less than the rabi output figure when we reckon with the fact that these beneficiaries were selling a substantial part of their outputs prior to the Kal project. This is borne out by the finding that the sample of control farmers sold two-fifths of their paddy output — and one-fifth of their 'nagli' output during the reference year. Were we to assume similar sales by the beneficiary farmers, these would amount to somewhere between 1391 and 1757 quintals.[1] Even then, at least two-

1. The lower estimate is on the assumption of 6.10 quintals of paddy sale for each of the 228 beneficiaries — this unit estimate is derived from the control sample. The upper estimate is obtained by assuming that 38.6 per cent of kharif output of the beneficiaries, namely, 4,552 quintals, was sold in 1984-85.

thirds of the additional production from the Kal project most probably was marketed. This is a significant result for high rainfall areas which happen to be often areas of high population density and tiny land holdings: Thus the planners need not worry unduly that additional production from irrigation schemes in such areas may be mostly absorbed in subsistence of the farmers and his farm hands who expect their wage payment in kind.

INCOME GAINS

Profitability of Crop Enterprise

There are more than one ways through which the income impact of an irrigation project can be analysed. One of the common ways is to measure the additional output due to irrigation, net of the incremental costs of cultivation. In this approach, the valuation of farmers' own inputs of land, labour, and capital is a problem. Hence, four different cost concepts are used by farm research scholars, namely, Cost A_1, Cost A, Cost B, and Cost C, giving rise to four different income concepts correspondingly. Of these, the income based on Cost C is a measure of pure profitableness of the crop enterprise because this cost is inclusive of all paid as well as imputed costs. On this reckoning, the Kal project did transform crop activity in the project area from one of a loss into a profitable one. Whereas farmers in the control sample incurred a loss of about Rs. 130 from each crop hectare devoted to crop activity, the beneficiary farmers reported a surplus of about Rs. 290 per hectare. But despite such transformation in the crop enterprise due to irrigation, these farmers are not able to overcome the fundamental imbalance in their household account, though there has been some reduction in their amount of annual dissavings.[1]

In the Indian conditions, the imputed costs of cultivation on account of resources of land and labour are actually incomes as these resources are mostly owned by small farmers themselves. Thus the farm income computed on Cost A_1 is a pertinent measure of income for such farmers. Adopting this measure, one finds the following picture of income from various crops in the Kal command during 1984-85.

1. For the sample as a whole, the reduction in dissavings is by a factor of half. Separate statistics of dissavings by cultivating households are not reported by Borude and Pawar.

	Control Sample	*Command Sample*
Unirrigated		
1. Kharif local paddy	Rs. 1853/ha	–
2. Kharif HYV paddy	Rs. 2258/ha	Rs. 2669/ha
3. Kharif 'nagli'	Rs. 799/ha	–
Irrigated		
4. Rabi HYV paddy		Rs. 3811/ha

Using the relevent crop area weights (vide Table 1), the average income on Cost A_1 basis for the control sample works out to Rs. 2055 for each hectare of 86.07 hectares under cultivation in 1984-85. The same for the command sample averaged Rs. 6,087 for each of 147.76 ha of the cultivated area of this sample. Thus the Kal project nearly trebled farm income from each cultivated hectare. This additional income of the order of Rs. 4,000 is primarily due to the Kal project enabling land owners to raise an additional crop of paddy during the otherwise fallow rabi season. Further, nine-tenths of this rise is due to rise in intensity of cropping (from 100 to 189) due to irrigation. The rest of the rise in income may be attributed to the two following factors: (1) abandonment of low value 'nagli' during kharif season and (2) realisation of internal cost economies as the fixed overhead of depreciation charge got spread over enhanced crop area.[1]

Private BC Ratio

For the farmers, public canal water, thanks to its high subsidisation by the state governments, is a very profitable proposition. In the present case, the farmers in the Kal command realise an income of about Rs. 3800 from using canal irrigation for rabi cropping alone. For this use, they pay Rs. 180/ha as canal charges to the state irrigation department. In addition, they incur cost to the tune of Rs. 240 on account of carrying out the irrigation operation, for which about 25 mandays labour is reported by the Kal farmers. From the farmers' angle, the cost of irrigation is Rs. 420, giving a private BC ratio of nearly 10 (Rs 420 + Rs. 3800 divided by Rs. 420). However, the project BC ratio would be far less than this. If 10 per cent interest cost on project investment of Rs. 78 million is reckoned, the interest cost alone amounts to Rs. 1691 per ha actually

1. Our computations reveal that, despite increase in investment in farm implements by the project beneficiary farmers, the depreciation cost averaged Rs. 114/ha for the beneficiary households as against Rs. 163/ha for the non-beneficiary farms.

irrigated. Assuming Rs. 150 on account of repair and maintenance cost/ha, the resource cost of Rs. 1,841 adds to farm income to the extent of Rs. 4,000 (Rs. 3,811 + Rs. 180).[1]

National Income Generation

An interesting income concept is that of the 'national income' computed on the 'value added' principle, whereby only the material costs of inputs are deducted from the value of output. Thus payments to hired labour (as well as imputed family labour cost), being a source of income to labouring class, are not akin to material inputs. Likewise, other factor payments in the form of interest on capital and rent paid for leased-in land, as well as payments of land revenue tax, or provision of notional cost of farm management (as is made in the present study by Borude and Pawar), are all treated as income generation activities of the economy. The addoption of this national income approach results in an income impact of Rs. 5,560 per irrigated ha. This impact is the result of an investment cost of Rs. 16,900 per ha actually irrigated, yielding a capital-output ratio of three for the Kal project. The ratio is undoubtedly biased downwards.[2] There is no escape from the conclusion that it is a rather high capital-output ratio for an activity belonging to the realm of agricultural sector for which the ratio is usually placed between 2.0 and 2.5.

Distribution of Income Gains

On-farm income gains of a rural household are primarily determined by two parameters, namely, its hold of irrigated acreage and the on-farm income gain from each unit of such area. Not all the sample households from the project benefited villages reported access to canal irrigation. For the 228 households the farm income gains by category of households are listed in Table 2. Nearly nine-tenths of the aggregate income gains from crop activity accrued to the cultivator households.

1. This gives rise to a BC ratio of 2.2 Even this level may shrink (possibly to unity) if needed adjustment in capital cost of the project is done and this cost is brought to the 1984-85 price level at which the on-farm benefits are assessed. No such adjustment is being attempted here as our interest is not in the issue of viability of the irrigation investment.
2. This capital-output ratio is seriously biased downwards as the project cost at historical instead of current (1984-85) prices has been used, notwithstanding the fact that we have ignored income benefits of the project construction phase, as well as the secondary income benefits from the establishment of this project.

Of the total income gain of about Rs. 0.5 million from canal irrigation, more than half was claimed by the marginal farmers having upto one hectare of land holding in the project command. Together with the small farmers (one to 2 ha of land holding), they accounted for four-fifths of the on-farm income generated by the Kal project. These respective shares in total income generation are primarily traceable to inter-household differences in canal irrigated acreage, as the inter-household differences in realised on-farm income per unit of irrigated area (vide column 4 of Table 2) are rather small, more so among the three categories of cultivator households.

Table 2

Relative Distribution of On-Farm Income Gains from Irrigation

Sr. No.	*Household category (number)*	*Average irrigated area per household with access to irrigation (ha)*	*Average on-farm income per irrigated hectare (Rs)*	*Per household on-farm income gains from irrigation (col 3 x col 4)*	*Total income gains by household category* (000 Rs)*
(1)	(2)	(3)	(4)	(5)	(6)
1.	Marginal farmers (150)	0.50 (86)	3789 (99)	1895 (86)	284 (56)
2.	Small farmers (29)	1.17 (202)	3546 (93)	4149 (188)	120 (24)
3.	Medium farmers (10)	0.97 (167)	4117 (108)	3993 (181)	40 (8)
4.	Agricultural labour households (5)	0.29 (50)	4786 (126)	1388 (63)	7 (1)
5.	Other non-cultivating households (34)	0.37 (64)	4089 (107)	1513 (68)	51 (10)
6.	All house holds (228)	0.58 (100)	3811 (100)	2210 (100)	504 (100)

* Obtained by multiplying column 5 by the number of sample households shown in parentheses in column 2.

Note : (1) In the columns 3 to 6, the bracketed figures are relative values to the sample of 228 households.

(2) The income is computed on Cost A_1 as the measure of cost of cultivation.

The agricultural labour households claim barely one per cent of the total income from the irrigated crop enterprise. This is, however, not a worrisome matter, as these are essentially landless households which primarily rely on income from their labour power. So, these benefit from irrigation through a rise in demand for their labour power. In the sample, each canal-irrigated hectare gave rise to an additional wage payment to hired labour of the order of Rs. 1100 during 1984-85. For the sample 133 ha of canal area the total additional wage payments would amount to nearly Rs. 150 thousand per year. Whether these accrued wholly to the 34 agricultural labour households in the command sample is not a pertinent matter. In fact, this additional wage income accrues also to the following households:

1. Marginal and small farmers who offer themselves for hired labour to other farmers.

2. Agricultural labour households of the selected as well as the non-selected villages, as also to the non-command labour households.

On the basis of the data for 21 sample labour households from the command villages and 34 from the control villages, one finds an income difference of Rs. 1600 per labour household on account of wage earnings (Rs. 2079 in total income from all sources) in favour of the households in the command sample. Since this difference is almost 50 per cent of the wage earnings per labour household in the control sample (Rs. 2500), one may say that the Kal project might have raised the income level of the labour class by 50 per cent (55 per cent if computed in relation to total income). In relative terms, this income increase from wage labour is much less than the increase in farm business income (from crop enterprise) in the case of landed class, that is, cultivator households, in whose case farm business income rose by nearly 200 per cent. But the reasons given below would suggest as if the disparity in gains between labour class and landed class is probably lesser than suggested by the above computations.

The hired labour in both the command and control villages is priced by Borude and Pawar at almost the same wage rate, namely, Rs. 9.73 per day for male labour in the control sample and Rs. 9.72 per day in the command sample. So, this way one would not capture the beneficial impact of the Kal project on wage rates because of rise in demand for farm labour. The prevalence of equal wage rates both within and outside the Kal command area in 1984-85 is due to absence of segmentation in the farm labour market in and around the Kal command area. Thus, the wage income gains of the labour class are probably underestimated.

Secondary Income Impact

It is very difficult to work out the secondary income generation of an irrigation project, though this is not of inconsiderable magnitude in comparison to the direct income impact of the project. The magnitude of the direct income impact is the national income addition through the application of canal water to crop activity. In the present case, this amounts to Rs. 5560 per irrigated ha, of which about Rs. 3800 accrue to the land owner and Rs 1100 to rural households hiring out their labour power to the irrigators. Since neither land is exclusively owned by cultivator households nor labour power is solely provided by the agricultural labour households, it is important to remember that only a substantial portion of Rs. 3800 accrues to the cultivator class and likewise a substantial portion of Rs. 1100 accrues to the labouring class. Some numerical idea about these two proportions can be obtained if we have information on class shares in land ownership as well as hired labour power.

From our sample data we find that 89.4 per cent of the irrigated area belongs to the cultivator households. Thus Rs. 3400 out of Rs. 3800 of farm business income may be deemed for the cultivator households. Of the rest, about Rs. 360 accrue to non-cultivator households other than argicultural labour households who get only Rs. 42. Unfortunately, a similar break up of Rs. 1100 of hired labour income cannot be accomplished as we do not know the class-wise breakup of hired labour used in irrigated agriculture of the area.

Some idea about the additional income generation from the secondary impact can be obtained by analysing the income increase of the non-cultivating households other than of agricultural labour. Such households number 54 in the command sample, and 55 in the control sample. Their income difference, on per household basis, was Rs. 2945 during 1984-85. Some of this difference is already counted when we computed direct income impact. In other words, we may leave out of reckoning the income differences due to crop activity (Rs. 1393) and wage earnings (Rs 338). This leaves us with a difference of Rs. 1214 per household. Multiply this figure by 54 and then dividing it by 132.52 ha of irrigated area in the sample, we obtain an estimate of about Rs. 500 of secondary income from each ha of irrigated area. This is only a local secondary income impact.

Anyway, we get an estimate that for each Kal irrigated hectare the total income impact within the Kal command area was of the order of Rs. 6000. For the Kal project as a whole the direct plus local indirect income impact amounted to nearly Rs. 28 million in 1984-85. (Possibly half of this accrued to the cultivating class, and one-fifth to the labouring class).

LABOUR ABSORPTION IMPACT

How much additional human labour gets employed as a result of irrigation is proposed to be worked out here. The assessment is primarily of labour used in the crop enterprise. The survey data reveals that under unirrigated conditions the farmers in the control sample used following quantum of human labour for each crop ha in their three main crop activities:

	Family	*Hired*	*Total*
1. Kharif local paddy	104 days/ha	130 days/ha	234 days
2. Kharif HYV paddy	109 days/ha	129 days/ha	238 days
3. Kharif 'nagli' crop	75 days/ha	82 days/ha	157 days
Weighted average	104 days/ha	123 days/ha	227 days

The labour use per hectare of cultivated area under rainfed conditions is about 227 person days, almost equally divided between the two sexes. It is noteworthy that despite the land holdings being small, the use of family labour was somewhat less than that of hired labour. This comparatively high use of hired labour in farm operations may be attributed to the paddy cultivation, in which timely completion of transplanting and harvesting requires the use of outside labour. Anyway, with the advent of the Kal project mono culture of paddy is further strengthened, and demand for labour rising substantially, more so in the rabi season during which canal irrigation is used in the command area. The actual labour use per ha during 1984-85 by the sample farmers of the command villages stood as follows:

	Family Labour	*Hired Labour*	*Total Labour*
1. Kharif HYV paddy (unirrigated)	130 days	122 days	252 days
2. Kharif HYV paddy (irrigated)	156 days	130 days	286 days

The labour use to the extent of 286 days for rabi irrigated paddy is the additional use of labour due to the Kal project. This alone constitutes 126 per cent of the labour use per ha in the control sample. It is noteworthy that this additional demand for labour was met more from family supplies than from hiring outside labour. Reckoning with the marginal rise of 25 days in the kharif season, the total additional use of labour due to one hectare of irrigation amounts to 311 days, almost equal to employment opportunity for one person per year per ha of irrigated area. On this reckoning, the Kal project may be deemed to have created on-farm employment for 4600 persons.

Let us see how elastic is demand for labour with respect to crop output. Without the Kal project, the output of each hectare of land stood at Rs. 4800, for which 227 days of human labour was used. With the project, these two numbers rise to Rs. 11,050 and 509 days, respectively. Thus, labour use rises by 140 per cent when the land productivity rises by 130 per cent, giving an employment-output elasticity of 1.08. But the value of this elasticity is below unity (0.72) for hired labour. A look at the farm assets of the sample households reveals that the beneficiary farmers had made no marked attempt to reduce the use of human labour by undertaking the mechanisation of agricultural operations.[1] This may largely explain the emergence of comparatively high magnitude of the employment-output elasticity in the Kal command — the typical value of this elasticity is 0.60.

Main Conclusions

The farmers of the Kal command have not utilised canal waters during the kharif season. Since two-thirds of the Kal irrigation potential are earmarked for use during this season, their non-use gives rise to the problem of underutilisation of irrigation capacity. But thanks to the storage reservoir, the unutilised waters are finally used in the ensuing rabi season, a dry season when paddy crop cannot be matured without the aid of artificial irrigation. While in apparent terms there is 42 per cent underutilisation of capacity of the Kal project, in real terms all the harnessed waters have been put to productive use by the farmers. As the irrigation requirements of rabi paddy are several times those of kharif crops, the crop area benefited turns out to be much smaller than that visulised by the project planners on the basis of irrigated farming in both kharif and rabi seasons.

1. Except for 27 threshers owned by the 280 households in the command villages, no other farm machine is reported.

Each hectare of canal irrigated area augmented crop output by about 2.7 tons of rice during the survey year 1984-85. Knowing as we do know that this is over and above about 1.9 tons of rice output under rainfed conditions, the foodgrains production augmenting role of the Kal project is quite impressive. For the entire project, the additional production per year amounts to over 12,000 tons of rice valued at nearly Rs. 29 million. A major part of the addition is due to increase in intensity of cropping in the wake of canal irrigation. While the intensity of cropping rose from nearly 100 to 188 per cent, paddy yield rose by 30 per cent — there was little contribution from the crop pattern effect as paddy dominates in both pre and post canal situations.

As a result of the Kal irrigation, crop enterprise no more remains a losing proposition for the farmers. It is found that each canal irrigated ha added to farm business income to the tune of Rs. 4000. As the Kal water is supplied to farmers at a low price of Rs. 180 per crop ha, the returns to irrigation are extremely high from farmers' own angle — the private BC ratio is almost 10. From the viewpoint of national income concept, each crop ha under Kal project generated income of the order of Rs 5,600 of which nearly Rs. 1,100 accrued to farm labour class. As for the farm income gains, about 80 per cent of them accrued to small and marginal farmers who predominate in the area.

In the wake of a tremendous rise in intensity of cropping, labour employment rose substantially. For each canal irrigated hectare it worked out to an additional on-farm job opportunity for a single person for about 300 days in a year. Despite the small size of the land holdings in the Kal command, there was substantial addition to demand for hired labour. In fact, the employment-output elasticity in this area is a little over unity, but around 0.72 for hired labour. This comparatively high value of the elasticity is *inter alia* due to low level of mechanisaton of the sample farms.

All in all, the public investment of nearly Rs. 78 million in the Kal irrigation project has yielded impressive results in the shape of (1) additional grain output of the order of 12,000 tons, (2) additional national income of the order of Rs. 26 million and (3) additional employment for 4,600 persons on the farms itself. While the private BC ratio for the project appears very favourable, one does not have enough data to say anything definite with regard to social BC ratio of the project. Probably, it is a shade above unity. The question is: how can it be enhanced further? Through greater use of canal water for rabi and summer vegetables?

Chapter 9

WATER MANAGEMENT IN THE MULA COMMAND*

SCOPE

I have first drawn brief attention to the nature of under-utilisation of surface irrigation potential and then assessed the land productivity on canal irrigated areas, and the resultant increase in output. Both the positive and the negative external diseconomies of canal seepage on crop output are also measured so as to compare the output augmentation effect of improvement in well water yield in the wake of canal seepage, and the loss of output due to waterlogging because of seepage from canal network. In some sense, this assessment constitutes the main core of the paper, and the reader must bear with both the argument and the fine statistical details. Finally, productivity per unit of canal water is estimated, which is then compared with the corresponding potential level that should have been reaslised as per the agronomists' research investigations in this area.

THE DATA BASE

The basic data are culled from a detailed techno economic investigation of the Mula Irrigation Project carried out by the Water and Land Management Institute (WALMI), Aurangabad, and brought out under the title *Evaluation Studies of Mula Irrigation Project, Maharashtra* in April 1984 (in mimeo. form).[1] Cropwise yield data given in this report were the handiwork of the Gokhale Institute of Politics and Economics,

* Published earlier in IJAE (Dhawan, 1987a)

1. At the very outset, the author wishes to put on record his gratitude to the WALMI and its staff for doing this painstaking, field-based enquiry. Appreciation, if any, for this short paper must be credited to them also.

Pune, who were entrusted with the task of socio-economic survey of the Mula command. These data are used by the author to estimate the overall irrigated yield in rice equivalent units[1]: the equivalence scale among the crops is worked out according to the crop prices recommended by the Agricultural Prices Commission (APC) in recent years (1980-81 to 1984-85). The author believes that the APC prices aptly reflect the weights which sould be attached to different crops in a wider, national perspective. Instead of expressing the overall yield in rupee terms, as is often done in research studies (including WALMI's), rice has been used as a numeraire, because price inflation renders the value in rupees dated in time. Though any crop could have been used as numeraire, rice is preferred, being the single most important crop of the country, notwithstanding its being a crop of marginal importance in the Mula command. The rice equivalence scale used in this paper is al follows:

one kg. of coarse grains	= 0.66 kg. of rice (dehusked paddy)
one kg. of seed cotton	= 2 kg. of rice
one kg. of sugarcane	= 0.1 kg. of rice
one kg. of gram	= 1.25 kg. of rice
one kg. of wheat	= 0.8 kg. of rice
one kg. of groundnut-in-shell	= 1.60 kg. of rice

RESULTS

Underutilisation of Irrigation Capacity[2]

Mula irrigation project has been in operation since 1971-72, when an irrigation capacity for about 20,000 hectares (ha) was created. Estimates of potential created and utilised in recent years are as follows:

While the phenomenon of under-utilisation of irrigation potential is understandable for a project during its construction phase, the high under-utilisation in the case of Mula project is a bit intriguing for a tract

1. This scheme of crop aggregation is different from the other scheme adopted by the author elsewhere, in which the segment of food crops are added up in terms of their calorific energy contents and finally expressed in 'foodgrain equivalent' units.
2. In writing this section I profited much from perusing Ashok K. Mitra's article ("Under-utilisation Revisited: Surface Irrigation in Drought Prone Areas of Western Maharashtra," *Economic and Political Weekly*, Vol. XXI, No. 17, April 26, 1986, pp. 752-756) which is also based on the Mula Project — the data base is the same, as Mitra, on behalf of the Gokhale Institute, was associated with the WALMI study. I am grateful to him for responding to my queries immediately after the article was published.

Year	Potential created (ha)	Potential utilised (ha)	Percentage utilisation of created potential
1976-77	59,750	33,962	56.8
1977-78	60,730	35,710	58.8
1978-79	65,500	33,430	51.0
1979-80	66,360	28,733	43.3
1980-81	73,320	30,816	42.0
1981-82	73,320	32,104	43.8

with rather low (594 mm.) and highly uncertain rainfall conditions that are typically encountered in the Deccan plateau. The picture of under-utilisation is not that ominous when viewed in terms of volume of water instead of area statistics. Excluding the 'dead' storage capacity of 4,500 million cubic feet (mcft.) of the Dyaneshwar reservoir, the 'surplus' water in the reservoir towards the close of an agricultural year varied as follows:

Year	Surplus (mcft.)	Date
1976-77	1,713	15th June 1977
1977-78	3,579	21st June 1978
1978-89	487	26th June 1979
1979-80	9,403	Ist June 1980
1980-81	1,076	27th June 1981
1981-82	13,189	23rd June 1982

For the six-year period 1976-77 to 1981-82 the surplus reservoir water at the end of an agricultural year amounts to an average level of 4,900 mcft. The average availability of water (as per inflows into the reservoir) during 1976-77 to 1981-82 was around 33,700 mcft. Accordingly, the under-utilisation would work out to 15 per cent only, much below the corresponding average of 51 per cent under-utilisation signalled by area statistics on irrigation potential and utilisation. Even this level of under-utilisation appears to be condonable if one were to duly reckon with the harsh reality of Indian public irrigation works that storage works are usually completed well ahead of the water distribution network. As against the ultimate irrigation potential of the order of 85,000 hectares,the average potential created during 1976-81 was 66,000 hectares, signifying one-fifth of the contemplated canal network to be incomplete.[1]

Thus, from the viewpoint of utilisation of irrigation potential, measured in terms of volume of water instead of irrigable area, the rate of capacity utilisation of the Mula project appears quite normal, that is, nearly full utilisation exists, thereby implying that gross under-utilisation, as indicated by the conventional area approach, does not mean correspondingly high quantum of tapped water being left unused in the reservoir at the end of an agricultural year. What is officially reported to be left in the reservoir can be satisfactorily accounted for by the following factors:

(1) A part of it is 'dead' storage that cannot technically flow into the main canal system.

(2) Some of it is not usable (though it is part of the 'live' storage) for want of an adequate delivery system, as in an on-going project the reservoir capacity for irrigation is much more than the canal network capacity established for delivering water to the farmers' fields.

(3) In some years, inflow into the reservoir is much more than the estimated flow of a given dependability assumed in a project. To illustrate, annual water yield of the Mula catchment ranges between a maximum of about 66,600 mcft. and a minimum of 13,500 mcft., with the 70 per cent dependable yield placed around 29,000 mcft.

Impact on Crop Yield

Since the inflow into the reservoir is, more or less, let out for irrigation purpose, the interesting question to ask is how much crop output is augmented through the use of such water in farmers' fields. The rainfed yield for four grain crops, namely, jowar, gram, bajra and wheat, averages 2.76 quintals (q)/ha in terms of rice equivalents (3. 83 q/ha in foodgrain units, i.e., without reckoning with grain prices). With the advent of canal irrigation, crop yields rise substantially, along with the emergence of new crops like sugarcane and summer groundnut that are not growable at all under rainfed farming. Canal irrigated yields for principal crops, based on sample data for 180 farmers, are listed in Table 1, both in normal units and in terms of rice equivalents, along with area weights as per the overall crop pattern for canal irrigated area for the Mula command

1. A part of the Mula Canal command has been submerged by the downstream construction of the Jayakwadi project, necessitating development of new command area under the Pathardi Branch Canal of the Mula Right Bank Canal.

as a whole (and not the observed crop pattern in the sample farms) in the recent years.

The aggregate crop yield comes to about 21 quintals of rice equivalents per crop hectare actually reported under canal irrigation —it would hardly amount to one ton/ha if adjudged with reference to created irrigation potential. As usual, foodgrains as a group yield far less (about ten quintals in rice units) than non-foodgrains (about 47 quintals), of which sugarcane, the premier crop of the Deccan in the matter of remunerativeness (especially when grown for sale to sugar factories) exhibits a towering yield level of the order of eight tons in rice equivalents. Before assessing the magnitude of output augmentation through each crop hectare area brought under canal irrigation, it may be worthwhile to size up the irrigated crop yields with the corresponding potential levels that appear to be realisable as per the agronomists' expectations based on intensive farming under recommended levels of irrigation. Assuming that experimental yields recorded by the water management experts at the Mahatma Phule Agricultural University (MPKV) at Rahuri (that is well

Table 1

Cropwise Yields on Canal Irrigated Areas in the Mula Command, 1982

Sr.No	*Crop*	*Area (per cent)*	*Yield (q/ha)*	*Yield in rice units (q/ha)*
1.	Hybrid jowar (kharif)	13.9	15.0	9.90
2.	Hybrid bajra	3.3	15.5 (3.0)	10.23
3.	Paddy	2.6	17.5[a]	11.55
4.	Summer groundnut	11.8	15.3	24.48
5.	Cotton	4.3	10.0[b]	20.00
6.	Rabi jowar	23.4	12.0 (4.2)	7.92
7.	Wheat	20.6	16.0 (5.5)	12.80
8.	Gram	2.6	10.0 (3.6)	12.50
9.	Sugarcane	11.8	800[c]	80.00
10.	Foodgrains	66.4		10.28
11.	Non-foodgrains	27.9		47.29
12.	All crops[d]	94.3		21.23

Note:—Bracketted yields refer to unirrigated yields.
(*a*) Unhusked. (*b*) Kapas (seed cotton). (*c*) Surgarcane. (*d*) The survey report also contains yield data for HYV maize (30q/ha), chillies (10q/ha) and vegetables (150q/ha). However, their area shares in irrigated crop pattern for the Mula command as a whole are not separately known.

within the Mula command area) are the potential yields for the Mula command as a whole, one finds that the observed aggregate yield during 1982 was about half the potential level of 43 quintals of rice equivalents. (We return to this question of yield gap later in the paper).

Direct Output Augmentation

The direct output impact of surface irrigation works (canals and tanks) connotes additional crop output on lands that acquire access to surface water flows. A broad reckoning of this additional output is provided by the simple difference between aggregate irrigated and aggregate rainfed yields. Using the more correct procedure (Yirr-k.Y o)[1]– 'K' is a fraction indicating the extent to which irrigated crop pattern is oriented towards crops that need irrigation during the wet season, viz., kharif season for most parts in India — the direct output impact from each of the 30,000 odd hectares irrigated by the Mula project in 1982 amounts to 19.82 quintals of rice equivalents.[2] Since the output impact for each hectare devoted to sugarcane cultivation is extremely high in comparison to all other crops, the magnitude of the overall (direct) output impact of canal irrigation vitally hinges on the relative share of sugarcane in canal irrigated crop pattern. The land productivity of 21.23q/ha is underpinned with a relative share of sugarcane being one-eighth (as against one-twenty-fifth envisaged by the project planners while reckoning the irrigation potential of the Mula at 85,000 hectares). There are reasons to believe that true share of sugarcane in total canal irrigated area in the Mula command is higher than the reported figure of 11.8 per cent. Farmers do not get easily the authorities' sanction[3] for raising sugarcane on canal water. Raising of sugarcane is restricted to the earmarked few perennial zones of the command subject to the overall restriction that sanctioned area under sugarcane would not exceed four per cent of the total potential irrigated area in the whole command.

1. The logical derivation of this formulation is given in the author's other study, titled Studies in Irrigation Impact: Issues of Productiviy, Stability and Equity, (mimeo, now published by Sage under the title *Irrigation in India's Agricultural Development* (1988)
2. The value of 'K' parameter used in computation is around 0.51. Summer groundnut in the Mula command is sown rather late and thus spills over to the kharif. It is, therefore, counted as a kharif crop. With the value of 'K' being half, it matters little for the estimate of output impact if rabi instead of kharif is deemed the main wet season.
3. In Maharashtra, farmers make formal application (about a forthnight before the commencement of each of the three crop seasons of a year) to the canal authority for using canal water for a particular crop in the coming season.

Whereas the sanctioning authority for crops other than sugarcane is usually the section officer (a junior engineer), sanctioning power in the case of sugarcane applicants rests with the Executive Engineer. In connivance with the canal functionaries at the lower level (e.g., the canal inspector who regulates the working of the minors/outlets), farmers grow sugarcane unauthorisedly — such area may be indicated to be under other crops like jowar and maize for which canal tariff is very low in comparison to tariff for sugarcane.[1] Thus, if a hectare under sugarcane is falsely indicated to be under jowar in both kharif and rabi seasons (that is, one hectare of kharif jowar and one hectare of rabi jowar are recorded in lieu of one hectare of sugarcane), the overall output impact of canal irrigation gets understated by 0.62 quintal (i.e., by about three per cent) for each crop hectare benefitted by canal irrigation as per the official records prepared by the canal functionaries. It is, however, difficult to assess the extent of under-assessment of output impact of canal irrigation on this count.

Indirect Output Augmentation

Critics of Indian canal irrigation have a two-fold reservation about the output-augmenting role of major irrigation works, namely, (1) the step-up in crop yield is well below expectations and (2) a part of the step-up needs to be discounted for the loss of output from waterlogging caused by canal irrigation. Within a decade of its operation, about 6,000 hectares of land in the Mula command is said to have got waterlogged (including land getting salinity). In addition to loss of crop output from this land, one has to reckon with the output lost from land submerged under the Mula reservoir. As against these output losses, one has to take due note of the increase in crop output from groundwater-based agriculture in the command that is otherwise characterised by poor conditions of groundwater availability. In what follows we bring out that the overall external effects on crop activity have been very substantial.

Ever since the introduction of canal irrigation, the seepage of canal water through the unlined canal network — as also field percolation —has substantially added to groundwater availability in the Mula command, there by giving a fillip to private investment in dug well irrigation. (With the spurt in dug wells in the command, the conniving canal functionaries and unauthorised users of canal water, in the event

1. The irrigation tariff for sugarcane is reported to be Rs. 750/ha as against Rs. 50/ha for jowar and maize, being thus quite conducive to both the conniving parties in the matter of illegal gratifications.

of a complaint or suspicion by higher canal authority, can get away by taking the standpoint that the real source of irrigation is well water, and not canal water). This powerful beneficial external economy of canals on the private rate of return on investment in a dug well has been analysed in detail by this author in his recent book (Dhawan, 1986a). Here, I would attempt to take account of the output increase via the rise in area under well irrigation within the Mula command.[1] For this purpose, let us look at the water losses in transit, the main source of improvement in groundwater availability.

The project designers envisaged that almost two-thirds of the water released from the canal headworks, namely, reservoir, would reach the farmers' fields. However, much less water is reaching the farmers' fields. As against 80 per cent conveyance efficiency envisaged for the main canal (from reservoir to distributary heads), WALMI's earlier studies revealed 62 per cent efficiency. Likewise, the assumed conveance efficiency of 80 per cent from the distributary to the field turned out to be only 35 per cent. Thus, only 22 per cent of the released water reached the fields as per WALMI's early studies.[2] The reasons for the transit losses being excessive are complex. Yet, it needs to be emphasised that unrealistic assumptions in this regard lower the output impact of canal irrigation to the extent the farmers' irrigation application to crops falls short of the assumed level (which is usually as per the agronomists' recommendations for obtaining good, if not maximum, crop yields).

The available information for the Mula command indicates (*a*) substantial increase in irrigated area per old well existing prior to the advent of canal irrigation in the command, (*b*) substantial change in crop pattern in favour of sugarcane crop under existing wells and (*c*) increase in the number of wells in the command area. These output-enhancing effects can be ascribed to canal seepage. Under natural conditions of groundwater recharge, the gross irrigated area per well would have averaged around 1.4 hectare of which sugarcane would account for nearly

1. The effect of seepage from canal network can spill over to areas adjoining the command boundary, thereby improving well irrigation even outside the canal command. To illustrate, the old Pravara Canal had substantially improved well water-yield within the part of the Mula Left Bank Canal command. This trans-command improvement in groundwater-based farming is not being assessed here.
2. In the project proposal to the World Bank in 1979, the overall conveyance efficiency of the Mula system is proposed to be enhanced from 24 to 38 per cent by way of lining of minors and field channels.

5.6 per cent only.[1] This vital information is based on a survey of 1,320 wells that existed in the Mula command area five years before the commissioning of the Mula project.[2] Assuming that (*i*) crop yields found on canal irrigated tracts during the course of the socio-economic survey of 180 beneficiary farmers, conducted during 1982-83, would have been realised in the case of well water also and (*ii*) the crop pattern observed on wells in the mid sixties also holds good for 1982-83 without the Mula project, the average crop yield on 1.4 hectare under well irrigation might have been around 16.70 quintals of rice equivalents per crop hectare in the absence of canal seepage of the Mula project.

The Mula project, in fact, increased the average gross irrigated area per well and induced a sharp change in crop pattern in favour of sugarcane.[3] The study of 255 wells, located within the command of six 'minors' investigated in depth by the WALMI investigators during 1982-83, indicates that the average area per well was 2.6 ha,[4] about 1.2 ha more than the average for the 1,320 wells surveyed in 1966. More importantly, a little over 50 per cent [5] of the benefitted area was used for raising sugarcane. Now, assuming the same estimational procedure as adopted earlier in the case of wells in the absence of canal irrigation (that is, crop yields on canal irrigated areas hold good for the area benefitted by the wells), the aggregate crop yield for wells augmented by the canal seepage averages at about 51.31[6] qunitals/ha, about thrice the level that would have obtained without the Mula project. The cause

1. This percentage for sugarcane pertains to wells in the command of the Mula Right Bank Canal. In contrast, the percentage for 147 wells in the future command of the Mula Left Bank Canal (MLBC) was 52 because of the high seepage from the adjoining Pravara Canal.
2. The survey data emerged during the course of a pre-project detailed soil mapping of the Mula tract.
3. This shift in favour of sugarcane is to be partly ascribed to the location policy of the Central Government, whereby Maharashtra State became a highly favoured State in the matter of grant of industrial licences for setting up sugar mills. The establishment of these sugar mills, especially in the co-operative sector, smoothens the change over from less intensive to more intensive farming
4. As part of the socio-economic survey, 26 wells located in seven villages were found to be irrigating, on the average, about 2.8 ha per well that compares well with 2.6 ha for the 255 wells, despite the fact that four out of the seven surveyed villages were situated outside the Mula command.
5. This percentage is slightly lower for the 26 wells referred to in footnote 4-44.7 as against 52.6 for the 255 wells.
6. If crop pattern, suggested by the data for 26 wells were adopted, the overall yield would amount to 47.79 q/ha, about 7 per cent below the adopted level of 51.31 q/ha.

of the large hiatus between the aggregate crop yield under well receiving canal seepage and the aggregate crop yield under wells not benefitting from canal seepage is the radical difference in the crop patterns on the two categories of wells (vide Table II).

Table II

Comparative Crop Patterns on Lands Irrigated by two Categories of Wells

Crop	*For wells without benefit of canal seepage*	*For wells having benefit of canal seepage*
Sugarcane	5.6	52.6 (52.0)
Wheat	11.0	9.5
Rabi jowar	43.5[a]	19.9
Summer groundnut	–	5.2
Cotton	21.0	– (16.0)
Kharif jowar	–	1.8
Kharif bajra	–	1.6
Other crops	18.9[b]	9.4 (32.0)[c]

a. Including kharif jowar.
b. 2.5 per cent under fruits, 3.5 per cent under vegetables and 4.4 per cent under lucerne grass.
c. 16 per cent under fruits and 3 per cent under vegetables.
Note:— Figures in brackets are based on 147 wells benefitting from the Pravara Canal on the border of the MLBC (see footnote 11 on p. 144.)

As per the records of the Director of Irrigation Research, Pune, the number of wells in the Mula Right Bank Canal command area stood at 5,934 in 1971-72, the year the Mula project was commissioned. Thereafter, the number steadily rose to 8,585 in 1981-82, the annual increment in numbers being of the order of 265 wells. Thus, for the reference year 1982-83 we have to work out the enhanced output based on canal seepage in respect of (*i*) the old 5,934 wells and (*ii*) the 2,916 wells established after the commencement of canal irrigation. For this purpose, we make the following assumptions:

(*a*) Area irrigated per old well rises from 1.4 to 2.6 hectares due to enhanced water-yield in these wells.[1]

1. These estimates are somewhat on the higher side compared to the corresponding estimates (1.2 and 2.1 hectares respectively) worked out by the author earlier in his book from secondary, talukawise data for canal and non-canal irrigated tracts of Ahmednagar district as a whole.

(*b*) Overall crop productivity, measured in terms of rice equivalents, is boosted for the old wells from 17 to 50 quintals/ha due to change in crop pattern (in favour of more remunerative crops like sugarcane and summer groundnut) due to well water-yield becoming more copious in the wake of canal water seepage, especially during the lean summer season.

(*c*) Each new well established after the advent of canal irrigation irrigates annually 2.6 hectares, each hectare recording a productivity of 50 qunitals in terms of rice units.

(*d*) There were 6,000 wells existing in the Mula command at the time of its commissioning, and 3,000 new wells had been established by 1982-83.

Thus, canal waters that seeped through the canal network and the canal irrigated fields helped in the additional production of the order of 0.61 million quintals of rice equivalents during 1982-83 (0.237 million quintals from the old wells and 0.377 million quintals from the new wells). This extra output is a shade less than the estimated output contribution of 0.62 million quintals from about 31,000 hectares of canal irrigated area (43 per cent of the created potential of 73,000 hectares). In other words, each crop hectare under canal irrigation made a direct output impact of the order of 20 quintals, and an equal indirect output impact through canal seepage used for well irrigation in the Mula command during 1982-83.

If water losses in transit have proved beneficial for well owners, these might have proved deleterious for other farmers in case their lands got waterlogged. Statistics of waterlogging and soil salinity, compiled by the Drainage Division of the Mula project, do indicate increase in the incidence of waterlogging and soil salinisation within the Mula command — such area rose from 259 hectares in 1970-71 to 7,382 hectares in 1978-79 but declined to 6,604 hectares in 1979-80 and 5,656 hectares in 1980-81.[1] In addition, the danger of waterlogging exists on 23,000 hectares of land in the command, as water table under these lands was found to be between 1.2 m and 3.0 m below the ground surface in 1980-81. Assuming output loss at the rate of 2.76q/ha from 6,000 hectares of waterlogged land and 5,300 hectares of area submerged by the reservoir, the output lost comes to about 32,000 quintals, or to about one quintal per hectare brought under canal irrigation in 1982-83.

1. These statistics pertain to areas with groundwater table being within 4 feet (1.2 m) of the surface level, or electrical conductivity of groundwater being above 4.0 mm. ohms/cm.

It is remarkable that the indirect output impact of the Mula project is a shade less than the direct output impact. (The sum total of the two impacts comes to about 39 quintals for each crop hectare served directly by the Mula reservoir, a level that compares favourably with the potential expected value of 43 quintals as per the water management experts' research work).

I have demonstrated earlier (in my recent book) that incremental output from a well, as a result of enhanced water-yield following the introduciton of canal irrigation, boosts up the rate of return on private investment in the well in Ahmednagar district of Maharashtra from a low level of 13 to about 50 per cent. Were we to credit this incremental output from wells existing prior to the commissioning of the Mula project to public investment in this major surface irrigation work, we would discover a corresponding boost up in the benefit-cost (B-C) ratio for this project. The WALMI report indicates a B-C ratio of 0.455 for this project (the ratio could be around 1.83 if the assumptions with regard to crop pattern and irrigation potential were to be fulfilled). Since the indirect output impact is of the same magnitude as the direct one that has been reckoned with while computing the B-C ratio of 0.455, one may broadly infer that the effective B-C ratio for the project may be twice the computed level. The author has discerned some minor faults in the computations of the WALMI, and if due corrections are made for the same, the correct B-C ratio becomes 0.60 instead of 0.455.[1] Doubling of this corrected B-C ratio — so as to take care of the indirect benefits of the project — gives rise to a value that exceeds unity by 20 per cent.

Productivity per Unit Volume of Canal Water

As part of its micro level studies, a couple of plots that fell under the command of the six selected 'minors' (that portion of the terminal segment of a canal network from which final outlets take off to the field channels) were chosen purposively by the WALMI investigators who made painstaking efforts to measure the volume of canal water used in irrigation. The number of such plots (54 to be exact) is too small to assess cropwise use of canal water during 1982-83: 15 observed plots were under wheat crop, 12 under groundnut, 9 under sugarcane, 7 each under bajra

1. The improvement in the B-C ratio is primarily due to our having rectified the WALMI error of computing on-farm income benefits net of the canal charges for various crops paid by the sample beneficiaries. There is no need for such netting if benefits are being compared with costs — yet this is not an uncommon error that unnecessarily biases downwards the B-C ratio for irrigation projects.

and rabi jowar, and 4 under kharif jowar. Cropwise estimates based on such purposively selected plots, especially in respect of crop yields, cannot be considered to be representative of the entire Mula command. On the other hand, we lack cropwise information on volume of water actually used by the 180 sample farmers whose yield data, based as it is on a stratified random sampling design, is otherwise representative for the whole command. Under the circumstances, we first use the 54 plot data to get an overall (for all crops together) picture of productivity per hectare-centimetre (ha-cm) of canal water reaching the farmers' fields. This is then compared with the corresponding estimate which is obtained by assuming that one-fourth of the water released from the reservoir reached these farmers' fields.

The relevant data on the sample of 54 plots, given in Table III, reveal an aggregate yield of the order of 17 quintals in rice units per hectare. Though this entire yield cannot be attributed to the use of irrigation input of the order of 53 cm/ha, yet it is worthwhile to appraise the use of very scarce resource like irrigation water by relating output to this very input in a production process—the scientists describe this

Table III

Cropwise Yields, Canal Water Use and Relative Area Share for 54 Plots in the Mula Command, 1982-83

Sr.	*Crop*	*Yield (q/ha)*	*Canal water (mm.)*	*Crop area (per cent*	*Production (kg/ha-cm)*	
					Original units	*Rice units*
1.	Sugarcane	574 (in terms of cane)	1811	11.8	316.95	31.70
2.	Summer groundnut	10.23 (nuts-in-shell)	628	11.8	16.29	26.06
3.	Wheat	15.93	384	20.6	41.48	33.19
4.	Rabi jowar	11.35	216	23.4	52.55	34.68
5.	Kharif jowar	14.30	175	13.9	81.71	53.93
6.	Kharif bajra	18.36	208	3.3	88.27	58.26
	Total (1 to 6)	17.45 (rice units)	529	84.8		32.99

Note:—Individual crop means, obtained from plotwise data, are simple arithmetic averages without regard to area under a plot.

productivity of water as 'water use efficiency.' Since this scarcity of a factor may not be true at an individual farmer level (e.g., a small farmer with a land holding of one hectare would find land more scarce than water), the resultant figure of production per unit of water — which comes to about 33 kg. of rice equivalents per ha-cm of canal water — cannot be used to comment on the farmers' efficiency in resource utilisation. Yet, this ratio is useful from the social perspective in the same way as land productivity in Asian agriculture and labour productivity in Western, industrial economies are meaningful ratios between output and scarce factor of production—land in the Asian case and labour in the industrial case.

The irrigation releases from the reservoir have been well above the planned level, averaging 130 cm, 143 cm and 252 cm per crop hectare under irrigation during kharif, rabi and summer seasons, respectively —the corresponding planned levels were 45 cm, 60 cm and 97 cm, respectivley. The water received by the farmers is estimated to be 33 cm during the kharif period, 36 cm during the rabi period and 63 cm during the summer period. When we reckon transit losses to be 75 per cent, these depths are adequate for carrying out intensive irrigated farming for most crops except sugarcane. They add up to 132 cm for the whole year as compared to 230 cm recommended for sugarcane crop—recommended applications for wheat, rabi jowar, gram, cotton and summer groundnut are 40 cm, 14 cm, 28 cm, 73 cm and 91 cm, respectively.

Dividing the recorded volume of water issued from the Mula reservoir by the corresponding area irrigated by this water, one obtains the irrigation delta (at canal head) of 211 cm,[1] of which 25 per cent, that is, about 52 cm probably reached the farmers' fields. Adopting these estimates, the land productivity per hectare of canal irrigated area for the year 1982-83 can be placed at 10.1 kg./ha-cm of canal water released from the reservoir but 40.8 kg./ha-cm of water actually delivered at the farm-gate, a magnitude that is about 8 kg. higher than the earlier estimate of 33 kg./ha-cm - the difference is traceable to crop yield differential in the two sets of data. In terms of output impact analysis, each ha-cm of water issued from the reservoir helped farmers to increase output to the extent of 9.4 kg. from their canal irrigated lands and 9.1 kg. from their dug well irrigated areas, that is to say, about 18.5 kg. in all.

1. This estimate is an average for the five-year period 1976-77 to 1980-81, during which about 68,800 ha-metres (10,000 cubic metres = one ha-metre) were annually released, thereby irrigating 32,530 ha (42,800 crop hectares if counted as per the departmental procedure, whereby annuals like sugarcane are counted thrice, and two-seasonals like cotton and chillies counted twice).

However, from canal irrigated areas they enhanced crop output to the extent of 38.1 kg. for each ha-cm of canal water reaching them through the canal network. Interestingly, the Mula farmers' output augmentation of 38.1 kg/ha-cm of canal water reaching them compares favourably with the performance of some other projects serving low rainfall tracts where water is an extremely scarce resource. As per this author's estimational work, the additional output, measured in terms of rice equivalents per ha-cm of canal water, was 37 kg. in Tungabhadra command (Karnataka), 42 kg. in Bhakra Nangal command (Punjab), 26 kg. in Jayakwadi command (Maharashtra, and 22 kg. in Nagarjuna Sagar command (Andhra Pradesh).[1]

In addition to about 38 kg./ha-cm from canal water entering into the farmers' fields, the water lost in transit (159 cm out of 211 cm released from the reservoir) contributed to additional production on areas served by well water. This output works out to 12.1 kg. (11.5 kg. if output lost on waterlogged lands, salinity-affected lands, and lands submerged under the Mula reservoir is taken into account) for each ha-cm of water issued from the reservoir.

1. These estimates are worked out by the author with the help of cropwise data from a recent study, entitled National Cropping Pattern Study in Irrigated Command Areas, prepared by the Operations Research Group, Baroda(July 1986, unpublished). The comparatively lower impact in Jayakwadi and Nagarjuna Sagar commands demands some comment. Whereas Jayakwadi has been commissioned recently, the irrigation deltas for crops assumed in the ORG study are on the high side (presumably these are at canal head, and not at field level). Both the irrigation level and the output impact level for the five projects are as follows:

Sr. No.	*Project*	*Irrigation (mm.)*	*Output impact per ha* (kg.)*
1.	Tungabhadra	762	2,786
2.	Nagarjuna Sagar	956	2,151
3.	Bhakra Nangal (Punjab)	489	2,071
4.	Rajasthan Canal	586	1,930
5.	Jayakwadi	736	1,921

Source: Dhawan (1989 c)

* 1984-85 level.

The observed water use efficiency of the Mula command farmers using canal irrigation, reckoned at 40.8 kg/ha-cm, is found to be one-third below the potential level of 62.5 kg./ha-cm which is computed from cropwise yield and irrigation data[1] (vide Table IV) generated by the MPKV, Rahuri for optimal farming under good water management conditions. The potential level is not realised, partly because the observed

Table IV

Cropwise Potential Values of Water Use Efficiency in the Mula Command Area

Crop (variety)	*Water use efficiency (kg/ha-cm)*	*Crop yield (q/ha)*	*Consumptive use of water (cm)*
Sorghum (CSH-5)	130.40	60	46
Sorghum (CSH-8R)	102.50	40	39
Wheat (HD-2189)	90.50	38	42
Bajra (CN-74)	64.00	16	25
Kharif groundnut	54.29	19	35
Summer groundnut (SB XI)	34.29	24	70
Gram (PG-2)	76.67	23	30
Safflower (Bhima)	56.41	22	39
Cotton (Savitri)	42.85	30 (kapas)	70
Sunflower (EC 68414)	53.85	14	26
Sugarcane (0-7219)	511.11	1,150 (cane)	225

Note:—Yield and water use efficiency in original units, that is, not converted into rice equivalents.

irrigation use (52 cm/ha) was about one-fourth less than the recommended level of 69 cm for all crops taken together and partly because the observed yield level (21.23 q/ha) was half the expected value of 43.32 q/ha. While we cannot say much on the irrigation deficiency at crop level, the cropwise yield deficiency vis-a-vis expected yields is as follows. The yield gap is negligible in respect of bajra, which however is a marginal crop in the canal irrigated tracts. It is in respect of sugarcane that the farmers

1. Strictly speaking, the experimental data on water use pertains to 'consumptive use' by plants. For low rainfall tracts, this is a good approximation to irrigation requirements, as the field percolation of water below the crop root zone and 'effective' rainfall balance each other in the following identity: consumptive use = irrigation + effective rainfall - field percolation.

have been able to come nearest to the expected yield level, with a yield deficiency of 30 per cent as against 70 to 75 per cent for cotton and kharif jowar, 57-58 per cent for wheat and gram, and 35 per cent for summer groundnut (overall yield deficiency being 51 per cent). It is not my purpose to dwell on the various factors that are responsible for potential yields being not realised in the field conditions. Yet, one observation may be in order. In a multi-crop enterprise a farmer may validly favour one crop over another in the matter of allocation of scarce resources and his managerial care. It appears that sugarcane crop benefits unduly from such discriminating behaviour of the farmer in the Mula command. Were its cultivation to be curtailed for reasons of spatial maximisation of benefits from public investments, it may give rise to better performance of other crops in the matter of yield deficiency.

SUMMARY AND CONCLUSIONS

As per the conventional area approach, a little under sixty per cent of the irrigation potential of the Mula project appears to be unutilised. Such substantial under-utilisation of irrigation capacity has been observed in many irrigation projects completed since the commencement of the planning era in India in 1951, and it has been a matter of concern and enquiry in both academic and other circles. While the phenomenon of under utilisation of capacity is to some extent unavoidable in on-going projects, yet two factors have been identified, namely, (1) the observed crop pattern deviating from the contemplated one and (2) in-transit losses of the canal network being much more than the expected levels while working out the project design — the latter factor being primarily pointed out in the writings of the engineers/administrators. In the particular case of the Mula project, the farmers' desire to grow sugarcane that consumes several times the water used by other crops like jowar and wheat has led to an apparent problem of under-utilisation of irrigation potential. Whereas the estimated irrigation potential of 85,000 hectares is underpinned by a four per cent share for this crop, the actual share is thrice this magnitude — in terms of the observed crop pattern the potential capacity is reduced to 44,000 hectares only. To put it briefly, there is no serious problem of under-utilisation of the tapped water. Whatever waters are left unused in the Mula reservoir at the end of the agricultural year are accountable by the fact that the reservoir has been constructed to its full capacity while the water distribution segment is still to be completed — this lagging of the distribution system has been a common phenomenon in several reservoir-based irrigation projects.

With losses in transmission being twice the contemplated level, only about 52 cm out of about 211 cm per hectare released from the Mula headworks reached the farm-gate level. The water reaching the farmers' fields, though about one-fourth less than the needed level as per the water management experts recommendations, boosted dry farm productivity from a little less than three quintals to about 21 quintals/ha in rice equivalents. This step-up in crop yield amounted to an additional crop output to the tune of 2 tons for each hectare brought under the direct benefit of canal irrigation. The losses in transit, notwithstanding the waterlogging caused by them in certain portions of the command, proved extremely beneficial for well owners as the seeped-in waters boosted the well water yield, enabling them to irrigate more area and also bringing substantial proportion of it under sugarcane. This indirect contribution of the Mula project to output augmentation works out to be of the same order as the direct one. Net of the output lost from waterlogged areas and from areas submerged by the reservoir, the final tally of addition to farm output comes to about 39 quintals for each hectare of crop area officially reported under canal irrigation. This tremendous contribution of canal irrigation irrigation should be instructive for critics of canal irrigation — some bitter ones among them (like B.B. Vohra) can be labelled as anti-canal and pro-groundwater protagonists. Once we recognise the vital interdependence between groundwater and surface water, it is easy to realise that a major factor behind the much-eulogised tubewells/dug wells is the seepage from surface irrigation works (canals and tanks), especially in low rainfall areas like the North-West wheat belt and the Deccan plateau. Without conjunctive use of surface and ground waters, exclusive emphasis on the development of one source of water can prove unproductive in the long run.

Given the extreme scarcity of water in relation to land resource in the Mula command that typifies the vast Deccan plateau (hardly one-third of the cropping can be done under irrigated conditions in this region if the limited waters continue to be pre-empted by heavily irrigated crops like sugarcane and paddy), it is instructive to ascertain the output impact per unit of water. This impact comes to about 38 kg. per hectare-centimetre of water received by canal irrigated fields, a level that compares favourably with some other irrigation projects located in low rainfall regions of the country. Yet, there is scope for further improvement in this productivity. This is suggested by looking at the potential level of water use efficiency that can be realised.

The observed water use efficiency of the canal users is about 41 kg/ha-cm (overall irrigated yield of 21 quintals divided by 52 cm). As per the recommended level of crop irrigation, the potential magnitude of water use efficiency comes to about 62 kg/ha-cm (overall potential yield of 43 quintals divided by 69 cm). The gap between the potential and the observed water use efficiencies is partly due to a yield gap (51 per cent) and partly due to irrigation gap (25 per cent). Keeping aside the linkage between the yield gap and the irrigation gap, the yield gap at the crop level is comparativley small for sugarcane crop, which is favoured by the farmers in a mutli-crop enterprise in the matter of resource allocation but to the detriment of yield of other crops.

Chapter 10

ANALYSIS OF SURVEY EVIDENCE ON IRRIGATED FARMING IN ANDHRA, U.P. AND GUJARAT*

1. Introduction

While the production-augmenting role of irrigation in Indian agriculture is widely recognised, empirical enquiries into the actual productivity per unit of irrigation water are lacking.[1] The cause of this dearth is the difficulty of obtaining information on quantities of irrigation water used by farmers in their crop activity. Such information is seldom available with Indian farmers, as they neither pay for the purchased water on volumetric basis nor practice irrigated farming with well-measured doses of water *a la* water management scientists at the farm research stations. So, compiling such information through a routine sample survey is out of question for a researcher interested in examining the production impact per unit of irrigation water. And it is a very costly proposition to gather such information through special surveys executed with the help of technically-trained personnel. Evidently, without liberal funding and collaboration from scientists/engineers, such surveys are not possible on a noteworthy scale.

In the absence of field data on irrigation water, information on number of waterings done for an irrigated crop can be easily gathered from farmers, and thus used as a surrogate for quantum of irrigation water. This is exactly what we are attempting in this paper, so as to get some insights into the productivity of irrigated farming in India. Admittedly, our enquiry lacks spatial coverage as the survey data at our

* Already published (Dhawan and Satya Sai, 1987)

1. This is not to detract from the valuable experimental work done by the research scientists at the Indian Agricultural Universities and other agricultural farm reasearch stations.

disposal pertain only to the three states of U.P., Gujarat and Andhra Pradesh. Also, the data related to the mid-seventies, and the position today well might be different in some important respects. Yet, the data have been explored for the following considerations. Firstly, even such survey data are rather scarce, especially according to source of irrigation. Secondly, our analysis can definitely serve a useful bench-mark to any future work that may be based on similar data for any subsequent period. Finally, some of the results may be valid for the irrigated agriculture of the day in the three states.

2. Hypotheses

We propose to test in this paper a couple of hypotheses about Indian irrigated farming. It is, however, difficult to specify the logic of the hypotheses because economic theory in this realm has yet to emerge in a definite form. These are partly suggested by the conventional wisdom in this area, and partly by some earlier (unpublished) work by the first author. Anyway, the main hypotheses are:

(1) Lightly-irrigated crops, like pulses and oilseeds, are more productive than heavily-irrigated crops, such as sugarcane and paddy, in water-scarce regions when produciton is assessed per unit of water.
(2) Productivity of irrigation water is positively related to both chemical fertilizers and volume of irrigation.
(3) Non-foodgrains as a group are superior to foodgrains.
(4) Indian farmers overirrigate their fields, especially while using low-price, public irrigation.
(5) Well irrigation is superior to surface irrigation - a variant of this is 'private irrigation is superior to public irrigation'- in creating production impact per unit of irrigation water.
(6) Conjunctive use of surface and ground waters produces superior output results to those obtaining under surface irrigation alone.
(7) Productivity of irrigated farming based on water purchased from other well owners is less than that under one's own well.

3. The Data Base

The National Council of Applied Economic Research (NCAER), New Delhi, conducted a nation-wide sample survey of about 22,000 farm households to study the determinants of demand for chemical fertilizers in India. Selected input-output data in respect of irrigated and unirrigated crops for three states of Andhra pradesh, Gujarat and

U.P. have been subjected to further analysis by S.P. Pal in his recent book, entitled *Contribution of Irrigation to Agricultural Production and Productivity* (NCAER, 1985). The detailed Appendix II (pp. 95-108) of this book lists the basic data in a bivariate format, the two variables being crop and category of irrigation. For a given crop that is irrigated by a specified mode of irrigation, mean sample magnitudes in respect of the following six characteristics are listed in the aforesaid Appendix:

... crop yield per ha;
... percent area under a crop fertilized with NPK;
... number of waterings done;
... crop area relative to total gross cropped area of the state sample;
... irrigation ratio for a crop;
... NPK application per ha

Irrigation is distinguished by the following nine types:[1]

(1) Canal irrigation;
(2) Canal plus tubewell/pumpset;
(3) Private tubewell;
(4) Private dugwell equipped with a pumpset;
(5) Owning a pumpset and lifting water from other's source;
(6) Purchase of water from tubewell/pumpset owner;
(7) Traditional well;
(8) Tanks and ponds;
(9) Other sources.

4. Methods of Analysis

The sample size for each of the three states under study in this paper was nearly 2,600 for U.P., 1,800 for Andhra Pradesh and 1,200 for Gujarat. The complete design of the survey is spelt out in Appendix I of Pal's book. Though the sample size is pretty large for obtaining reliable state-wide estimates, we do bear in mind that the survey was designed with the primary objective of estimating consumption of the three chemical fertilizers (N, P and K) for the decadal period 1976-86, and not for studying the characteristics of irrigated farming for each state. However, this is no serious limitation. After all, irrigation and fertilizers are highly complementary inputs in the non-temperate climate of the three states. Yet, one must remember two points, namely, (1) marked soil-climatic heterogeneity within the states of Andhra Pradesh,

1. The authors have rechristened some of the categories of irrigation so as to make them more intelligible to the reader less familiar with irrigation literature. However, the serial numbers have been left untinkered.

Gujarat and U.P. and (2) the survey being not designed to compare the performance of the nine types of irrigation in each state. In short, differences between any two types of irrigation need to be viewed circumspectly, as these could also be due to sampling and non-sampling errors on the one hand and may be confounded by the intra-state heterogeneity factor on the other hand — S.P. Pal duly cautions us in this regard while analysing the differences in Andhra Pradesh. Our endeavour to conduct the analysis within broad aggregate of crops and sources of irrigation is partly conceived with a view to surmounting such limitations of the data at our disposal.[1]

It is imperative to point out in what respect our enquiry differs from that of Pal who partly based his book on the data base which we use in our paper. Firstly, whereas he concentrates on inter-source comparisons in respect of yield by taking up one important crop *at a time*, we cover all crops together. To attain the needed crop aggregation we have adopted the crop prices *recommended* by the Agricultural Prices Commission (APC). Aggregation of diverse crop outputs has been expressed in terms of rice equivalent units, for which the APC prices constitute the relevant price set. Under this scheme, one kg. of cotton (kapas) equals 2 kg. of rice; one kg. of chillies/tobacco equals 4 kg. of rice; one kg. of wheat = 0.8 kg. of rice; one kg. of paddy/coarse cereals = 0.66 kg. of rice; one kg. of sugarcane, = 0.1 kg. of rice; one kg. of groundnut = 1.6 of rice. one kg. of pulses = 1.3 kg. of rice.[2]

Secondly, we concentrate on broad sources of irrigation that have figured in the debates on irrigation in India. By combining the data for canal irrigation and for tanks/ponds, we obtain the data for surface irrigation works. Likewise, groundwater irrigation consists of the four categories: private tubewell; private dugwell equipped with a pumpset; traditional well and purchase of water from tubewell/pumpset owners. Conjunctive irrigation, though it covers (*i*) simply owning a pumpset, (*ii*) canal plus tubewell irrigation, and (*iii*) other sources, is preponderantly of type (*ii*) in Andhra Pradesh and U.P. Relative positions

1. Some crass discrepancies came to our attention during the course of analysis, especially in the case of cotton and sugarcane crops in the Gujarat sample. Many of these could be rectified. We hope these have had no telling impact on our aggregative analysis.
2. For a discussion on this scheme of rice equivalents, interested readers' attention may be drawn to first author's work (Dhawan, 1988c).

of the three derived categories of irrigation in the sample are given in Table 1.

Table 1

Share of Main Categories of Irrigation in Three States, 1975-76

State	*Surface Irrigation*	*Groundwater*	*Conjunctive Irrigation*	*All Sources*
Andhra Pradesh	48.9	31.8	19.3	100.0
Gujarat	17.4	77.0	5.6	100.0
U.P.	31.6	58.7	9.7	100.0

Thirdly, we try to bring into the reckoning the inter-source differential with regard to intensity of cropping effect of irrigation. After all, the conventional view of one source of irrigation being rated higher than another rests on the triple consideration of yield effect, crop pattern effect and intensity of cropping effect of irrigation. In the absence of source-wise sample data on cropping intensity, we take recourse to source-wise intensity of irrigation (i.e. ratio of gross irrigated area to net irrigated area), a variable having a positive bearing on intensity of cropping as per Dharm Narain and Roy's research into determinants of intensity of cropping in India.[1] Fourthly, Pal, unlike us, makes no assessment of yield or output impact of irrigation per irrigated ha or per watering per irrigated ha.

The incremental output impact per irrigated hectare is computed by the following formula:[2]

$$O = Y^1 - KY^\circ \qquad \text{................(1)}$$

where:- O stands for output impact per irrigated hectare;

Y^1 stands for overall irrigated yield per ha;

Y° stands for overall irrigated yield per ha;

K is a fraction indicating to what extent irrigated area is oriented towards crop needing kharif irrigation.

1. Dharm Narain and Shyamal Roy, *Impact of Irrigation and Labour Availability on Multiple Cropping*. IFPRI, Washington D.C., 1980.
2. The rationale for this formula, which is modified version of the conventional procedure of simple differencing (Y1-Yo), is developed elsewhere in first author's recent book (Dhawan, 1988c).

While overall unirrigated yield is assumed to be the same for all sources of irrigation in a given state, 'K' parameter is allowed to vary with the source of irrigation. The 'K' values for the three broad categories of irrigation are as listed in Table 2.

Table 2

'K' Values for Various Categories of Irrigation in Three States, 1975-76

State	*Surface Irrigation*	*Groundwater*	*Conjunctive Irrigation*	*All Sources*
Andhra Pradesh	0.93	0.69	0.23	0.71
Gujarat	0.73	0.55	0.73	0.61
U.P.	0.50	0.46	0.56	0.48

The field data on NPK application refers to fertilizer use per ha of area fertilized (i.e. it is not an average of all sample fields, including the unfertilized ones). By making the assumption that NPK fertilizers are used wholly on irrigated fields only, one can easily derive a broad estimate of NPK intensity on irrigated fields. This is achieved by first multiplying the reported intensity by percent area fertilized, and then dividing this product by percent irrigated area under a crop. Each kg. of fertilizer is valued equal to 2.4 kg. of rice for the purpose of netting out the output impact of irrigation for the added expenditure incurred on fertilizers following a change from rainfed to irrigated farming.

Finally, a few words about crop grouping are necessary. The dichotomy foodgrains-non foodgrains is well established in the Indian literature on agricultural economics, whereby cereals and pulses constitute the foodgrains group and the remaining crop categories (oilseeds, fibres, fodders, fruits and vegetables) comprise the non-foodgrains group. The same cannot be asserted about the distinction between lightly-irrigated and heavily-irrigated crops. One line of distinction is in terms of a crop requiring light or heavy depth of watering in a single irrigation operation. Another connotation is in terms of more or less water-using crops. In this context, pulses, oilseeds and coarse cereals are usually deemded to be lightly-irrigated crops, whereas paddy, sugarcane and fruits are considered heavily-irrigated crops. In this paper, we have opted for this criterion for categorising crops into lightly and heavily-irrigated ones.

5. Results Based on Total Irrigated Segment

Aggregate crop yield rises substantially following the advent of irrigated farming in each of the three states where agro-climatic conditions are, on the whole, not conducive for high level of land productivity under unirrigated conditions. In Gujarat state, where normal rainfall is around 725 mm and where groundnut, cotton and bajra are main rainfed crops, the sample average yield under unirrigated conditions during 1975-76 was of the order of 6 quintals/ha (expressed in rice equivalents) which rose to about 18 quintals/ha under irrigated conditions, an impressive step-up by about 185 per cent. In Andhra Pradesh, with a normal rainfall of 890 mm that is still not adequate for sustaining rainfed paddy (groundnut and jowar are the main rainfed crops here), the overall rainfed yield was of the order of 9 quintals/ha, which got boosted by over 125 per cent to 21 quintals/ha in the wake of irrigation. In U.P., which recorded a rainfed yield of the order of 10 quintals/ha because of its somewhat better agro-climatic conditions which permit the cultivation of raifed paddy in its eastern and the sub-Himalayan plains, the step-up in land productivity is comparatively lower, both in absolute terms (irrigated level –16.7 quintals/ha) and relative terms (67 per cent). That the comparative rise in overall crop yield in the three states, following the introduction of irrigation, is somewhat inversely related with rainfall level of a state is in harmony with the general perception of the discerning scholars of Indian irrigation - the first author of this paper found in an early study a negative coefficient of correlation minus 0.52 between normal rainfall and absolute yield differential due to irrigation across a cross section of eleven states of India.

Needless to add, the observed level of overall crop yield in irrigated agriculture is governed by a number of factos, of which the irrigators' ability (as well as inclination) to apply chemical fertilizers intensively is of crucial importance. This ability, in turn, depends on his resource position, his access to credit insitutions; availability of irrigation and its quality; his choice of crops and their varietal aspect; etc. Inter-state variation in overall irrigated yield is, in fact, positively linked with inter-state disparity in respect of fertilizer use and quantum of irrigation. More specifically, as against an NPK level of 99 kg. per irrigated ha in Andhra Pradesh, the corresponding levels for Gujarat and U.P. samples were; 63 kg. and 32 kg. Likewise, the number of waterings in Andhra averaged about 4.1 per irrigated ha in comparison to only 3.3 in Gujarat and 2.4 in U.P. These comparative statistics are set out below, both in absolute and relative terms (relative to Andhra Pradesh magnitude = 100).

	Andhra Pradesh	*Gujarat*	*U.P*
I. Absolute levels:			
a. overall irrigated yield	2115 kg/ha	1790 kg/ha	1666 kg/ha
b. NPK	99 kg/ha	63 kg/ha	32 kg/ha
c. No. of waterings	4.14	3.28	2.42
II. Relative levels:			
a. overall irrigated yield	100	85	79
b. NPK	100	64	32
c. No. of waterings	100	79	58

The formula (1) indicates that the output impact of irrigation tends to exceed the absolute yield differential due to irrigation to the extent crop pattern under irrigated conditions tends to be oriented more to crops of the dry seasons of the year (i.e. as 'K' parameter approaches zero). The sample value of 'K' is 0.48 for U.P. state, 0.61 for Gujarat state, and 0.71 for Andhra Pradesh. Consequently, the output impact per gross (crop) hectare of irrigation amounts to about 12 quintals of rice equivalents in U.P., and about 14 quintals in both Andhra Pradesh and Gujarat. It would thus be noticed that the inter-state disparity in yield differential due to irrigation is considerably narrowed when the seasonal orientation of irrigation in a state is duly reckoned with. This noteworthy result emerges effectively when relative positions of U.P. and Gujarat vis-a-vis Andhra Pradesh (the state with the highest yield differential between irrigated and unirrigated farming) are compared as shown below:

	A.P.	*Gujarat*	*U.P.*
1. Relative position in respect of yield differential	1.00	0.99	0.56
2. Relative position in respect of output impact for irrigated ha	1.00	0.99	0.83

In each of the three states, irrigation resource is quite scarce in relation to land resource. Therefore, it is quite meaningful to examine to what extent irrigation water is used so as to achieve maximum output impact per unit of water resource. From this perspective, the U.P. farmer overtakes both the Andhra and the Gujarat farmer. The comparative magnitudes for the three states, which are set out below, are suggestive of an inverse relationship between output impact and irrigation use, a relationship that is consistent with movement along yield-irrigation response curve for a single crop of given variety. In short, the law of variable factor proportions appears to operate even for aggregate data across 3 states.

	A.P.	*Gujarat*	*U.P.*
1. Average no. of waterings	4.14	3.28	2.42
2. Average output impact per irrigated ha (kg of rice units)	1426	1408	1187
3. Output impact of irrigation per watering (kg. of rice units/ha)	344	429	491

Needless to add, the above-mentioned estimates of productivity of irrigation water, as conveyed by the measure output impact per watering of irrigation, do not connote the contribution of irrigation input alone but of all factors whose use in production rises in the wake of a changeover from dry to irrigated farming. Of all these factors, the incremental step-up is most marked in the case of chemical fertilizers. Assuming (*a*) the entire amount of NPK application on irrigated areas consitutes an incremental usage due to irrigation (i.e. we assume tacitly that the intensity of NPK use is nil in rainfed farming), and (*b*) deducting its value in rice equivalents from the output impact of irrigation, one gets the following estimates of output impact that are net of NPK cost:

	Net output impact per irrigated ha	*Net output impact per watering per ha*
Andhra Pradesh	1188 kg	287 kg
Gujarat	1257 kg	383 kg
U.P.	1110 kg	459 kg

How foodgrains and non-foodgrains fare in the irrigated agriculture is listed in Table 3. Non-foodgrains as a group do exceed the foodgrains group by a substantial margin in all the three states both in respect of overall crop yield and yield per unit of irrigation water — this is true, with the singular exception of surface irrigation works in Andhra Pradesh, for every source of irrigation in the three states. This better yield performance is positively linked with a corresponding differential in the use of chemical fertilizers and also in the quantum of irrigation. And yet farmers' area allocative behaviour is not in harmony with the performance of non-foodgrains which occupy much less share in total irrigated area than do the foodgrain crops. This is indicative of some serious constraints that prevent farmers from moving away from foodgrains to non-foodgrains. Besides constraints of resources for cultivating non-foodgrains, and their own subsistence requirements, it is important to realize that the design as well as operation of an irrigation system can constrain the farmers in choosing crops.

Table 3

Foodgrains versus Non-Foodgrains in Irrigated Agriculture, 1975-76

crop group and its characteristics	Andhra Pradesh	Gujarat	U.P.
I. Foodgrains			
1. Average yield (kg/ha)	1737	973	1419
2. No. of waterings	3.60	2.80	2.31
3. Output per watering per ha (kg of rice units)	483	347	614
NPK (kg/ha)	91.8	54.8	27.5
5. Relative share in total irrigated area (%)	85	68	89
II. Non-Foodgrains			
1. Average yield (kg/ha)	4917	2838	3615
2. No. of waterings	8.07	3.89	3.26
3. Output per watering per ha (kg of rice units)	609	729	1107
4. NPK (kg/ha)	154.5	72.8	69.7
5. Relative share in total irrigated area (%)	15	32	11

Thus in the absence of field channels, field-to-field irrigation in tank/canal commands is not conducive for growing crops other than paddy. Likewise, unlike in the northern canals, there is canal zoning in much of the Deccan, whereby sugarcane cultivation is deliberately restricted to perennial and wet zones.

In Table 4 are presented the comparative position of heavily-irrigated crops vis-a-vis lightly-irrigated crops in the matter of (*a*) yield per unit of watering and (*b*) incremental output impact per unit of watering. The measure (*b*) reckons with the seasonal aspect of a crop; otherwise, productivity comparison is unduly biased in favour of crops grown in the main wet season when rainfall meets the main water requirements of crops in contrast to dry season crops whose water needs are met primarily from irrigation. In this paper, heavily-irrigated crop group consists of paddy and sugarcane; lightly-irrigated crop group covers coarse cereals, pulses and oilseeds; and all other crops (wheat, cotton, tobacco etc.) are in medium irrigation category. It is only in U.P. that the hypotheses of lightly-irrigated crops being more productive per unit of irrigation water than heavily-irrigated crops appears tenable. In Andhra Pradesh, the two crop groups are equally productive, and in Gujarat heavily-irrigated group has an edge over the lightly-irrigated group. Crops needing medium irrigation appear to be using more water than heavily-irrigated crops in U.P., and thus reveal productivity per unit of water below that of the latter. To an extent the same is true for Gujarat — in both these states the medium irrigation group preponderates in total irrigated area in contrast to Andhra Pradesh where this group shows the best performance because of its lowest use of irrigation vis-a-vis other two groups.

Table 4

Comparative Productivities of Crops Irrigated to Different Intensities, 1975-76

Crop category by irrigation intensity	*Area (%)*	*Yield (kg/ha)*	*No. of waterings*	*NPK (kg/ha)*	*Yield per watering (kg/ha)*
Andhra Pradesh					
1. lightly-irrigated crop	2.3	1321	2.72	15	486
2. Heavily-irrigated crop	94.0	2076	4.25	99	488
3. Medium-irrigated crop	3.7	3599	2.28	150	1579
4. All crop	100.0	2115	4.14	99	511
Gujarat					
1. Lightly-irrigated crop	5.3	777	1.47	37	529
2. Heavily-irrigated crop	15.3	1219	2.14	88	570
3. Medium-irrigated crop	79.2	1970	3.62	60	544
4. All crop	100.0	1790	3.28	63	546
Uttar Pradesh					
1. Lightly-irrigated crop	14.7	1083	1.01	14	1072
2. Heavily-irrigated crop	36.3	2138	2.38	40	898
3. Medium-irrigated crop	49.0	1491	2.88	32	518
4. All crop	100.0	1666	2.42	32	688

The above results are in better harmony with the proposition that productivity per unit of water, with the exception of Gujarat[1] is inversely related to extent of irrigation. While we have found no conclusive evidence

1. The source of this exception could be the data discrepancies to which an allusion has been made in footnote 1 on page 158.

on the hypotheses in question, it would be more meaningful from the policy viewpoint if either (*a*) a specific lightly-irrigated crop is contrasted with another specific heavily-irrigated crop, or (*b*) a long duration crop like sugarcane is contrasted with a combination of seasonal crops growable in the same season. While an illustrative comparison of the type (*a*) is provided below with the help of Andhra data, the other type (*b*) is examined for U.P. In Andhra Pradesh summer groundnut appears to be superior to summer paddy both from the viewpoint of output per unit of watering and per unit of NPK use. Thus, if area under summer paddy were reduced and that under summer groundnut increased in Andhra pradesh, production per unit of irrigation as well as chemical fertilizers would be enhanced. (The relevant data for the two crops is given below):

	Summer groundnut	*Summer paddy*
1. Percent share in total irrigated area	1.1	25.6
2. Yield per irrigated ha (kg of rice units)	1760	1794
3. No. of waterings	3.00	4.33
4. Yield per watering (kg)	587	414
5. NPK (kg/ha)	13	92
6. Yield per kg of NPK	135	19

In U.P. sugarcane occupies the field for 9 to 10 months during which farmer can take paddy plus wheat crops. The following data shows that output per watering per ha in sugarcane averaged about 1,100 kg. of rice units as compared to about 600 kg of rice units (about 690 kg. in foodgrain units when we treat a kg of wheat to be equal to a kg of rice) for paddy-wheat sequence.

	Sugarcane	*Wheat*	*Paddy*	*Wheat + paddy*
1. Per cent share in total irrigated area	11.1	49.0	25.2	74.2
2. Yield per irrigated ha (kg of rice units)	3629	1491	1479	2970
3. No. of waterings	3.30	2.88	1.98	4.86
4. Yield per watering (Kg)[8]	1100	518	747	611
5. NPK (kg/ha)	70	32	27	59
6. Yield per kg of NPK (kg of rice units)	52	47	55	51

8. The differential in yield per watering would be further widened if one were to reckon with the fact that depth of watering in paddy is more than in groundnut.

6. Comparative Performance by Sources of Irrigation

Relevant statistics on irrigated farming based on surface water on groundwater exclusively, as also on a conjunctive use of both of them, are shown in Table 5. These certainly do not sustain the hypothesis of groundwater being superior to surface water from the viewpoint of output-augmenting aspect of irrigation. It will be argued later that the validity of this hypothesis probably hinges on an assessment of the output augmentation per unit of *net* instead of *gross* irrigated area.

Table 5

Comparative Performance of Surface Irrigation, Groundwater Irrigation and Conjunctive Irrigation, 1975-76

Irrigation category	*Andhra Pradesh*	*Gujarat*	*U.P.*
I. Surface Water			
1. Overall crop yield (kg/ha)	2111	1397	1784
2. No. of waterings	3.79	3.25	2.61
3. Output impact per crop ha (kg)	1245	939	1285
4. Output impact per watering per ha (kg)	329	289	492
5. NPK per irrigated crop ha (kg)	102	81	30
II. Groundwater			
1. Overall crop yield (kg/ha)	2353	1898	1552
2. No. of waterings	5.01	3.42	2.45
3. Output impact per crop ha (kg)	1711	1553	1093
4. Output impact per watering per ha (kg)	341	454	446
5. NPK per irrigated ha (kg)	96	57	30
III Conjunctive			
1. Overall crop yield (kg/ha)	1935	1481	1761
2. No. of waterings	4.06	3.81	2.61
3. Output impact per crop ha (kg)	1721	1023	1202
4. Output impact per watering per ha	424	269	461
5. NPK per irrigated ha (kg)	98	47	54

When we compare the two sources of irrigation by taking into account only crop-wise yields and crop pattern, one finds that the overall crop yield per gross (crop) ha in respect of groundwater irrigation in the state of U.P. in 1975-76 was about 1,552 kg., about 13 per cent below the corresponding level of 1,784 kg. recorded on surface water-irrigated lands in the state. While the level of fertilizer intensity on both types or irrigated lands was indeed the same (about 30 kg/ha), the yield advantage of surface irrigation in this state appears to be positively linked with the quantum of irrigation because average number of waterings on groundwater-irrigated areas was 2.45 (6 per cent below the corresponding figure of 2.61 for surface irrigation). In all probability, the two sources of irrigation do not differ significanty if we duly reckon with the fact of considerable sampling and non-sampling errors being present in the estimates based on survey data gathered through a questionnare that relied on memory recall by the respondents.

It is true that both in Andhra pradesh and Gujarat groundwater comes ahead of surface water, and the margin in overall crop yield is accountable in terms of corresponding margins in the number of waterings, though not in the NPK level. More specifically, the average crop yield in surface water irrigation is found to be 10 per cent below the corresponding magnitude for groundwater irrigation in Andhra Pradesh, a difference that is too small to generate any confidence in any conclusion of groundwater being, on a crop ha basis, more productive than surface water. It is only in Gujarat that the difference of 26 per cent is substantial enough to sustain the hypothesis under testing. This difference is further widened to 40 per cent if reckoned in terms of output impact instead of yield differential - for Andhra Pradesh the difference widens from 10 to 27 per cent.

Though it is widely felt (mainly on the basis of micro level studies) that intensity of irrigation in well irrigation is higher than under surface irrigation, state-wide estimates are lacking as secondary statistics of gross irrigated and net irrigated area are not published according to type of irrigation. It is only in respect of Andhra Pradesh that its *Season and Crop Report* carries such data since the early seventies - the Centre has been urging upon other States to do so for quite some time. For this State we find that the intensity of irrigation for all groundwater sources averages 146 per cent, well above the level of 131 per cent for canal irrigation and 114 per cent for tank irrigation — the weighted average for surface irrigation works out to 124 per cent. It we adopt these values for the sample data, the superiority of groundwater over surface water in the matter of output impact does emerge markedly. More specifically, the relative magnitudes of the two categories of irrigation in Andhra Pradesh compare as follows:

	Ground water	*Surface water*
1. Overall crop yield per net irrigated ha	100	76
2. Output impact per net irrigated ha	100	62

As regards the hypothesis of conjuctive irrigation being superior to surface irrigation, the available evidence is not conclusive. Leaving aside the case of Gujarat for the reasons given earlier in the methodology section, one observes that both in Andhra Pradesh and U.P. conjunctive irrigation is a shade less inferior to surface irrigation in the matter of overall crop yield. It is in respect of output impact that in Andhra Pradesh the advantage shifts in its favour by a two-fifth margin. But no such turnabout occurs in U.P.

When we compare canal irrigation with canal plus tubewell/pumpset irrigation, we still get a mixed picture. Whereas in Andhra Pradesh and Gujarat the output impact of canal irrigation is unmistakably less than that of combined use of canal and tubewell/pumpset, it is the other way found in Uttar Pradesh, as is testified by the following data:

	A.P.	*Gujarat*	*U.P.*
1. Output impact per irrigated gross ha (kg):			
(*i*) canal	1359	1043	1273
(*ii*) canal + pumpset/tubewell	1722	1613	859
2. No of waterings:			
(*i*) canal	4.02	3.47	2.63
(*ii*) canal + pumpset/tubewell	4.07	1.63	2.22
3. Output impact per watering per irrigated ha (kg):			
(*i*) canal	338	300	484
(*ii*) canal + pumpset/tubewell	423	989	387

It is quite possible that intensity of irrigation on lands receiving both canal and tubewell/pumpset water is higher than the corresponding level on purely canal-irrigated lands. In that event, conjunctive use of public canal water and private well water may generate more output per unit area on net irrigated basis than from wholly canal-irrigated lands, with the possible exception of tail reaches of a canal system where canal supplies happen to be inadequate in comparison to the head reach areas.

Farmers owning their own tubewells exhibit the best productivity performance in comparison to all other eight modes of irrigation in the State of Andhra Pradesh only but not in the other two states. The comparative statistics according to each source of irrigation are listed in Table 6. Needless to caution the reader, the comparative picture of Table 6 is partial as it does not reckon with that part of the output impact that is attributable to higher intensity of irrigation of a given source, say private tubewell, over another source, say tank irrigation. Anyway, the hypothesis that productivity of irrigated farming based on water purchased from other well owners is less than that from one's own well is not tenable for Gujarat, and also for Andhra Pradesh if we restrict the comparison to owned dugwells only. In U.P., farmers depending on water purchased from other well owners perform somewhat better than owners of traditional wells.

Table 6

Inter-Source Relative Positions (Canal = 100) in Output Impact of Irrigation in Three States, 1975-76.

S.N.	*Category of irrigation*	*Andhra Pradesh*			*Gujarat*			*Uttar Pradesh*		
		I	*II*	*III*	*I*	*II*	*III*	*I*	*II*	*III*
1.	Canal irrigation	100	4.02	100	100	3.48	100	100	2.63	100
2.	Canal plus tube-well pumpset	127	4.07	125	155	1.63	330	67	2.22	80
3.	Private tubewell	219	6.43	137	102	3.51	101	78	2.61	79
4.	private dugwell equipped with a pumpset	113	5.06	90	110	4.19	91	94	2.29	108
5.	Owning a pump-set and lifting water from other source	54	4.56	48	92	4.67	69	137	3.16	114
6.	Purchase of water from tubewell/pumpset owner	127	4.43	115	232	2.11	382	87	2.41	95
7.	Traditional well	91	4.12	89	75	2.34	112	64	2.48	68
8.	Tanks and ponds	76	3.40	90	40	2.14	66	83	2.15	102
9.	Other Sources	82	2.67	124	38	1.29	102	105	3.36	82
10.	All Sources	102	4.14	104	135	3.28	143	93	2.42	101

I Stands for output impact per irrigated ha.
II Stands for no. of waterings
III Stands for output impact per unit of watering/ha.

7. The Problem of Overirrigation

A strong impression exists that the Indian irrigator overirrigates his crops, especially when he is using the highly subsidised water from public irrigation works. The impression has been partly based on the following kinds of visible wastage of water in the fields:

(*i*) Overflow from an irrigated field, either because of lack of field levelling, or lack of supervision during the irrigation operation;

(*ii*) Overflowing field channels that connect the field to the water outlet point in a canal system;

(*iii*) Prevalance of field-to-field irrigation because of the absence of a field channel network below the canal outlet.

Table 7

Irrigation Deltas Adopted for Different Crops

S.N.	*Crop*	*Andhra Pradesh*	*Gujarat*	*Uttar Pradesh*
			(in milli metres)	
1.	Rice	680	680	750-910
2.	Bajra	150	200	–
3.	Maize	–	–	225-275
4.	Jowar	300-450	140	300
5.	Ragi	300-450	–	–
6.	Groundnut	655	350	–
7.	Sugarcane	680	1960	660
8.	Wheet	–	600	220
9.	Gram	–	150	75
10.	Average for all crops	646-652	566	397-443

Our enquiry is limited to testing one aspect of over-irrigation, namely, number of waterings exceeding the recommended level. We have no data to test the other aspect, namely, irrigation delta (depth being so excessive that a good deal of it percolates below the crop root zone). A little reflection would bring out that the hypothesis of overirrigation cannot be tested satisfactorily even if one has data both on actual volume of irrigation water applied to a field and the volume recommended by the soil scientists. When we observe the actual number of waterings to be less than the recommended level, as we do in our data set, we do recognize that the phenomenon of *overirrigation in a single watering* may have been masked.

Since we could not locate very firm data on recommended[1] levels of waterings for various crops for each state, we are desisting from carrying out a crop by crop examination of the extent of overirrigation/underirrigation. Instead, we test the hypothesis for all crops taken together. To do so, we compile *weighted averages* for both actual and recommended number of waterings separately for *each source for each state*, the weights being the irrigated areas under a source in each state. Knowing as we do know the limitations in our data base, we would caution the reader against attaching too much cardinal significance to the final numbers that have been thrown up by our computations.

Table 8

Actual and Normative Number of Waterings for Different Sources of Irrigation, 1975-76

Category of Irrigation	*No. of waterings in Andhra Pradesh*		*No. of waterings in Gujarat*		*No. of waterings in U.P.*	
	Normative	*Actual*	*Normative*	*Actual*	*Normative*	*Actual*
1. Canal	8 to 9	4.02	10	3.48	6	2.63
2. Canal + tubewell pumpset	9	4.07	7	10.63	5	2.22
3. Private tubewell	8	6.43	7	3.51	5	2.61
4. Private dugwell with pumpset	9	5.06	9	4.19	5	2.29
5. Ownership of pumpset only	9	4.56	11	4.67	6	3.16
6. Purchase of water from tubewell/ pumpset owner	9	4.43	7	2.11	6	2.41
7. Traditional well	9	4.12	8	2.34	5	2.48
8. Tanks/ponds	9	3.40	8	2.14	7	2.15
9. Other sources	9	2.67	7	1.29	6	3.36
10. All sources	9	4.14	8 to 9	3.28	5 to 6	2.42

1. In Dhawan (1987d) the first author painstakingly built up crop-wise figures of recommended irrigation deltas for each of the eleven states (including Andhra Pradesh, Gujarat and U.P.). To deduce the number of waterings, these crop-wise figures of delta are divided by 7.5 cm, the usual recommended irrigation depth in a single watering for most crops.

Both the observed and the normative (recommended number of waterings are listed in Table 8, source-wise and state-wise. Instead of overirrigation, sizable underirrigation emerges in all categories of irrigated farming in each of the three states. It is noteworthy that farming based on private means of irrigation also exhibits underirrigation. For such farming one may not visualize the phenomenon of overwatering in a single irrigation operation to the same extent[1] as in the case of farming based on public irrigation, where desire to overirrigate in a single irrigation operation partly stems from the uncertainties of a public supply system.

Summary and Conclusions

Irrigation, irrespective of its denomination, is found to change both crop pattern and crop yields of rainfed farming so impressively in each of the three states that overall, or aggregate, yield per crop hectare gets boosted up from a little over 6 quintals to a little under 18 quintals (in terms of rice units) in Gujarat; from about 9 to about 21 quintals in Andhra Pradesh; and from about 10 to a bit below 17 quintals in U.P. In all likelihood, these levels of irrigated yield, based as they are on the NCAER survey data of the mid-seventies, would be somewhat higher today, yet remaining substantially below the potential of 40-50 quintals/ha indicated by agronomical findings in India.

The yield hiatus between promise and performance is mainly accountable in terms of a substantial input gap between the recommended and the actual doses of the two leading but complementary inputs of irrigated farming viz chemical fertilizers and irrigation water. Looking at the requisite number of waterings for various crops in each state and assuming an NPK application of 150 kg. per average irrigated crop ha as the recommended dose for chemical fertilizers, we find that irrigated crops were seriously underfertilized and underirrigated in the mid-seventies. More specifically, crops were underfertilized to the extent of 80 per cent in U.P., 60 per cent in Gujarat, and 33 per cent in Andhra Pradesh. Likewise underirrigation, not to mention lack of its timeliness, amounted to 55-60 per cent in these three states.

It is not our purpose to delve into the myriad factors responsible for the non-realisation of the crop yield potentials even under irrigated

1. Normally, one would not expect overirrigation in a plot irrigated from one's own source of irrigation. Yet, overirrigation occurs, not so much because of lack of scientific knowledge on the part of the irrigator but because of (*a*) the pernicious electricity tariff in many states that encourages overpumping and (*b*) farmers' inability to gauge the extent of depth of watering.

farming. As the input gap diminishes over time, the crop yields are bound to rise further. It is prudent to let the gap be bridged in a gradual manner, and not to think in terms of a policy of intensive agriculture, whereby both chemical fertilizers and irrigation are deployed in such a concentrated manner that each ha is irrigated/fertilized to the recommended level. Economists, being highly conscious of relative scarcity of irrigation vis-a-vis land resource in a macro context (this is true for the three states under study), have favoured a policy of extensive irrigation, in which crop area is lightly-irrigated —and consequently lightly fertilized because of the well-known complementarity between the two inputs. This policy not only enhances spatial equity in gains from irrigation but also produces more crop output from the available resources of land, irrigation water and capital (fertilizers) than is realisable under the alternative policy of intensive farming that is favoured by the scientists, especially the agronomists. The source of the extra output is the inexorable fact that per hectare productivity of irrigation water is inversely related to volume of irrigation used per ha.

Productivity of irrigation water, as conveyed by the ratio of output impact of irrigation per irrigated hectare to number of waterings, was about 340 kg. of rice equivalents in Andhra Pradesh, about 430 kg. of rice equivalents in Gujarat, and about 490 kg. of rice equivalents in U.P. In this regard, non-foodgrains as a group do perform better than foodgrains, irrespective of the type of irrigation. The evidence on lightly-irrigated crops being more productive per unit of water than heavily-irrigated crops is far from conclusive: while the proposition is true for U.P., the two crop groups are equally good in Andhra Pradesh, and heavly-irrigated crops do carry an edge over lightly-irrigated crops in Gujarat. For more meaningful results in this fruitful area of investigation, it is better to have specific crop comparisons. Thus between summer groundnut and summer paddy in Andhra Pradesh, the former reveals much higher productivity of irrigation (as well as per unit of chemical fertilizers) than the latter. This suggests an advantage in shifting irrigated acreage from summer paddy to summer groundnut. The observed area shares of these two crops in total irrigated acreage are far from being commensurate with their comparative advantage - this is a particular case of the general case of non-foodgrains occupying a position in total irrigated area wholly incommensurate with the comparative advantage in productivity per unit of watering.

Because of serious shortcomings in respect of data for certain crops in the Gujarat sample we have desisted from comparing any oilseed/pulse crop with any heavily-irrigated crop. In the case of the U.P.

sample, the areal coverage on oilseeds/pulses is too small to warrant any confident conclusions — the yield of pulses per unit of watering was twice that of wheat, one half times that of paddy but marginally (6 per cent) higher than that of sugarcane. What is noteworthy here is that sugarcane turns out to be superior to wheat-rice sequence in terms of output per unit of water — output per unit of fertilizers is of comparable magnitude in either alternative. We have reasons to believe that this result holds good for both Punjab and Haryana also. Therefore, those scholars who have been recommending the reduction of sugarcane cultivation in the Deccan canals, especially in Western Maharashtra and Marathwada regions of Maharashtra state, may note this comparative advantage of Northern India in sugarcane cultivation.

Our investigation into the comparative performance of irrigation sources does not affirm that groundwater irrigation is invariably superior to surface irrigation in the matter of overall crop yield, or output impact per crop hectare of irrigated area, or productivity of irrigation water. In all likelihood, the proposition of groundwater (primarily under public ownership) in the matter of increasing farm output is true when output comparisons are envisaged per hectare of *net* instead of *gross* irrigated area. This is suggested by our finding for Andhra Pradesh which shows that the intensity of irrigation, as measured by the ratio of gross irrigated area to net irrigated area, in the case of groundwater is decisively higher than that of canal or tank irrigation. Our inability to observe clear-cut superiority of conjunctive irrigation over surfact irrigation may be due to our inability to adjust for the differential on account of intensity of irrigation. Finally, irrigated farming based on water purchased from other farmers owning tubewells is somewhat better than that based on traditional, self-owned dugwells.

Chapter 11

PRODUCTIVITY OF WATER IN TEN CANAL COMMMANDS*

Introduction

In the absence of crop output compilation acording to land under each source of irrigation in a State, the author had earlier used the powerful statistical technique of multiple regression to decompose, state-wise, aggregate crop output into its main components, namely, source-wise outputs on the one hand and output from rainfed or dry farming on the other. This enabled him to assess for nine States the production impact of each principal source of irrigation for the late seventies. Results of this indirect method were quite satisfactory for four States, namely, Punjab, Haryana, Tamil Nadu and Andhra Pradesh (Dhawan, 1986c). For other States, infirmities in the basic agricultural statistics gave rise to results of questionable reliance. Moreover, this approach does not provide estimates at crop group level. And one does not know how much irrigation water goes into producing the estimated output impact as a result of changing one dry ha into a wet ha. The present paper permits us to overcome some of these limitations in respect of the single most important source of irrigation viz canal irrigation, though project-wide instead of state-wide results emerges. Also, inter-project comparative analysis through correlation approach provides some insights into factors that enhance or inhibit productivity impact of canal irrigation in India.

Two additional points about the present work may be stated here. First, data on capacity utilization of an irrigation project has been used to assess the output impact per ha of *created* irrigation potential–this is simply accomplished by multiplying the observed output impact per ha of actual area under canal irrigation by a fraction equal to the rate of utilization of created irrigation potential. Such an adjustment

* Already published (Dhawan, 1989c)

takes care of the phenomenon observed in some canal commands, whereby canal beneficiary farmers tilt their crop pattern in favour of heavily-irrigated crops like sugarcane and paddy much more than the provision made for these crops while working out the estimate of irrigation potential. Second, the scheme for aggregating diverse crop outputs has been modified: instead of calorie content of food crops we use crop prices as the basis for aggregation. This modification, besides bringing in the price angle, helps in extending the crop set by bringing fibres, fodders, fruits and vegetables within the fold of our aggregative analysis. Since the rupee is quite dated in time — because of persistence of price inflation -, crop-wise price set is converted into crop-wise rice equivalents set, rice being the single most important crop of the country. It is believed that communicative value of numbers in units of rice equivalents is better than in monetary units.

Methodology and the Data Base

The crucial information that we need for purpose of our enquiry pertains to (*a*) project level data on crop yields under irrigated and unirrigated conditions, alongwith crop-wise irrigation requirements, (*b*) crop pattern data for canal-benefitted acreage, (*c*) crop pattern data for the command in the absence of the project and (*d*) set of crop prices for deriving the rice equivalence scale. Information with regard to (*a*) and (*b*) is obtained from a recent study by the Operation Research Group (ORG 1986). The pre-project crop pattern is not available in this study. The crop pattern under unirrigated acreage during 1982-83 (the latest year for which the national estimates of total crop area and total irrigated crop area for different crops are available) for the state in which a project is located is used as a proxy for 'without canal' crop pattern. The prices *recommended* by the Agricultural Prices Commission (now known as the Costs and Agricultural Prices Commission) for various crops for the period 1980-81 to 1984-85 are essentially used for working out the rice equivalence scale listed in Table 1. The author believes these prices aptly reflect the weights that one should attach to different crops in a wider, national perspective.

Productivity of irrigated farming has been computed by the following formula:

$$Y^I = \Sigma P_i \,.\, Y_i \,.\, W_i$$

where: Y_i is irrigated yield for ith crop;

W_i is relative share in irrigated crop pattern during 1982 -83 to 1984-85;

P_i is rice equivalent for ith crop

Table 1

Mean Prices for Various Crops Recommended by APC during 1980-84 and the Rice Equivalence Scale Based on them

Crop	*Mean Price (Rs/quintal)*	*Rice equivalence scale*	
		computed	*adopted (Pi)*
Rice	183[1]	1.00	1.00
Wheat	146	0.80	0.80
Other cereals	117	0.64	0.66
Gram	228	1.25	1.25
Other pulses	235	1.28	1.30
Cotton	374 (for kapas)	2.04	2.00
Groundnut	285 (nuts-in-shell)	1.56	1.60
Mustard	329 (seed)	1.80	1.80
Soyabean	229	1.25	1.25
Potatoes	75	0.41	0.40
Chillies	750[2] (dry weight)	4.10	4.00
Sugarcane	17.47[3]	0.10	0.10
Tobacco[4]	8.08 (per kg)	4.42	4.00

1. paddy price divided by 0.66
2. this author's estimate
3. for 10% sugar recovery
4. This crop is not reported in the selected ten project commands.

Likewise, productivity of unirrigated farming has been computed. The output impact of one irrigated crop ha is given by

$$(Y^I - K.Y^O)$$

where: Y^I stands for overall irrigated yield;

Y^O stands for overall unirrigated yield; K is a fraction that indicates the extent of kharif orientation of the irrigation crop pattern in a canal command.

The ten irrigation works covered in the ORG study are listed below, alongwith the names of the States in which their commands are located and the agro-climatic nature of these commands.

I. **Paddy Region**

1. Mayurakshi, West Bengal, high rainfall (1285 mm)
2. Gandak, Bihar, high rainfall (1200-1400 mm)
3. Mahanadi Delta, Orissa, high rainfall (1405 mm)

II. **Wheat Region**

4. Rajasthan (Indira Gandhi) Canal, Rajasthan, scanty rainfall (300 mm) that is not enough for crop farming in the arid climate of western Rajasthan.
5. Bhakra Nangal, Punjab, low rainfall (600 mm)
6. Tawa, Madhya Pradesh, varied rainfall (750-1000 mm in Zone C, 1000-1250 mm in Zone B, and 1250-1500 in Zone A).
7. Sarda Sahayak, U.P, good rainfall (1000 mm).

III. **Coarse Grains Region**

8. Nagarjunasagar, Andhra Pradesh, low to medium rainfall (680-1100 mm).
9. Tungabhadra, Karnataka, low rainfall.
10. Jayakwadi, Maharashtra, low to medium rainfall (650 to 1100 mm).

Before presenting the results, two observations on the data base (vide Appendix I) are imperative. One is about the yield data and the other is about the irrigation data for crops. The yield data (nor for that matter the crop-wise irrigation data) are not an outcome of any statistically well-designed survey of farmers done by ORG in each project command (such time-consuming surveys were ruled out by the short time frame available for preparing the study). These are essentially obtained from the Command Area Development Agency (CADA), whose field data in this regard may not be truly representative of the position in the whole command - in the absence of CADA, recourse was made to the state directorate of agriculture. Likewise, the irrigation deltas indicated for the various crops lack comparability across projects; to the extent these are (*i*) at field gate level for some projects and at distributory/outlet level for other projects, and (*ii*) based on actual irrigation practices for crops in some other projects. Therefore due caution should be exercised in drawing conclusions based on inter-project comparisons.

Finally, what has been assessed in this paper is the *direct* output impact of canal water without reference to the *indirect* output effects, some being negative and some positive. Environmental groups have been deeply concerned with the twin problem of waterlogging and soil salinity emerging within the command of major irrigation works. The loss of output on this account needs to be assessed, as also the loss from fertile lands submerged by a reservoir. In contrast to these adverse output effects, one has to duly reckon with the beneficial effects in the shape of improved groundwater availability in the wake of canal introduction in low rainfall tracts. This seepage of canal water to the groundwater table becomes a source of substantial addition to output that otherwise gets ascribed to development of well irrigation. That this indirect contribution of canal water can be as high as the direct one has been brought out by the author for the low rainfall command of the Mula project in Maharashtra (chapters 6 and 9). This same may be true for the Bhakra Nangal project whose waters sustain the private tubewell irrigation of Punjab and Haryana, the most-applauded source of irrigation. But then these very waters become problemetic in the cotton tracts of the two states by bringing to the surface saline waters lying underground - these cotton tracts have naturally poor drainage. Wherever the seepage is excessive and does not get duly removed through horizontal or vertical drainage, waterlogging ensues, especially in good rainfall regions, thereby eroding production gains of direct canal irrigation — among the ten projects Sarda Sahayak (U.P.) most likely belongs to this category.

Table 2

Project-wise Enhancement in Land Productivity and Output Impact (in Rice Equivalents) per Ha of Irrigation

S.N. Project	*Land productivity (kg/ha)*			*Percent rise in land productivity*		*Output impact (kg/ha)*		*Percent rise in output*	
	Yo	Y_I	Y^*_I	Y_I	Y^*_I	Y_I	Y^*_I	Y_I	Y^*_I
1. Mayurakshi	1053	3638	3492	245	232	2690	2582	255	245
2. Tungabhadra	1031	3353	2112	225	105	2786	1755	270	170
3. Nagarjunasagar	1022	3077	2215	201	117	2157	1553	211	152
4. Bhakra Nangal	1167	2596	1947	122	67	2071	1553	177	133
5. Rajasthan Canal	Nil	1930	1428	NC	NC	1930	1428	NC	NC
6. Gandak	1053	2498	1699	137	61	1761	1197	167	114
7. Tawa	834	1986	953	138	14	1969	945	236	113
8. Sarda Sahayak	700	1734	1040	148	49	1580	948	226	135
9. Jayakwadi	437	2109	1076	383	146	1921	980	440	224
10. Mahanadi Delta	834	1398	1342	68	61	956	918	115	110

Yo - unirrigated i.e. rainfed yield
Y_I - observed irrigated yield
Y^*_I- adjusted downwards for capacity utilisation
NC - not computable.

EMPIRICAL RESULTS

Step-up in Productivity

The rise in the level of land productivity, measured as overall crop yield per crop hectare, is substantially boosted by canal irrigation in relative, if not absolute, terms. It is only in the Tawa project that the relative boost-up in crop yield turns marginal in nature when canal-irrigated productivity is adjusted downwards for the low level of capacity utilization of this project (vide Table 2). For all the ten projects, the simple mean value of productivity of canal-irrigated lands is about 21 quintals/ha, which becomes about 15 quintals when computed per hectare of irrigation potential created. In contrast, the simple average value of rainfed yield comes to about 8 quintals/ha. The yield step-up is accompanied by perceptible reduction in inter-project (i.e. spatial) disparity in land productivity, because the coefficient of variation of unirrigated yield across projects is 42 per cent as compared to 22 per cent in respect of irrigated yield (30 per cent if the yield is scaled down for the capacity utilization factor).[1].

Productivity of canal-irrigated farming per ha of actual irrigated area during the mid-eighties is found to vary between 14 quintals in Mahanadi Delta (Orissa) and 36 quintals in Mayurakshi Project (West Bengal). Nagarjunasagar (A.P.) and Tungabhadra (Karnataka) projects in the Deccan plateau reveal high productivity level (above 30 quintals), whereas Sarda Sahayak (U.P.) and Rajashtan Canal (Rajasthan) fall in the low productivity (below 20 quintals/ha) category. Bhakra Nangal (Punjab) falls in the intermediate range with a level of the order of 26 quintals/ha. A correlation analysis across projects shows that level of land productivity under irrigated conditions bears a positive relation with two aspects of crop pattern, namely, (1) the relative area devoted to non-foodgrains (r = 0.32), and (2) the relative area of crops requiring kharif irrigation (r = 0.38). However, it is negatively related to rainfall level of the project command (r = minus 0.33) and the rate of capacity utilization factor (r = minus 0.21).

Direct Output Impact

In terms of output impact per (actual) irrigated hectare, Tungabhadra tops the list with about 28 quintals but closely followed

1. Compare this role of canal irrigatioon in reducing spatial disparity in land productivity with another empirical finding by some scholars that inter - farmer disparity in respect of crop yield is much less under irrigated than rainfed conditions for the same canal command

by Mayurakshi (vide Table 2). Mahanadi Delta still remains at the bottom, with output impact of the order of 10 quintals. Now, five projects (Rajasthan Canal, Tawa in M.P., Nagarjunasagar, Jayakwadi in Maharashtra, and Bhakra Nangal) reveal output impact in the range of 19-22 quintals.

When due account is taken of irrigation water used in creating the output impact, Mayurakshi displaces Tungabhadra at the top of the ladder, recording about 51 kg per ha-cm (acre-inch) of irrigation water. Bhakra and Tawa, because of low irrigation delta of the order of 49 cm (19 inches), record 42 and 40 kg, respectively, per cm of irrigation delta. The project with the highest impact, namely, Tungabhadra, averages about 37 kg/ha-cm. Though Mahanadi Delta continues at the bottom of the list (about 14 kg/cm), Jayakwadi, Sarda Sahayak and Gandak (Bihar) reveal productivity impact of 26-28 kg per ha-cm of water.

The rate of capacity utilization, measured as a ratio of gross irrigated area to created irrigation potential, is found to be highly variable across the ten projects. Among the ten projects, Mahanadi Delta and Mayurakshi appear to have attained almost full utilization of their irrigation potential. Tawa and Jayakwadi appear to have gross underutilization that almost equals half the irrigation potential. Other six projects fall in the range of 60-75 per cent capacity utilization. The estimated irrigation potential created so far in these projects (a majority of them are still under construction phase), alongwith the rate of capacity utilization, is listed below.

	Potential (ooo ha)	*% utilization*
1. Sarda Sahayak*	1,350	60
2. Nagarjunasagar*	729	72
3. Rajasthan Canal*	571	74
4. Gandak*	896	68
5. Bhakra Nangal (Punjab portion)	566	75
6. Mahanadi Delta	536	96
7. Tungabhadra (Karnataka portion)	363	63
8. Mayurakshi	246	96
9. Tawa*	192	48
10. Jayakwadi*	73	51

* under progress

Mayurakshi has nearly full capacity utilization of irrigation potential and it turns up with topmost position in the matter of productivity of irrigated land. At the other end, Mahanadi Delta, owing to near-capacity utilization level, undergoes a perceptible improvement and no more remains at the downmost position in the matter of land productivity under irrigated conditions. Anyway, the output impact per ha of created irrigation potential now amounts to 9 to 11 quintals of rice equivalents for Tawa, Jayakwadi, Sarda Sahayak and Mahanadi Delta; 13-14 quintals for Gandak and Rajasthan Canal. Nagarjunsagar, Tungabhadra and Bhakra Nangal record about 17-18 quintals with about 26 quintals in Mayurakshi. Statistics of land productivity and output impact of irrigation, with and without adjustment for capacity utilization factor, are set out project-wise in Table 2, which also gives the irrigation impact of land productivity and output relative to rainfed level.

The output-augmenting role of canal irrigation is lower in high rainfall areas than in low rainfall areas. The coefficient of correlation between output impact per actually irrigated ha and rainfall is of the order of minus 0.65. Since the rate of utilization of canal irrigation potential is also positively, though weakly, related to rainfall level in the canal command of a project (r = 0.24), the output impact per ha of created irrigation potential remains negatively related to rainfall variable (r = minus 0.59). The output impact of canal irrigation is heightened in canal commands with more emphasis on growing non-foodgrain crops (r = 0.44). However, it is lowered in canal commands where irrigation is used primarily for the crops needing kharif irrigation (r = minus 0.34). The complete matrix of correlation is set out in Table 3.

Table 3

Correlation Matrix

	Productivity (all crops) (1)	*Output impact* (2)	*Rainfed yield* (3)	*Rainfall* (4)	*Kharif orientation* (5)	*Irrigation level* (6)	*% Nonfoodgrains* (7)	*Food-grains product-ivity* (8)
1.	1.00							
2.	0.72	1.00						
3.	0.34	-0.20	1.00					
4.	-0.33	-0.65	0.53	1.00				
5.	0.38	-0.34	0.66	0.44	1.00			
6.	0.22	-0.04	0.04	-0.08	0.48	1.00		
7.	0.32	0.44	-0.49	-0.71	-005	0.67	1.00	
8.	0.76	0.59	0.51	-0.13	0.12	-0.40	0.25	1.00

Foodgrains versus Non-Foodgrains

The government's dominant motive in expanding irrigation facilities in India is to enhance grain production. Area-wise, foodgrains acreage preponderates in total irrigated area in the country, and the data from the ten canal commands corroborates this; in the case of Tawa, Gandak, Mayurakshi, Bhakra Nangal, Sarda Sahayak and Mahanadi Delta foodgrains account for over 85 per cent of the benefitted area. It is in the dry crop regions (the Deccan plateau and Rajasthan where millets/jowar are the main grains under rainfed conditions) that the per cent share share of foodgrains under irrigated conditions range between 61 and 68 per cent.

The productivity of lands under foodgrains in terms of rice equivalents is found to range between 9 quintals and 24 quintals per irrigated hectare. Only Bhakra Nangal, Tungabhadra and Mayurakshi projects appear with foodgrains productivity level above the national average of 19 quintals (in terms of foodgrains) for all irrigation sources taken together. Calorie for calorie, all grains are practically of equal value for meeting human energy needs. Calorie gap being a major nutritional deficiency of Indian population at the lower rungs, one may ignore the price tags on different grains and simply adjudge the productivity of goodgrains under canal-irrigated lands in terms of their weight alone. In this perspective, the level of foodgrains productivity per irrigated ha witnesses a perceptible rise (in comparison to rice equivalents), the extent of rise varying (*a*) positively with the proportion of wheat and coarse cereals in the foodgrains basket in a canal command and (*b*) negatively with the share of high-priced pulses in the grain basket. The comparative figures of yield in two units of mesasurment are set out in the first column of Table 4.

By and large, the two fine cereals viz. wheat and rice, predominate in the foodgrains basket raised under irrigated conditions. Compared to coarse cereals, these are today both high-valued and high-yielding crops. In contrast, pulses are high-valued but low-yielding crops. In comparison to the fine cereals, pulses require much less use of irrigation and chemical fertilizers. These therefore attract attention of two categories of farmers within a canal command, namely, (1) those who are not sure of canal supplies and (2) the resource-poor. For, both the irrigation needs and resource requirements for growing pulses are much less than for the fine cereals. It is widely observed that farmers located at the tail-ends of a canal system (outlet, distributory, branch canal and main canal) are not so well supplied with canal water as those located in the upper and the middle reaches of a canal network.

Table 4

Comparative Performance of Foodgrains and Non-foodgrain Crops under Canal Irrigation

S.N. Project	*Yield (kg/ha)*		*Irrigation (mm)*		*Percent excess of NFG over FG*		*Yield per ha-cm*		
	FG	*NFG*	*FG*	*NFG*	*yield*	*irrig-ation*	*FG*	*NFG*	*% excess of NFG over FG*
1. Rajasthan Canal	1500 (1598)	2565	482	756	71	57	31.1	33.9 (33.2)	9
2. Tawa	1977 (2279)	2524	487	753	28	55	40.6	33.5 (46.8)	- 17
3. Gandak	1789 (1941)	4191	607	866	134	43	29.5	84.4 (32.0)	64
4. Nagarjunasagar	1729 (1743)	4435	1084	682	157	-37	16.0	65.0 (16.1)	306
5. Tungabhadra	2219 (2431)	3842	761	763	73	Neg	29.2	50.4 (31.9)	73
6. Jayakwadi	1072 (1463)	4332	301	1653	304	499	35.6	26.2 (48.6)	-36
7. Mayurakshi	2434 (2437)	4279	521	619	76	19	46.7	69.1 (46.8)	48
8. Sarda Sahayak	1390 (1677)	4634	504	1226	234	143	27.6	37.8 (33.3)	37
9. Bhakra	2161 (2553)	3576	476	649	65	36	45.4	55.1 (53.6)	21
10. Mahanadi Delta	911 (890)	2002	752	400	120	-47	12.1	50.1 (11.8)	314

FG — Foodgrains (cereals and pulses).
NFG — Non-foodgrains (oilseeds, cotton, sugarcane, potatoes and chillies).
Note — Figures in brackets are in terms of physical weight without reckoning with differences in foodgrain prices. Unbracketed figures are in terms of rice equivalents.

As a group, foodgrains do not compare favourably with non-foodgrains in the matter of productivity per unit irrigated area. However, the yield disparity varies from project to project, recording a low of 28 per cent in Tawa command to a very high of over 300 per cent in the case of Jayakwadi (vide Table 4). To a large extent, this disparity is linked with a corresponding disparity in irrigation level in the two crop groups. That is to say, non-foodgrains as a group absorb more of the irrigation resource than do foodgrains.

When due note is taken of irrigation factor, and the yield performance of foodgrains vis-a-vis non-foodgrains is adjudged in terms of yield per ha-cm of irrigation water, the comparative picture becomes somewhat diffused. To begin with, the yield disparity widens in the case of Nagarjunasagar and Mahanadi Delta commands as non-foodgrain crops in these two commands are raised with lesser use of irrigation water than used in the case of foodgrain crops. Next, the yield differential per unit of water turns in favour of foodgrains in the case of such projects as Tawa and Jayakwadi where the observed yield differential per ha is less than the disparity in irrigation application. Finally, the yield differential is narrowed in the case of Rajasthan Canal (9%), Bhakra Nangal (21%), Gandak (64%), Tungabhadra (73%) and Sarda Sahayak (37%). In view of this varied nature of the findings it is not possible to categorically conclude that one crop group is more productive than the other in the matter of yield per unit of water. Probably, one explanation for this state of affairs is the crop heterogeneity within each group. Having already but briefly alluded to crop heterogeneity within the foodgrains group, one may now delve into the same in respect of non-foodgrains in what follows.

Sugarcane occupies a pre-eminent position within the non-foodgrains group, not so much in terms of its share in total irrigated area but for its high productivity level, as also for its irrigation needs for the year as a whole. No wonder, Indian irrigators have shown a marked preference for raising this crop once they get access to a low-priced irrigation source like canal water, more so if they are in a position to sell their prroduce to sugar factories at a government-guaranteed price. If its relative share in total irrigated acreage is incommensurate with its high remunerativeness, the explanation is to be sought (*a*) in the binding constraint of irrigation availability during summer period by which time reservoirs/rivers are at their lowest level of the year, and (*b*) the planners' desire to restrict area under this crop so as to promote extensive farming with lightly-irrigated crops in water-scarce regions like the Deccan plateau. Anyway, the high productivity level for irrigated non-foodgrains in Jayakwadi, Sarda Sahayak and Gandak commands is mainly accountable in terms of relatively substantial share of sugarcane in the non-foodgrains crop-mix. Likewise, the comparatively lower levels attained in Rajasthan Canal, Tawa and Mahanadi Delta commands is traceable to the low share of this crop in the non-foodgrains crop-mix in these commands.

In the Nagarjunasagar and Tungbhadra commands the source of high productivity level of non-foodgrains is the predominant place of cotton which turns up with exceptionally high yield in these two commands. More specifically, the cotton yield here, measured in 'kapas', is reported to be 2230 kg/ha in Tungabhadra and 2041 kg/ha in Nagarjunasagar command in contrast to 1200-1300 kg/ha in Rajasthan Canal, Tawa and Bhakra Nangal commands, and 718 kg/ha in Jayakwadi area. Potatoes, another high tonnage crop, play significant role in raising productivity of the non-foodgrain group in Mayurakshi, Sarda Sahayak, and Bhakra Nangal commands. Since their rrigation requirements are markedly lower compared to cotton, it scores over other crops in the matter of productivity per unit of irrigation water. It is its perishable nature, coupled with high price uncertainty, that holds down its relative share in irrigated agriculture. In public canal-irrigated tracts, its cultivation gets discouraged as farmers find canal system inadequate for this crop that requires, as do all vegetables, frequent but light irrigation.

Among non-foodgrains, oilseeds constitute an important component under rainfed farming but not so in irrigated farming. In the main wet season, these respond to irrigation much more in the shape of yield stabilization than in yield step-up, notwithstanding the fact of their having low irrigation requirements. It is in the rabi season that irrigation impinges perceptibly on their yield also, though the level attained is not striking either in comparison to the wet-season yield of the same crop under dry farming conditions, or in relation to other rabi crops (excluding gram). Because the irrigation needs are neither exacting like those of HYV wheat nor high, their cultivation under rabi irrigation is rewarding to farmers without assured supply of canal irrigation. It is in the summer season that good irrigation becomes a per-requisite for oilseeds like groundnut. But, then, summertime availabiliy of irrigation is not an easy proposition. Among the ten projects, summer groundnut is cultivated on a considerable scale in the commands of Tungabhadra, Jayakwadi and Nagarjunasagar (all reservoir-based irrigation works), and rabi groundnut is coming up in Mahanadi Delta command, as also elsewhere in Orissa state. As for mustard/rapeseed, it attracts in a noteworthy manner the Rajasthan canal farmers.

A summary view of productivity per unit of irrigation water for six crop categories of pulses, oilseeds, fibres (cotton), vegetables (potatoes and chillies) and sugarcane is as follows. It is found that pulses and oilseeds are not superior to cereals/fibres everywhere in the matter of yield (in rice units) per ha-cm of irrigation water. The two exceptions, where cereals perform better in the matter of water economy, are Bhakra

Nangal and Jayakwadi. While vegetables top over all other crop groups, sugarcane, with comparatively low productivity per unit of water, is not at the bottom in all projects. In Nagarjunasagar and Jayakwadi (dry crop region) and Gandak (rice region), it does better than cereals. (While the summary data are in Table 5, the detailed data are in Appendix II)

Table 5

Crop Group-wise Output per Hectare-Centimetre of Canal Water in Selected Commands

Command/region	*cereals*	*pulses*	*oilseeds*	*fibres*	*vegetables*	*sugarcane*
I. **Wheat Region**						
Rajasthan	30(37)	33	54	29	–	24
Tawa	35(43)	117	–	43	–	11
Bhakra Nangal	46(54)	37	67	42	143	16
Sarda Sahayak	27(33)	41	–	–	98	26
II. **Dry Crop Region**						
Nagarjunasagar	15(15)	24	34	55	161	31
Tungabhadra	29(32)	54	40	64	–	29
Jayakwadi	36(50)	31	32	64	–	42
III. **Rice Region**						
Gandak	35(38)	48	51	–	121	43
Mayurakshi	47(49)	–	76	–	133	45
Mahanadi Delta	11(11)	42	35	–	64	–

* Rice equivalents; figures in brackets are physical grain units.

Summary

The output-augmenting role of public canal irrigation in India, as revealed by the analysis of data for the ten irrigation works for the mid-eighties, turns out to be quite substantial when compared to the yield level prevailing under purely rainfed conditions. Without regard to the size of an irrigation work, the simple mean value of output impact of canal irrigation is of the order of 16 quintals of rice equivalents for each crop hectare brought under irrigation, almost twice the magnitude of output level without irrigation. Even when due account is taken of the fact that barely 70 per cent of the created irrigation potential of the ten projects was actually utilized during the 3-year period 1982-83 to 1984-85, the output-enhancing role of canal irrigation appears impressive, namely, about 10 quintals of rice equivalents for each hectare of irrigation potential brought into existence. In point of fact, in none of the ten projects studied canal irrigation fails to augment output of rainfed farming by at least a factor of two for each hectare of created irrigation capacity.

Since farmers within the selected commands devote a major share of canal-irrigated acreage to foodgrain crops, investments in canal irrigation works play a vital role in realizing the objective of expanding the domestic supply of foodgrains in India. The land productivity under canal irrigation ranges between 8 and 24 quintals of rice equivalents per irrigated ha, with an overall average (simple mean) of 17 quintals/ha (19 quintals if measured in grain units, that is, without reckoning with the price vector for different foodgrains). Of course, the land productivity for non-foodgrain crops as a group under irrigated conditions is much higher than that for foodgrains group. By and large, non-foodgrains as a group absorb more irrigation resource than do foodgrains. Yet, water for water, non-foodgrains appear more economical than foodgrains, as production per unit of irrigation water for 8 out of 10 projects is higher for non-foodgrains than for foodgrains. Crop category-wise, vegetable crops have the highest productive impact per unit of irrigation water. On the same reckoning, sugarcane comes out with the poorest rating vis-a-vis other crop categories like fibres, pulses, oilseeds and cereals, with the notable exception of the projects located in the Deccan plateau, the region known for high yield of sugarcane. By and large, the productivity of pulses and oilseeds, the two crop categories which are not favoured by farmers once they get access to irrigation, is, with the exception of Punjab, higher than that of cereals when reckoned in terms of output per unit volume of irrigation.

A brief probe into factors that inhibit or promote land productivity under canal irrigation reveals its negative association with rainfall level within a canal command. The productivity is, however, positively related to quantum of irrigation, and the share of non-foodgrains in total irrigated area. The above propositions hold good with still greater force in respect of output impact of canal irrigation.

Appendix I

Basic Crop-wise Data on Area Share, Yield and Irrigation

I. WHEAT REGION

S.No.	*Crop/Season*	*Area share (%)*	*Irrigation (mm)*	*Yield (kg/ha)*	*Area share (%)*	*Irrigation (mm)*	*Yield (kg/ha)*
	Kharif		**Rajasthan Canal**			**Tawa**	
1.	Paddy	1.8	1100	4280	0.5	575	1628
2.	Jowar				0.1	75	475
3.	Bajra	0.8	272	710			
4.	Maize						
5.	Pulses	14.2*	265*	1040*	0.7	100	
6.	Groundnut	1.7	495	1814	0.9	600	1277
7.	Cotton	20.3	937	1338			
8.	Chillies						
9.	Total Kharif	38.80	666		2.2	412	
	Rabi/Summer						
0.	Wheat	25.6	618	2380	72.7	600	2584
.1.	Gram	14.5	388	655	23.5	150	1407
12.	Jowar						
13.	Maize						
14.	Pulses						
15.	Paddy						
16.	Groundnut						
17.	Mustard	11.9	417	1050			
18.	Potatoes						
19.	Total Rabi	52.00	508		96.20	490	
20.	Sugarcane	0.6	2119	50000	0.1	2125	22550
	Kharif		**Bhakra Nangal**			**Sarda Sahayak**	
1.	Paddy	27.0	710	3670	14.7	710	1222
2.	Jowar	3.3	330	1861			
3.	Bajra	3.3	330	1364			
4.	Maize	6.3	330	1905	0.1	142	1704
5.	Pulses	0.1	280	877			
6.	Groundnut	0.1	330	750			
7.	Cotton	3.7	635	1342			
8.	Chillies						
9.	Total Kharif	43.8	590		14.8	707	
	Rabi/Summer						
10.	Wheat	45.0	420	3093	72.9	468	1787
11.	Gram	5.1	216	629	1.7	280	926
12.	Jowar	2.3**	216**	1913**			
13.	Maize						
14.	Pulses						

S.No.	*Crop/Season*	*Area share (%)*	*Irrigation (mm)*	*Yield (kg/ha)*	*Area share (%)*	*Irrigation (mm)*	*Yield (kg/ha)*
15.	Paddy						
16.	Groundnut						
17.	Mustard	0.7	254	875			
18.	Potatoes	1.7	560	20000	3.7	559	13750
19.	Total Rabi	54.8	395		78.3	468	
20.	Sugarcane	1.4	1016	16000	6.9	1583	41700

* For guar. ** For barley.

Appendix I (Contd.)

II. DRY CROP REGION

Sr.No.	*Crop/Seasons*	*Area share (%)*	*Irrig-ation (mm)*	*Yield (kg/ha)*	*Area share (%)*	*Irrig-ation (mm)*	*Yield (kg/ha)*	*Area share (%)*	*Irrig-ation (mm)*	*Yield (kg/ha)*
	Kharif	**Nagarjuna Sagar**			**Tungabhadra**			**Jayakwadi**		
1.	Paddy	63.4	1119	2671	21.9	890	3530	1.9	391	1015
2.	Jowar	1.7	648	1164	3.9	285	1500	7.6	49	1915
3.	Bajra				3.9	188	1500	14.1	49	1600
4.	Maize									
5.	Pulses	03	320	800	3.9	318	1310			
6.	Groundnut									
7.	Cotton	24.1	701	1936	20.5	700	2230	4.0	224	718
8.	Chillies	4.9	506	2041						
9.	Total Kharif	94.4	969		54.1	683		27.6	98	
	Rabi/Summer									
10.	Wheat							21.9	486	1585
11.	Gram							13.8	245	600
12.	Jowar	1.8	648	1164	5.5	365	2500	14.9	400	1200
13.	Maize				5.5	365	3000			
14.	Pulses	1.0	643	1100						
15.	Paddy				16.8	1200	4500			
16.	Groundnut	2.7	760	1591	10.9	760	1800	13.0	781	1541
17.	Sesamum				6.0	590	1260			
18.	Potatoes									
19.	Total Rabi/ Summer	5.5	702		44.7	806		53.6	517	
20.	Sugarcane	0.1	2743	85000	1.2	2740	80000	14.9	1674	70000

III PADDY REGION

Sr.No.	Crop/Seasons	Area share (%)	Irrigation (mm)	Yield (kg/ha)	Area share (%)	Irrigation (mm)	Yield (kg/ha)	Area share (%)	Irrigation (mm)	Yield (kg/ha)
	Kharif	**Gandak**			**Mayurakshi**			**Mahanadi Delta**		
1.	Paddy	65.0	597	2314	89.9	438	3526	51.3	925	1500
	Rabi/Summer									
2.	Wheat	19.6	579	3198	0.7	720	2143	0.6	700	2000
3.	Gram	1.7	393	1500						
4.	Maize	1.5	450	3000						
5.	Pulses							22.7	125	400
6.	Paddy	3.0	1167	2680	7.5	1500	5000	6.1	1350	2500
7.	Groundnut							5.2	450	1000
8.	Mustard	1.1	286	700	0.9	250	900	2.6	200	500
9.	Sesamum									
10.	Potatoes	0.8	498	15000	0.7	450	15000	5.2	450	7200
11.	Total Rabi/ Summer	27.0	616		9.8	1254	–	42.4	434	–
12.	Sugarcane	5.0	1053	45000	0.3	1500	68000			

Note: Yield data are in original units, namely, "kapas' for cotton; nuts-in-shell for groundnut; dry weight for chillies, cane (and not gur) weight for sugarcane, and grain weight for foodgrain crops other than paddy.

Appendix II

Crop Group Data on Area, Yield and Irrigation

I. WHEAT REGION

	Crop group	Percent share in area	Irrigation (mm)	Yield (kg/ha)	Yield per ha-cm (kg)	Percent share in area	Irrigation (mm)	Yield (kg/ha)	Yield per ha-cm (kg)
		Rajasthan				**Tawa**			
1.	Cereals	28.2	639	1925 (2364)	30.1 (37.0)	74.0	594	2046 (2556)	34.5 (43.0)
2.	Pulses	28.7	327	1083	33.1	23.5	150	1703	117.3
3.	Oilseeds	13.6	427	2292	53.7	–	–	–	–
4.	Fibres	20.3	937	2676	28.6	0.9	600	2554	42.6
5.	Vegetables	–	–	–	–	–	–	–	–
6.	Sugarcane	0.6	2119	5000	23.6	0.1	2125	2255	10.6
		Bhakra				**Sarda Sahayak**			
1.	Cereals	87.2	491	2243 (2667)	45.7 (54.3)	87.7	508	1394 (1692)	27.4 (33.3)

Appendix II (Contd.)

Crop Group Data on Area, Yield and Irrigation

	Crop group	*Percent share in area*	*Irrigation (mm)*	*Yield (kg/ha)*	*Yield per ha.cm (kg)*	*Percent share in area*	*Irrigation (mm)*	*Yield (kg/ha)*	*Yield per ha-cm (kg)*
2.	Pulses	5.2	217	793	36.5	1.7	280	1158	41.3
3.	Oilseeds	0.8	264	1758	66.6	–	–	–	–
4.	Fibres	3.7	635	2684	42.3	–	–	–	–
5.	Vegetables	1.7	560	8000	142.9	3.7	559	5500	98.4
6.	Sugarcane	1.4	1016	1600	15.7	6.9	1583	4170	26.3

Note: Yield data are in rice equivalents; bracketed figures pertain to foodgrain units (physical grain units unadjusted for prices).

II DRY CROP REGION

	Crop group	*Percent share in area*	*Irrigation (mm)*	*Yield (kg/ha)*	*Yield per ha-cm (kg)*	*Percent share in area*	*Irrigation (mm)*	*Yield (kg/ha)*	*Yield per ha-cm (kg)*
		Nagarjunasagar				**Tungabhadra**			
1.	Cereals	66.9	1158	1736	15.0	57.5	791	2254	28.5
				(1757)	(15.2)			(2507)	(31.7)
2.	Pulses	1.3	568	1340	23.6	3.9	318	17.03	53.6
3.	Oilseeds	2.7	760	2546	33.5	16.9	700	2797	40.0
4.	Fibres	24.1	701	3872	55.2	20.5	700	4460	63.7
5.	Vegetables	4.9	506	8164	161.3		–	–	–
6.	Sugarcane	0.1	2743	8500	31.0	1.2	2740	800	29.2
		Jayakwadi							
1.	Cereals	60.4	305	1092	35.8				
				(1517)	(49.7)				
3.	Pulses	3.8	245	750	30.6				
4.	Oilseeds	13.0	781	2466	31.6				
4.	Fibres	4.0	224	1436	61.1				
5.	Vigetables	–	–	–	–				
6.	Sugarcane	14.9	1674	7000	41.8				

Chapter 12

ERADICATING POVERTY IN WATER ABUNDANT EASTERN INDIA
Lessons From Three Case Studies*

Introduction

The carrying capacity of land is inter alia governed by both the natural fertility of the soil and the quantum of rainfall. The plains portion of eastern India is very fortunate in these two respects. Today, the east Gangetic plains (including Bangladesh) is a densely populated region of the world. As the economy of the region, unlike in densely populated European countries and Japan in the Far East, is land based, the proportion of the population below poverty line is very high here. There is a widely-shared feeling that poverty of the region can be eradicated if the region's abundant water resources are properly developed.

Development of water resource here has two distinct, though highly inter-linked, aspects, namely, irrigation and flood control and drainage. So far, the progress in these areas has not been sufficient enough to lead to a rate of growth of agriculture ahead of the rate of growth of population. Leaving out the comparatively better growth of east U.P. (3.01 per cent per annum), the rate of growth of crop output in south Bihar plains, north Bihar and West Bengal during the two-decade period 1960-80 averaged 0.41, 1.19 and 2.16 per cent, respectively. As for the progress in irrigation development in the same two-decade period, the irrigation coverage (measured as a ratio of gross irrigated area to total area) rose from about 26 to 31 per cent in West Bengal; 8 to 27 per cent in north Bihar; 48 to 63 per cent in south Bihar plains, and 29 to 41 per cent in east U.P. — the corresponding changes in more rapidly growing regions were 46 to 75 per cent in Punjab–Haryana region (rate of agricultural growth 5.77 per cent), and

* Results about Bihar already published (Dhawan, 1989d).

from 30 to 57 per cent in western U.P. (rate of agricultural growth 3.90 per cent).[1] With the exception of Bihar, one observes a close relationship between the rate of agricultural growth and the pace of irrigation development.

Irrigation being land augmenting, its establishment is tantamount to expanding the land base of a region. Among irrigation sources, private tubewell irrigation is considered to be the most land augmenting. And the east Gangetic plains are bountifully endowed with groundwater that can be very efficiently exploited through the tubewell technology. What stands in the development of tubewell-based agriculture in the region has been explored by the author earlier in his work *Development of Tubewell Irrigation in India*. This paper carries forward the same exploration.

Scope and Outline

The concern here is with the issue of eradicating rural poverty through the development of groundwater irrigation. The context is that of the east Gangetic plains region of Indian subcontinent, and the focus is on marginal farmers with land-holding upto one hectare. The optimistic feeling, both in academic and non-academic circles, is that tubewell irrigation can sufficiently raise the farm output of the land-poor farmers so as to enable them to cross the poverty line. Does the ground reality warrant this feeling? If not, under what conjunctive conditions can tubewell technology do the job of poverty alleviaton?

The text that follows is in three sections. In the first section we have brief expositions on the following three aspects:

...... various institutional arrangements by which the indivisibility of a tubewell investment can be overcome for the benefit of the marginal farmers;

.... the particular role of irrigation in the agriculture of the east Gangetic plains;

.... a discussion on the viability of flood control through building reservoirs.

The section II analyses the economics of private tubewell irrigation in a tract of Bhojpur district of Bihar state. The tract suffers from the twin natural hazard of waterlogging and flood damage during the main (kharif) crop season. In the survey year it additionally suffered from a power famine that adversely affected the performance of the electric

1. These statistics are from Bhalla and Tyagi (1988), as quoted in Alagh (1989).

tubewells. The working of the groundwater market in this tract is briefly examined.

It is in section III that we analyse in some depth the two separate experiences of the asset-poor farmers who opted for investment in tubewell borings which were operated with diesel pumpsets taken on rental. While the most satisfying experience is from Purnia district of north Bihar, the unfavourable one pertains to a tract in West Dinajpur district in northern West Bengal.

I

Tubewell Indivisibility

Tubewell being a lumpy investment, marginal farmers do not find it a viable proposition to invest in their own tubewells. This indivisibility is further heightened because of the phenomenon of landholdings being fragmented in space. Over time, the intrinsic indivisibility of tubewell has declined, partly due to technical advances in the minimum size of components of a tubewell and partly due to the advent of high yielding varieties (HYV) of crops. Wherever the process of land consolidation has been completed, the indivisibility due to land fragmentation has also fallen sharply. These téchnological and land reform changes sharply reduced the minimum farm size for investment in a singly-owned tubewell in the western parts of the Indo-Gangetic alluvium between 1950 and 1975 (Dhawan, 1982, p. 54). But in the east Gangetic plains this minimum size stood at 19 acres in West Bengal, 13 acres is Bihar and 5.5 acres in east U.P. - the progress in land consolidation in east U.P., though inferior to that of Punjab and Haryana, has been much better than that in West Bengal and Bihar. These farm sizes of the mid-seventies might be perceptibly smaller today but still above the one hectare mark.

When this author wrote the tubewell monograph, he thought that the institution of government tubewells was intrinsically best suited for the development of groundwater-based agriculture in the east Gangetic plains. For one, he did not visualize any noteworthy development either of cooperative/community tubewells or of groundwater market, both of which, like government tubewells, could surmount the twin-disability of small land holdings and their fragmentation in space. For another, in public tubewell irrigation one could also exploit the economies of scale of tubewell irrigation. Nor, for that matter, he could anticipate the possibility of overcoming the tubewell lumpiness via installation of tubewell borings only, to be operated with mobile pumpsets. While a resourceful farmer can surmount the fragmentation hurdle by installing low-cost borings on his parcels of land and operate them through his own diesel pumpset, an asset-poor farmer would depend on renting in a pumpset for drawing water from his own boring.

Two other institutional developments in tubewell irrigation are worth mentioning. First, from Bangladesh, where a variety of institutional developments relating to tubewell irrigation have occurred, one hears of rural banks having financed the practically landless groups to instal tubewells as an agri-business that caters to the irrigation needs of all classes of farmers. Ahmed and Sampath (1988) have econometrically investigated the working of this particular groundwater market (as far as I know, there is no such development in India), in which the monopolistic exploitation of the buyers of water was rather small (one-fifth of the monopoly surplus extractable under pure monopoly situation). Second, the Comprehensive Area Development Corporation (CADC) of the government of West Bengal has been carrying out a variety of experiments over the last twelve years in involving rural people in the management of CADC-owned tubewells. Sarkar (1989) gives a descriptive account of these experiments.

As an alternative to public tubewell irrigation which other institutional arrangement is best for the marginal farmers can be ascertained by reviewing experiences from various parts of the eastern subcontinent. Towards this end, I offer in section III of this paper some results about promoting the installation of low-cost borings by marginal and small farmers in northern parts of West Bengal and Bihar states.

Role of Irrigation

Irrigation has been widely perceived as a major prerequisite for enlarging crop production the in Indian subcontinent. There is hardly any differences of opinion that its prior development is a must if the scarce-most resource of land of this subcontinent is to be put to productive use during the non-monsoon period of the year. A similar view can also be taken of its relevance for land use during the monsoon or kharif period for the highly arid, western parts where monsoon rain is inadequate for sustaining crop enterprise. In the absence of crop intensification with modern inputs like chemical fertilisers and HYV seeds, the main role of kharif irrigation remains protective in nature, more so in high rainfall areas like those of the east Gangetic plains. Thus one may say that irrigation has a double role to play in these plains: primarily productive during the winter and the summer seasons, and primarily protective during the kharif season.

For discharging such a twin role, an irrigation resource ought to have some desirable attributes. First, it must be copious and dependable enough to meet bulk of the water needs of the rabi crops grown in relatively rainless period of the year — this is particularly important if 'boro' paddy rather than wheat is being visualised for the rabi season.[1] Second, it must be flexible enough to serve the purpose of protective irrigation whenever there is failure of monsoons. Evidently, such irrigation has to be primarily reservoir based. The question is: will it be a surface or underground reservoir? This brings us to tubewell irrigation on the one hand and the reservoir-based surface irrigation on the other. Before sorting out this issue in the particular context of the east Gangetic plains and its rural poor, let us look at the linkages between irrigation and poverty reduction.

Both the spatial and temporal investigations have brought out the existence of an inverse relation between the poverty ratio and the agricultural growth/productivity. Since the latter is positively determined by irrigation, one may infer that the poverty ratio is also inversely related with irrigation. The strength of this inferred relationship is governed by the level of output expansion resulting from irrigation. If irrigation turns out to be highly output augmenting, the poverty alleviation is likely to be more. This brings us to (1) the factors and forces that maximise production impact of irrigation, especially tubewell irrigation, and (2) the determinants of the rate of expansion in irrigation development.

The production effect of irrigation in the east Gangetic plains, when compared to the rest of the Indian subcontinent, has been comparatively low. This is partly because of lower output impact consequent upon bringing each hectare here under irrigation, and partly because of lower pace of development of irrigation resource. Compared to the national average of 1.8 tons of foodgrains equivalents addition resulting from one crop hectare area brought under irrigation in 1983-84, the corresponding estimate for Bihar and West Bengal states was of the order of one ton — the separate estimate for east U.P. is not available, though it may be somewhat above one ton (Dhawan, 1988a). In the case of West Bengal the low addition is partly accountable by the fact that irrigation resource here is mainly oriented to kharif season, in which the yield differential due to irrigation (i.e., the excess of irrigated over unirrigated yield) is found to be a small fraction of the corresponding yield differential for crops of the non-kharif seasons.

1. Irrigation needs of 'boro' paddy are 40 to 50 inches delta as compared to 15 to 20 inches delta for. wheat crop.

Many scholars have studied the diffusion of HYV seeds of wheat and paddy in the Indian subcontinent. While the diffusion has been an unqualified success in the case of rabi wheat, it has not been so in the case of paddy. Like rabi wheat, rabi or summer cultivation of HYV paddy has been adopted wherever farmers have had good access to irrigation. However, they have shown disinclination for HYV seeds for the main kharif season (with the notable exception of Punjab and Haryana States where farmers have found the kharif climate somewhat similar to th dry rabi climate of the east Gangetic plains). Lack of control on water during the kharif season is generally identified as a major factor militating against the adoption of HYV paddy during the kharif season. This brings us to the flood-cum-waterlogging hazard, in which the east Gangetic plains would undoubtedly rank the worst in the Indian subcontinent.

Flood-cum-Waterlogging Hazard

Subsistence farmers are known for their risk aversion. This aversion becomes stronger when they face the clear prospect of uncertainty in realising high crop yields attainable only via the use of modern farm inputs financed through interest-bearing loans. Leaving aside the risk to paddy yield arising from comparatively higher incidence of pests and diseases during kharif than during rabi season, the east Gangetic plains farmer has to reckon also with crop damage from floods and from prolonged periods of waterlogging of fields during the monsoon season. This risk is comparatively less in the east U.P. plains, where the serious risk from flood damage is said to be confined to only one-fourth area. In east U.P., the natural risk from waterlogging is also much less, though man-made constructions like river embankments, railways, roads and canals have certainly added to the waterlogging problem. In contrast, both the problem of natural water congestion (i.e. poor drainage) and the threat of flood aggravate in areal extent as one moves eastwards from east U.P. to Bangladesh - in the lower reaches, the cyclonic storms at the maturing stage of 'Amman' paddy are an added source of risk to kharif cropping.

The agronomic potential of HYV seeds of paddy is realiseable in the east Gangetic plains only when this crop is cultivated during the non-monsoon period. Under most favourable circumstances, the monsoon rice yield can touch 30-35 quintals per hectare, a level which is indeed well above the current irrigated yield of about 15 quintals or so. Still, it would stay 15-20 quintals/ha less than the potential yield of HYV rice under good agronomical practices. The farmers' prior need for realising this kharif potential of HYV paddy is for effective protection against flood hazard through the following two inter-linked measures as against the present policy of extending (and strengthening) the network of embankments along the rivers in east U.P. and Bihar. First is the construction of big reservoirs for storing flood waters in the mountains of the Himalayas, Vindhyas and the Chotanagpur hills. Second is the detention of these mountainous waters through greater afforestation work in the upper catchments of all rivers of the region. Together these two measures might improve the drainage in the plains (both water flow and silt in the rivers get reduced).

The option of detention reservoirs raises several questions, of which the following ones need stating.

1. Do we have enough safe dam sites for building reservoirs in the hilly areas surrounding the plains region?
2. If answer to the question (1) is in the affirmative, will investments in such reservoirs be economically justifiable? In short, will the production gains by a factor of two to three from kharif cropping under the aegis of flood protection - and other incidental gains (e.g., protection to assets, both public and private) - be commensurate with the huge costs of such reservoirs?
3. How do we go about apportioning reservoir costs (as also those of afforestation programme) among the riparian countries of the eastern subcontinent on the one hand and among the riparian states of the Union of India on the other?

The conventional thinking on flood control apears to be that investment in reservoirs are economically worthwhile only when such reservoirs are conceived for multipurpose use, including irrigation and hydel power generation (Government of India, 1980). If that be so, one worrisome question arises about the usability of the stored waters for irrigation purpose. Evidently, such waters have per force to be released during the non-monsoon period, so as to create storage for inflow of fresh flood waters in the succeeding monsoon season. Such releases can generate hydel power, which can be transmitted for pump operation for lift irrigation (groundwater mainly) in the plains down below. This power should go a long way in eradicating the chronic power shortages of northern and eastern India, as also play a useful role in meeting the growing power needs of these two regions. But to what good use can we put the released water? Their being let in a network of canals, so as to meet irrigation needs of the plains during the rabi/summer period, appears to be of doubtful merit from the long-run aspect of sustained growth of agriculture. For, such canals appear unwarranted in flat, high rainfall areas where their development would further impede the natural drainage system, not to mention their potential for raising groundwater table to within crop root zone (i.e., create waterlogging conditions for crops).

Thus one has to investigate the viability of investments in detention reservoirs under the assumption that their irrigation component may be small — and possibly the enormous hydel power potential from the conceivable reservoirs for controlling the floods in the Brahmputra river basin may not be fully used in the eastern subcontinent. This also calls for commencement of studies which bring out the magnitude of pure benefits from controlling the flood-cum-waterlogging problem. While in the next section I do a case analysis of tubewell benefits being eroded in the presence of this twin hazard, here I may briefly present some statistics from a canal command enjoying a modicum of flood protection from the reservoir which supplies irrigation water to this command.

Mayurakshi project is basically an irrigation project, although some element of flood control, besides hydel generation, is part of the reservoir at Masanjore on the river Mayurakshi. Its canal command is mainly in the southern West Bengal districts of Burdwan, Mursheedabad and Birbhum. Despite high rainfall (1285 mm), kharif irrigated paddy here has performed better than elsewhere in the state. According to Operation Research Group (ORG), Baroda, the 'Amman' and 'Aus' yields in the mid-eighties in this command were about 35 and 33 quintals per hectare, respectively — the 'boro' paddy averaged about 50 quintals/ha (wheat averaged about 21.5 quintals/ha). Though the corresponding data for the same period for the state of West Bengal are not available, yet the following state level data suggests as if the benefit from flood control in Mayurakshi command could be considerable.

	Range of irrigated paddy yield between 1978-79 and 1983-84
'Aus' Paddy	between 20 and 26 quintals/ha
Early 'Amman'	between 18 and 27 quintals/ha
'Amman'	between 20 and 27 quintals/ha

II

Bhojpur Tubewells

The case analysis that follows is about shallow tubewells of

Bhojpur district in South Bihar plains. The erstwhile Agricultural Refinance and Development Corporation (ARDC, now NABARD) did an evaluation of their performance on the basis of a sample survey. The results of this study (ARDC, 1982) are reviewed and its survey data on 57 tubewell owners, 28 farmers buying water from these owners, and 21 farmers of the 'control' sample are reanalysed to draw attention to natural and man-made factors giving rise to rather modest returns to investments in private tubewells. Besides landholdings being small and fragmented in space, the survey tract suffers from the natural hazard of severe flood-cum-waterlogging. This is because it is located at the junction of the mighty Ganga and the Sone rivers. Among the man-made factors, the power famine in the ARDC survey year (1978-79) affected the performance of sample electric tubewells so adversely that these turned out with lower returns than even diesel tubewells.

As it is, crop entreprise in the survey tract (Barahara and Arrah blocks) is a very risky proposition. While the kharif crop is threatened by the twin hazard of flood and waterlogging, rabi cropping is risky because October-March rainfall is low (4.5 inches), though the latter risk can be overcome through investment in irrigation. Land use under purely rainfed conditions is more oriented to the rabi season when low water requiring pulses and some local wheat are grown. Thus the control farmers having no access to irrigation devoted almost three-fourths crop area to rabi cropping. Under such circumstances, the area impact of perennial irrigation like tubewells will remain modest till kharif cropping can be ensured through flood control and drainage measures. Otherwise, the principal impact of introducing tubewell irrigation gets restricted to changes in crop mix and crop yields of the rabi season.

Impact Results

The survey results bring out the following main changes in the farm economy. The intensity of cropping on tubewell owning farmers' fields stood at 154 per cent in the survey year. In fact, the enlargement of crop area per tubewell averaged just about one hectare. HYV wheat displaced both pulses and local wheat in the wake of tubewell irrigation. This beneficial development occurred also on the fields of farmers dependent on market in tubewell water. Whatever limited cultivation of lowyielding local paddy and maize existed during the kharif season, the advent of tubewell irrigation shifted it to HYV seeds. However, the enhanced paddy yield (about 16 quintals of rice/ha) remained far below the agronomical potential yield of HYV paddy. No sample farmer reported raising higher yielding rabi/summer paddy. Yet, the relative step-up in overall crop yield was impressive, especially in the case of wheat whose yield rose be 113 per cent. The overall crop yield, as measured by the value of gross output per crop hectare, on tubewell-irrigated areas did become twice of that under unirrigated conditions.

On the whole, each crop hectare brought under tubewell irrigation augmented crop output by about 1.5 tons (in rice equivalents) on tubewell owners' farms (as well as on the farms of buyers of tubewell water). As the crop area irrigated per tubewell is about 4.2 ha, the total output addition per tubewell is of the order of 6 tons in rice equivalents, about two-thirds of this occurring on the farm of a tubewell owner and the rest on the farms of buyers of surplus tubewell water. If all the irrigation potential of a shallow tubewell could somehow be utilised, the output addition per tubewell would have been much more. For, hardly one-third of the potential had been used in the survey area.

In the present case, no marginal farmer installed his own tubewell. The average size of a sample tubewell owner is about 11.43 acres (4.6 ha). But because of fragmentation the average net area benefited by a tubewell is only 4.78 acres (1.9 ha), a little over two-fifths of the farm size of the tubewell-owning farmers. Thus fragmentation of landholdings leaves unexploited the irrigation capacity of a tubewell. Over the period of planning, the problem of fragmentation has been substantially resolved in the western Indo-Gangetic plains. But no noteworthy progress has been made in this regard in Bihar and Weat Bengal despite a widely felt need for such a land reform. Though the ARDC report does not give any data on the rate of discharge of the sample tubewells, this author feels that a sample tubewell could potentially command 15 acres (about 6 ha) with seasonal crops like paddy in the kharif and wheat during the following rabi season. That is, 30 crop acres as against about 10 crop acres benefited in the sample area by each tubewell.

Despite gross underutilisation of tubewell capacity, the aggregate impact of the ARDC scheme for private tubewell irrigation in Bhojpur district was substantial, more so in the case of availability of foodgrains. Under the ARDC scheme, 467 tubewells were installed during the first half of the seventies. As against an investment cost of Rs. 5.70 million, the value of additional crop production amounted to about Rs 4.60 million per year. The foodgrains output expanded four-fold, the addition being of the order of 38 thousand quintals — primarily in the form of wheat and rice but partly at the expense of pulse crops whose output diminished by about 5 thousand quintals. (This adverse change in the nutritive content of food supplies must be viewed alongwith improved availability of vegetables and potatoes by about 8 thousand quintals). It may be clarified that these estimates are inclusive of output effects on farms irrigated with tubewell water purchased from farmers who installed tubewells under the ARDC scheme.

BC Results

First we present benefit-cost results for a farmer buying tubewell water. For an average net area of 2 acres with an intensity of cropping of 170 per cent, the gross crop area under purchased tubewell water amounted to 3.4 acres. In the absence of irrigation, the net output from 2 acres would have been around Rs 627 at 1978-79 prices. It rose to Rs 2190 with purchased tubewell water costing about Rs 447, the water price being Rs 5 per hour in most cases and Rs 4 in some cases. Thus, the private BC ratio for purchased tubewell water is rather attractive, namely, 4.5. This indicates that water needs of the buyer farmers were met adequately. In fact, "bulk of the purchasers stated that they received waterings as previously agreed upon at the right time and in the required quantity" (ARDC, p. 42).

To what extent there was monopolistic exploitation by the tubewell owners in their water selling agri-business cannot be correctly gauged from the ARDC report, which mentions no data on average and marginal costs of operating a tubewell per hour — the two costs are usually equal in the case of diesel-operated pumpsets. For the sample diesel tubewells, the marginal cost might be placed between Rs 3 to Rs 4 per hour. In that case, the sale price of Rs 5 per hour does not appear to be exploitative. In fact, the ARDC report categorically states: "According to the buyers of water, the water charges were quite reasonable though some of them would like the government to regulate the charges" (p. 43. This lack of evidence of exploitation in the groundwater market goes well with two other facts: (1) high level of the BC ratio for the buyers and (2) the income from sale of surplus tubewell water being about one-tenth of a sample tubewell owner's income from crop enterprise.

Still, there is need to investigate further the working of the water market from the viewpoint of marginal farmers during years of water stress i.e., drought years. In fact, the above results do need firming up in two following respects. First, these pertain to buyer farmers with an average landholding of two hectares. One would like to see how marginal farmers, who otherwise predominate in the east Gangetic plains, fare in the water market, more so during years of drought. Second, the ARDC evaluators' assumption of equality in farm crop enterprise between tubewell owners and tubewell water buyers needs further probing.[1] Whether this equality will hold good during drought time needs testing, especially with regard to crop yields.

As for a tubewell-owning farmer, he did enlarge his net farm income by about Rs 1258-1298 from each crop hectare brought under tubewell irrigation (the lower estimate is for an electric tubewell, and the higher for a diesel one). For this he incurred the following irrigation costs: (1) operational and maintenance cost of the tubewell, and (2) interest and depreciation charges on the tubewell investment. The ARDC report does not contain any explicit details about such costs. However, it is not all that difficult to arrive at reasonable estimates in this regard. For a 5 HP electric tubewell in Bihar, the fixed or flat charge for 1978-79 amounted to Rs 891. This amount is much less than Rs 1432 shown as irrigation cost against an electric tubewell in Annexure 5 of the ARDC report. The difference of Rs 541 is really the depreciation amount on the nominal investment of Rs 8950 per electric tubewell in the scheme.

Taking Rs 1000 as the annual interest cost, the total cost per crop hectare for tubewell irrigation is about Rs 775-734 (the lower figure being for electric tubewell owners). Thus the private BC ratio for a tubewell owner, even without engaging in water selling activity, averaged around 2.0 for electric tubewell owners and about 2.2 for diesel tubewell owners - the ARDC report mentions an internal rate of return (IRR) of 29 per cent for electric tubewells and 31 per cent for diesel tubewells.

It has to be borne in mind that these BC ratios (or IRRs) are for a tubewell owner who could benefit two hectare area of his land holding and achieve about 155 per cent intensity of cropping on this benefited area. Evidently, the BC ratio would shrink more than proportionately as the area benefited per tubewell diminishes in magnitude. In fact, the ratio for an electric tubewell owner becomes unity when the benefited area is 1.07 ha (1.66 ha in gross terms) - for a diesel tubewell the same is reached at 0.68 ha (1.05 ha in gross terms).

III

West Dinajpur Survey

Bulk of this section III is devoted to close analysis of survey results

1. In another survey, the output per acre on lands irrigated with purchased water from other tubewell owners was observed to be 30 per cent below the level prevailing on tubewell owners' fields (NABARD, 1988B).

on private tubewell irrigation in West Dinajpur district in northern region of West Bengal state. Towards the end of the section we present a brief account of similar tubewell irrigation in north Bihar. The evaluation study on tubewell irrigation in West Bengal was conducted by the Evaluation and Monitoring Cell of the State Bank of India (SBI). Admittedly, it is a decade old work, and its findings may not fully reflect the state of affairs as of today. Yet, it is insightful from three angles.

First, it permits analysis by farm categories. Socond, it provides information on pre-and-post tubewell investment situations in respect of income and assets of the sample farmers. (In recent years, the pre-and-post project approach to project evaluation has been almost given up in favour of with-and-without project approach). Third, one can examine the results of promoting mainly the installation of low cost tubewell borings by the marginal farmers. These farmers were expected to draw water through these borings by hiring in diesel pumpsets from other farmers, mostly small farmers who were visualised to augment their farm income by hiring out their SBI-financed diesel pumps.

The SBI sample consists of 84 farmers, 30 of whom took the SBI loan for constructing tubewell borings only. Of the 12 marginal farmers in the sample, 10 opted for borings, only one for a pumpset only and one for a complete tubewell. 15 out of the 44 small farmers in the sample opted also for boring only, 6 for pumpsets only and 23 for complete tubewells. Most sample farmers (80 out of 84) at the time of the survey (1977-78) had borings on their farms, which were highly fragmented in space (6 fragments per sample farmer). Because of the preponderance of small and marginal holdings in the sample, the average farm size is a little over 5 acres (2 ha). In the survey year, the average size of operated area in the four size classes stood as follows:

marginal farmers (less than 2.5 acres)	2.0 acress
small farmers (2.5 to 5 acres)	4.2 acres
medium farmers (5.1 to 10 acres)	6.4 acres
large farmers (above 10 acres)	12.1 acres
all sample farmers	5.1 acres

Before focussing on the impact of groundwater irrigation on marginal and small farmers separately, a few points about the sample as a whole may be noted. First, in the pre-investment period (1972-74), the sample farmers enjoyed little access to irrigation, the irrigation ratio being only 4 per cent. Following the investment, they did not enter wholly in to the stage of irrigated farming either, as the irrigation ratio obtaining in 1977-78 was only 32 per cent.

Second, the average per farmer investment in groundwater irrigation was Rs 3900. Purposewise, this averaged about Rs 5600 for a complete tubewell, Rs 1300 per boring and a little over Rs 4100 for a diesel pumpset. All the sample pumpsets were of 5 horse power rating and the average depth of boring was 87 feet and in 50 per cent cases the low-cost coir filter was used. Third, since the actual investment costs turned out to be lower than the SBI loan and since the borrowers were expected to put up only 5 per cent of the investment, one may say that the groundwater investment was wholly financed by institutional funds. Fourth, since the depth of boring was almost one-fourth less than that provided for in the SBI scheme, it is quite possbile the expected discharge of 6000 gallons per hour per tubewell was not wholly realised in practice.

Fifth, the incremental income from crop enterprise as a result of the investment in groundwater irrigation was about Rs 1035 per sample farmer. This rises to Rs 1214 when we reckon with the small agri-business income of Rs 131 from hiring out of the diesel pumpset and Rs 48 from sale of tubewell water. It needs pointing out that this income is not inclusive of additional wage income accruing to landless class from selling labour power to the farmers whose demand for hired labour rose following increased crop activity due to tubewell irrigation. But it is also not net of cost of depreciation and interest on capital cost of tubewell irrigation. According to this author's computations, the values of these three omitted items may be reckoned as shown below.

1.	Additional cost of hired labour at the rate of Rs 89 per irrigated crop acre	Rs 219
2.	Depreciation at the rate of 7 per cent on the reported value of assets (about Rs 2600) relating to borings, pumpsets and tubewells at the time of the survey	Rs 182
3.	Interest at the rate of 9.50 per cent on the average loan amount of Rs 3900 per farmer	Rs 370

Thus, from the strict angle of national income generation, the investment of Rs 3900 in tubewell irrigation generated annual income worth Rs 1251 (Rs 1214 + Rs 219 - Rs 182), which implies a capital-output ratio of a little over 3. Net of both depreciation charge and cost of hired labour, the incremental income of the sample farmers constitutes 26 per cent of their investment in well irrigation. To put it differently, the private benefit-cost ratio for the investing farmers is about 1.5. This is worked out from the following data:

1. Irrigation cost per crop acre	Rs 419
variable portion	Rs 199
fixed portion (depreciation and interest)	Rs 220
2. Incremental income benefit from each crop acre under tubewell irrigation (without netting out the variable portion of irrigation cost)	Rs 620
3. Benefit-cost ratio(2 divided by 1)	1.5

Finally, there was limited development of groundwater market in the survey tract. Sale and purchase of water was not very common among the sample farmers. Only eight of the 84 farmers reported sale of water by allowing the use of their borings at about Rs 2 per hour, which brought in income of Rs 243 annually per selling farmer. Of the four farmers who reported such purchase via the use of other farmers' borings, the price paid was even less than Rs 2 per hour for reasons of social consideration e.g. relationship and friendship. The average price for 1300 hours of transaction in this market comes to Rs 1.86 per hour of boring use. For the sample farmers, the income from water selling activity was just a little under five per cent of their incremental income from crop enterprise under irrigated conditions. In comparison, the income from pumpset hiring out was much more. The average price for hiring a diesel pumpset was Rs 5 per hour. The sample farmers hired out their pumpsets for about 2300 hours, earning Rs 11,651. (There was hiring in of pumpsets by sample farmers with borings to the extent of 1100 hours). On the average, the sample farmers' income from custom hiring of their pumpsets was about one-eighth of their incremental income from crop enterprise.

Changes in Marginal Farmers' Economy

Prior to the investment in ground irrigation, a sample marginal farmer derived six-tenths of his income from cropping on his 3-acre land base (2.75 acres owned and about 0.25 acres rented in). His value of gross output at 1977-78 prices from crop enterprise was around Rs 2350, which rose by only 12 per cent in the wake of tubewell irrigation. This marginal production gain is totally out of alignment with substantial improvement in his irrigation ratio from 9 to 49 per cent. While the quality of irrigation at his disposal, dependent as it was on the availability of pumpsets for hiring, was certinly not of a high rating, yet this factor alone is not a major factor behind his making low production gains from tubewell irrigation. The main factor was the marked reduction in his land resource during the intervening period between tubewell investment and the survey year.

More specifically, their farm operated area declined by one-third in this intervening period. While two-thirds of the reduction in the operated area could be traced to dimunition in land ownership itself, the rest is traceable to reduced availability of land for renting purpose. The germane question is: could these two sources of reduction in land base be linked, directly or indirectly, with the very advent of tubewell-based farming in the survey tract? A correct answer to this question is very imperative. If the reduction in land base of the marginal farmers is, historically or otherwise, inevitable, the alleviation of their poverty through the development of groundwater resources would remain unresolved.

Net of incremental cost of cultivation (but without providing for imputed cost of family labour and interest-cum-depreciation costs of tubewell irrigation), the farm income of the sample marginal farmers actually contracted by 12 per cent. The contraction of about Rs 209 per marginal farmer was almost made good by Rs 192 addition to income from five following sources which can be indirectly linked to SBI tubewell scheme:

income from agricultural labour	Rs 110
dairying	Rs 29
sale of water	Rs 17
income from hiring out of pumpset	Rs 17
income from hiring out of bullocks	Rs 19

One may rightly ask which class of farmers acquired the land lost by the marginal farmers. In our sample, a perceptible rise is noticed in land area of medium farmers. Their operated area expanded by about one-tenth during the pre-and-post tubewell period, with little change in respect of small as well as large farmers. Because of such increase in land area, this category of farmers gained the most from their investments in groundwater irrigation. In percentage terms, their production and income gains vis-a-vis other farm categories compare as follows:

	Per cent increase in	
	crop output	*income from crops*
marginal farmers	12	(-) 12
small farmers	54	22
medium farmers	84	65
large farmers	60	31
all farmers	60	34

In order to isolate the income/output effect due to change in land base, one needs looking at changes in farm parameters like land productivity, crop pattern, and intensity of cropping. In respect of landproductivity per unit area of the operated holding, the marginal farmers do reveal an encouraging performance as per the following statistics:

	increase in land productivity	
	amount	*in percentage*
marginal farmers	Rs 531/acre	68
small farmers	Rs 424/acre	54
medium farmers	Rs 519/acre	65
large farmers	Rs 409/acre	60
all farmers	Rs 456/acre	60

The marginal farmers' gains in land productivity were more due to faster improvement in intensity of cropping which rose by 44 points as against the sample average of 23 points only during the pre-and-post tubewell situations. But they made lower gains in overall crop yield, none at all in paddy (vide Table 1) but comparatively more in the case of wheat. While inter-group changes in crop pattern due to tubewells differed little (vide Table 2), the absence of yield gain in respect of paddy in the case of marginal farmers in primarily due to their inability to intensify the cultivation of this crop. In fact, there adoption of HYV seeds of both wheat and paddy was extremely low

Table 1

Impact of Tubewells on Crop Yields in West Dinajpur

	Marginal farmers	*Small farmers*	*Medium farmers*	*Large farmers*	*All farmers*
1. Overall yield (Rs/acre)					
(*i*) pre-tubewell	445	524	577	528	531
(*ii*) post-tubewell	597	685	810	724	723
(*iii*) incremental	152	161	235	196	192
2. Paddy yield (q/acre)					
(*i*) pre-tubewell	6.5	6.4	6.8	6.0	6.5
(*ii*) post-tubewell	6.5	7.4	8.2	6.9	7.4
(*iii*) incremental	nil	1.0	1.4	0.9	0.9
3. Wheat yield (q/acre)					
(*i*) pre-tubewell	3.0	4.8	5.3	3.9	4.8
(*ii*) post-tubewell	6.8	7.6	8.2	6.9	7.6
(*iii*) incremental	3.8	2.8	2.9	3.0	2.8
4. Percent increase in					
(*a*) overall yield	34	31	40	37	36
(*b*) paddy yield	nil	15	20	15	14
(*c*) wheat yield	126	57	54	78	58

Source: Based on data in SBI (1980)

Table 2

Crop Pattern Changes Due to Tubewells in West Dinajpur

	Marginal farmers	*Small farmers*	*Medium farmers*	*Large farmers*	*All farmers*
1. Incremental change in percent share of crops:					
Paddy	(-) 17.0	(-) 11.0	(-) 9.4	(-) 3.10	(-) 11.1
wheat	12.3	12.6	12.0	14.4	12.7
jute	8.4	0.4	(-) 1.5	(-) 1.0	(-) 0.2
pulses	(-) 5.7	(-) 2.9	(-) 1.6	(-) 1.0	(-) 2.4
mustard	2.5	1.4	1.1	1.6	1.3
2. Percent crop area under HYV seeds in 1977-78 :					
paddy	nil	2.1	6.31	5.45	3.87
	(nil)	(nil)	(3.20)	(nil)	(0.8)
wheat	21	93	89	92	87
	(nil)	(29)	(80)	(40)	(40)

Source: SBI (1980)
Note : Figures in parentheses pertain to pre-tubewell period.

Among other factors, the quality of irrigation at the disposal of marginal farmers might have hampered their adoption of HYV seeds -and cultivation of 'boro' paddy. Though all the four categories of farmers did depend to some extent on other farmers for meeting their irrigation needs, this external dependence was far more in their case. Their expenditure on purchased tubewell water and pumpset hiring amounted to 69 per cent of their total variable irrigation cost, whereas this percentage was 31 for small farmers, 33 for medium farmers, and 41 for large farmers. As the diesel pumpsets are liable to breakdown, their owners were reported to have been more eager to meet first their own irrigation needs than to hire them out to others for earning some income at a rental rate which was moderately above the operational cost of a pumpset.

Whatever be the reasons for low adoption of HYV technology by the marginal farmers, their extent of input intensification per acre of operated area vis-a-vis other farmers in the wake of tubewell irrigation changed a as shown in Table 3.

If the marginal farmers could use more of chemical fertilisers on their irrigated crops despite poorer quality of irrigation, they would have certainly further enhanced their land productivity. After all, they were

Table 3

Incremental rise (Rs/acre)

	variable irrigation	*chemical fertilisers*	*manures*
marginal farmers	96	62	22
small farmers	97	47	17
medium farmers	112	38	21
large farmers	67	45	27

applying chemical fertilisers worth Rs 31 per crop acre in the survey year (as compared to Rs 27 by small and marginal farmers and Rs 32 by large farmers). And the relationship between incremental land productivity and incremental fertiliser application in the present sample is rather high (r = 0.87).

Had there been no shrinkage in their land base, the marginal farmers would have realised an income benefit of about Rs 350 from each crop acre brought under tubewell irrigation at an estimated cost of about Rs 280. These statistics indicate a benefit-cost ratio of a little over 1.2 for the option of tubewell borings operated by rented pumpsets —to what extent they depended in the present case on purchased tubewell water from other farmers is not known. Though the BC ratio is evidently much below the sample average of 1.5, it is higher than the corresponding BC ratio of unity for the small farmers. After benefits in the case of medium and marginal farmers are duly adjusted for changes in the operated land area, the BC ratios for the samle farmers are listed in Table 4.

Table 4

Costs and Benefits of Tubewell Irrigation in West Dinajpur

Cost/Benefit	*Marginal farmers*	*Small farmers*	*Medium farmers*	*Large farmers*	*Whole sample*
1. Cost of tubewell irrigation (Rs/crop acre irrigated):					
variable	124	208	209	132	199
fixed	160	295	185	155	219
total	284	503	394	287	418
2. On-farm income benefit from tubewell irrigation (Rs/ crop acre irrigated)	352	501	821	538	620
3. BC ratio (2 ÷ 1)	1.24	1.00	2.08	1.87	1.48

In the case of small farmers, the BC ratio is understated as we have not reckoned with (*i*) their rental income from hiring out the pumpset and (*ii*) their income from sale of water. But despite reckoning with this omitted income the correct BC ratio of 1.17 remains low. A look at Table 4 reveals that this category of farmers had high cost of irrigation, largely because of comparatively high incidence of fixed costs of depreciation and interest charges. In their case, the gross irrigated area benefited by their investments in pumpsets as well as borings was comparatively smaller (2.2 acres as against 5.4 acres for large farmers and 3.4 acres for medium farmers). Qualitatively similar differential in returns between farmers investing in borings only and farmers investing in both borings and diesel pumpsets was observed in the following NABARD study from north Bihar.

Purnia Tubewells

Purnia in north Bihar is near northern West Bengal. It has become known all over the world to the intermediate technology enthusiasts for its bamboo tubewells. (These are shallow tubewells in which piping material for borings is fabricated out of bamboo strips. This enables the use of a local resource viz bamboo in lieu of metallic pipes produced by modern industry sector). During the decade 1969-79, both the Land Development Bank (LDB) of Bihar and the Kosi Regional Rural Bank (RRB) promoted the development of private tubewell irrigation. Under the LDB schemes, 2000 conventional shallow tubewells, 4000 bamboo tubewells and 4000 pumpsets were proposed for Purnia and the adjoining Saharsa districts. Though the RRB scheme was much less ambitious, it envisaged the installation of bamboo tubewell borings also. NABARD has come out with an evaluation report (NABARD, 1988A) on the comparative performance of conventional and bomboo tubewells on the one hand, and of the bamboo tubewell borings only.

NABARD's survey results pertain to 40 conventional tubewells, 40 bamboo tubewells and 33 bamboo borings for the agricultural year 1981-82. The small and marginal farmers alone opted for the low cost bamboo boring. For the sample of 33 farmers, the average farm size comes to 2.87 acres (1.16 ha), of which over nine-tenths benefited from tubewell watering in the survey year. They enhanced their farm income by over Rs 1150 per year by incurring an investment of Rs 600 (Rs 720 at 1981-82 prices) in a bamboo boring. Acre for acre, their incremental income per unit irrigated area was comparable with the average level for all the 80 owners of complete tubewells. But if we restrict the comparison to bamboo tubewell which were primarily installed by small farmers (average size of operated holding = 4. 15 acres i.e. 1.68 ha), the farmers with borings did one-sixth better. For, their incremental income from each irrigated acre was Rs 449 as compared to Rs 388 of the bamboo tubewell owners.

As per NABARD's assessment, the IRR was over 50 per cent for bamboo borings, about 18 per cent for bamboo tubewells (each costing Rs 5500 or so) and about 36 per cent for conventional tubewells (each costing in the sample about Rs 7700). Evidently, the farmers who invest in diesel pumpsets confer a beneficial external economy on others having borings only. Without their investments, the marginal and samll farmers having borings only would be at a loss. In short, the option of encouraging marginal farmers to invest in borings only cannot be a meaningful course of action so long as other farmers (or landless groups like artisans) are not forthcoming to bear the risk of investing in pumpsets also.

Concluding Remarks

The water endowment of eastern India is indeed bountiful. But, harnessing these waters for poverty alleviation is very problematic. To control the flood waters and to improve the drainage here are two formidable problems that require joint action with both the upper and lower riparian countries of Nepal, Bangladesh and Bhutan. Groundwater explotation suffers because of problems of small and fragmented landholdings. The states here have miserably failed in running public tubewell irrigation system. Some recent success in community run tubewells and private tubewells engaged in water selling activity need watching and further analysis. Likewise, surmounting tubewell indivisibility by allowing installation of low-cost borings only for marginal farmers has given encouraging results in raising farm incomes. This route to poverty eradication can faulter if the historical process of decrease in land base of the poor is not countered through other means.

Chapter 13

TOWARDS A NEW WATER POLICY*

The government has lately been releasing official documents on important policy areas. The latest one to emerge is on India's water resources. Though it was approved at the second meeting of the National Water Resources Council on September 9, it has yet to be circulated outside limited government circles. This is a bit surprising as it is a small document of only 15 pages (see Appendix).

The Press Information Bureau has instead concentrated on publicising the Prime Minister's eloquent speech on the occasion. In a way, it is good. For, the PM's eloquence gives some clue to the newness of the water policy. The policy document makes rather drab reading, notwithstanding its comprehensiveness in touching upon various pertinent issues. It is, of course, not very fair to expect effusiveness in a policy document. Nor one should quarrel with it because it fails to give an inkling into the practical difficulties of operationalising the policy prescriptions.

Strictly speaking, there is hardly anything new about the policy prescriptions which are already to be found in various reports of committees, commissions, study groups, individual scholars, etc. If at all there is anything new, it is the idea of transferring water from one river basin to another. Though the issue is mentioned in a low key in the main document (para 3.4, p 6), the Prime Minister spotlighted it as follows in his speech: Another significant *conceptual achievement* is the recognition that the development of river basins need not always be directed only at the people living within that basin. Our rivers are bountiful and if properly harnessed many of these rivers can meet adequately the requirements of the people living in the basin and still have something left over for others less fortunately placed (emphasis added).

* Appeared in *Economic and Political Weekly*, October 31, 1987, but without the appendix.

In India, we already have a few examples of inter-basin transfer of water. The Beas-Sutlej link diverts some Beas water to Sutlej river because in the upper reaches Beas happens to flow about 1,000 feet above the Sutlej level. Likewise, there are three/four cases in the Western Ghats, in which the streams have been diverted eastwards to the water-deficit Deccan. I think the most promising scope for inter-basin transfer exists in the Western Ghats whose west-flowing streams carry over 21 million hectare-metres, of which only 3 m hectare-metres can be utilised in the narrow (but long) coastal region of Malabar and Konkan. It is true that there is likewise a lot of water available in eastern India. But it cannot be transferred to the water-deficit Deccan plateau situated about 2,000 feet above the river levels of the east. This is a pipe dream. In point of fact, the whole idea of transfer of Himalayan waters to the southern peninsula, either via the Ganga-Cauvery link or the Garland Canals of Captain Dastoor, is outside the practical realm, notwithstanding its political appeal in terms of the north supplying water to water-short south. Actually, it is symptomatic of an inadequate understanding of our water bounty even in well-educated circles. The author was astounded to hear from a well meaning agricultural scientist (with some claim to eminence in agricultural economics) when he suggested at a meetting of senior scientists that all the river waters of Punjab be allocated to Rajasthan, and Punjab be made to depend on its groundwater reserves only. While he showed awareness that productivity of water is greater the more dry a region is, he revealed an absymally poor understanding of the nature and sources of groundwater resources. It is such people with inadequate knowledge about the resources who are a great obstacle in resolving problems of water sharing even within the same river basin, not to mention of inter-basin transfer.

The policy document emphasises water resource planning at river basin level rather than in terms of state or district boundaries. Since the basins of major rivers of India cover more than a single state, problems of reconciling inter-state interests arise. The greater the scarcity of water in relation to land, the more intense can be the conflict in sharing the waters among the states of the basin. Here, as a result of the past history of water disputes, such as that in the United States, rather acceptable principles for sharing river waters have emerged. For example, sharing water in proportion to the contribution to river flow by the catchment area of each state is a good working principle. Yet, negotiations in practice can be quite acrimonious, partly for genuine reasons (eg, unequal burden of disruption costs due to submergence of land by a reservoir) and partly for lack of a correct understanding of the complex nature of the water resource on the part of people at large.

The bountifulness of our water resources, especially groundwater resources, needs a clearer appreciation. When it comes to inter-basin transfer of surplus waters, the very concept of surplus water needs proper understanding. About half the river flows in India are not tappable for techno-economic reasons, an assessment that has been reaffirmed in the policy document (para 1.2, p 1). The states, whose waters are contemplated for diversion to other states, may readily condescend if unexploitable waters constitute a large fraction of their water resources. Unfortunately, rivers with such abundance of unexploitable water as the Brahmaputra and Gandak in the east are mis-situated with respect to water deficit basins of the west and south. Within the water deficit basins, the estimated proportion of unexploitable water is very low, that is, they cannot be deemed to be bountiful enough to spare substantial quantities for other water-deficit basins even if technical possibilities do exist.

The insufficiency of our water resources needs some expounding, especially for the benefit of those readers who think there is plenty of groundwater underneath the land. Groundwater is indeed more plentiful in natural occurrence than is surface water (excluding sea water that is unfit for irrigation purpose). But this comparative ranking of the two water sources is in *stock* terms. In order to sustain irrigated farming in perpetuity the *stock* concept of groundwater resources is irrelevant. Instead, we have to go by the *flow* concept, whereby groundwater potential for irrigation purpose is assessed in terms of annual additions to the stock of groundwater. Evidently, depletion of groundwater resource can be avoided when annual withdrawals of groundwater tend to equal annual replenishment. That is to say, we overdraw on groundwater reserves during bad rainfall years but underdraw during good rainfall years so as to compensate for the excessive withdrawals during bad rainfall years.

In flow terms, our endowment of groundwater is far less bountiful than that of surface water. Official estimates reveal that the ultimate irrigation potential of groundwater in India is for about 42 million hectares of crop area, which constitutes about 35 per cent of the total irrigation potential of the country that is attainable with full exploitation of our exploitable water resources. Those who plead for according high priority to the development of groundwater-based irrigation must appreciate the limits in this regard. Firstly, there is the natural paucity of this resource. Secondly, we have already tapped nearly three-fourths of the ultimate groundwater potential of 42 million hectares. In other words, the untapped groundwater potential is now barely one-fourth of the total untapped irrigation potential of the country. Therefore, irrespective of the superiority of groundwater over surface irrigation, we have to persist with the development of surface irrigation works for meeting our irrigation needs.

To conclude, there is no doubt that a fair implementation of the water policy is going to be no easy task. Water being a state subject in the Indian Constitution, states may resist, more for political than for genuine economic considerations, central interventions at implementation stage. Success in this area cannot be ensured by argument and tribunals. The outcome will be shaped by the extent of give-and-take spirit among states. To foster such a spirit we have to work on a wide front, including 'extension' education in the realm of water resources. No less important is the professional engineers' will to assert themselves in the face of their political masters.

Appendix

National Water Policy

1.1 Water is a prime natural resource, a basic human need and a precious national asset. Planning and development of water resources need to be governed by national perspectives.

1.2 It has been estimated that out of the total precipitation of around 400 million hectare meters in the country, the surface water availability is about 178 million hectare meters. Out of this about 50% can be put to beneficial use because of topographical and other constraints. In addition there is a ground water potential of about 42 million hectare meters. The availability of water is highly uneven in both space and time. Precipitation is confined to only about three or four months in the year and varies from 10 cm in the western parts of Rajasthan to over 1000 cm at Cherrapunji in Meghalaya. Further, water does not respect state boundaries. Not merely rivers but even underground aquifers often cut across state boundaries. Water as a resource is one and indivisible: rainfall, river waters, surface ponds and lakes and groundwater are all part of one system; water is also a part of a larger ecological system.

1.3 Floods and drought affect vast areas of the country, transcending state boundaries. A third of the country is drought-prone. Floods affect an average area of around 9 million hectares per year. According to the National Commission on Floods, the area susceptible to floods is around 40 million hectares. The approach to the management of drought and floods has to be coordinated and guided at the national level.

1.4 Even the planning and implementation of individual irrigation or multi-purpose projects, though done at the State level, involve a number of aspects and issues such as environmental protection, rehabilitation of project-affected people and livestock, public health consequences of water impoundment, dam safety, etc. On these matters common approaches and guidelines are necessary. Moreover, certain problems and weaknesses have affected a large number of projects all over the country. There have been substantial time and cost overruns on projects. In some irrigation commands, problems of water-logging and soil salinity have emerged, leading to the the degradation of good agricultural land. There are also complex problems of equity and social justice in regard to water distribution. The development and exploitation of the country's groundwater resources also give rise to questions of judicious and scientific resource management and conservation. All these questions need to be tackled on the basis of common policies and strategies.

1.5 The growth process and the expansion of economic activities inevitably lead to increasing demands for water for diverse purposes: domestic, industrial, agricultural, hydro-power, navigation, recreation, etc. So far, the principal consumptive use of water has been for irrigation. While the irrigation potential is estimated to have increased from 19.5 million hectares at the time of Independence to about 68 million hectares at the end of the Sixth Plan, further development of a substantial order is necessary if the food and fibre needs of a growing population are to be met. The country's population which is over 750 million at present is expected to reach a level of around 1000 million by the turn of the century.

1.6 The production of foodgrains has increased from around 50 million tonnes in the fifties to about 150 million tonnes at present, but this will have to be raised to around 240 million tonnes by the year 2000 A.D. The drinking water needs of people and livestock have also to be met. In keeping with the objectives of the International Drinking Water Supply and Sanitation Decade Programme (1981-1991), adequate drinking water facilities have to be provided to the entire population in both urban and rural areas and sanitation facilities to 80% of the urban population and 25% of the rural population by the end of the decade. Domestic and industrial water needs have largely been concentrated in or near the principal cities, but the demand from rural society is expected to increase sharply as the development programmes improve economic conditions in the rural areas. The demand for water for hydro and thermal power generation and for other industrial uses is also likely to increase substantially. As a result, water which is already a scarce resource will become even scarcer in future. This underscores the need for the utmost efficiency in water utilization and a public awareness of the importance of its conservation.

1.7 Another important aspect is water quality. Improvements in existing strategies and the innovation of new techniques resting on a strong science and technology base will be needed to eliminate the pollution of surface and ground water resources, to improve water quality and to step up the recycling and re-use of water. Science and technology and training have also important roles to play in water resources development in general.

1.8 Water is one of the most crucial elements in developmental planning. As the country prepares itself to enter the 21st century, efforts to develop, conserve, utilise and manage this important resource have to be guided by national perspectives. The need for a national water policy is thus abundantly clear: water is a scarce and precious national resource to be planned, developed and conserved as such, and on an integrated and environmentally sound basis, keeping in view the needs of the States concerned.

2. The prime requisite for resource planning is a well-developed information system. A standardised national information system should be established with a network of data banks and data bases, integrating and strengthening the existing Central and State level agencies and improving the quality of data and the processing capabilities. There should be free exchange of data among the various agencies and duplication in data collection should be avoided. Apart from the data regarding water availability and actual water use, the system should also include comprehensive and reasonably reliable projections of future demands for water for diverse purposes.

3.1 The water resources available to the country should be brought within the category of utilizable resources to the maximum possible extent. The resources should be conserved and the availability augmented by measures for maximising retention and minimising losses.

3.2 Resource planning in the case of water has to be done for a hydrological unit such as a drainage basin as a whole, or for a sub-basin. All individual developmental projects and proposals should be formulated by the States and considered within the framework of such an overall plan for a basin or sub-basin, so that the best possible combination of options can be made.

3.3 Appropriate organisations should be established for the planned development and management of a river basin as a whole. Special multi-disciplinary units should be set up in each state to prepare comprehensive plans taking into account not only the needs of irrigation but also harmonising various other water uses, so that the available water resources are determined and put to optimum use having regard to existing agreements or awards of Tribunals under the relevant laws.

3.4 Water should be made available to water short areas by transfer from other areas including transfers from one river basin to another, based on a national perspective, after taking into account the requirements of the areas/basins.

3.5 Recycling and re-use of water should be an integral part of water resource development.

4.1 Water resource development projects should be as far as possible be planned and developed as multipurpose projects. Provision for drinking water should be a primary consideration. The projects should provide for irrigation, flood mitigation, hydro-electric power generation, navigation, pisciculture and recreation wherever possible.

4.2 The study of the impact of a project during construction and later on human lives, settlements, occupations, economic and other aspects should be an essential component of project planning.

4.3 In the planning, implementation and operation of projects, the preservation of the quality of environment and the ecological balance should be a primary consideration. The adverse impact, if any, on the environment should be minimised and should be off-set by adequate compensatory measures.

4.4 There should be an integrated and multi-disciplinary approach to the planning, formulation, clearance and implementation of projects, including catchment treatment and management, environmental and ecological aspects, the rehabilitation of affected people and command area development.

4.5 Special efforts should be made to investigate and formulate projects either in, or for the benefit of, areas inhabited by tribal or other specially disadvantaged groups such as Scheduled Castes and Scheduled Tribes. In other areas also, project planning should pay special attention to the needs of Scheduled Castes and Scheduled Tribes and other weaker sections of society.

4.6 The planning of projects in hilly areas should take into account the need to provide assured drinking water, possibilities of hydro-power development and the proper approach to irrigation in such areas, in the context of physical features and constraints such as steep slopes, rapid run-off and the incidence of soil erosion. The economic evaluation of projects in such areas should also take these factors into account.

4.7 Time and cost overruns and deficient realization of benefits characterising most irrigation projects should be overcome by upgrading the quality of project preparation and management. The under-funding of projects should be obviated by an optimal allocation of resources, having regard to the early completion of on-going projects as well as the need to reduce regional imbalances.

5.1 Structures and systems created through massive investments should be properly maintained in good health. Appropriate annual provisions should be made for this purpose in the budgets.

5.2 There should be a regular monitoring of structures and systems and necessary rehabilitation and modernisation programmes should be undertaken.

6. There should be proper organisational arrangements at the national and state levels for ensuring the safety of storage dams and other water-related structures. The Central guidelines on the subject should be kept under constant review and periodically updated and reformulated. There should be a system of continuous surveillance and regular visits by experts.

7.1 There should be a periodical reassessment on a scientific basis of the ground water potential, taking into consideration the quality of the water available and economic viability.

7.2 Exploitation of ground water resources should be so regulated as not to exceed the recharging possibilities, as also to ensure social equity. Ground water recharge projects should be developed and implemented for augmenting the available supplies.

7.3 Integrated and coordinated development of surface water and ground water and their conjunctive use should be envisaged right from the project planning stage and should form an essential part of the project.

7.4 Over exploitation of ground water should be avoided near the coast to prevent ingress of sea water into sweet water aquifers.

8. In the planning and operation of systems, water allocation priorities should be broadly as follows:—

- Drinking water
- Irrigation
- Hydro-power

– Navigation
– Industrial and other uses.

However, these priorities might be modified if necessary in particular regions with reference to area specific considerations.

9. Adequate drinking water facilities should be provided to the entire population both in urban and in rural areas by 1991. Irrigation and multipurpose projects should invariably include a drinking water component, wherever there is no alternative source of drinking water. Drinking water needs of human beings and animals should be the first charge on any available water.

10.1 Irrigation planning either in an individual project or in a basin as a whole should take into account the irrigability of land, cost-effective irrigation options possible from all available sources of water and appropriate irrigation techniques. The irrigation intensity should be such as to extend the benefits of irrigation to as large a number of farm families as possible, keeping in view the need to maximise production.

10.2 There should be a close integration of water-use and land-use policies.

10.3 Water allocation in an irrigation system should be done with due regard to equity and social justice. Disparities in the availability of water between large and small farms should be obviated by adoption of a rotational water distribution system and supply of water on a volumetric basis subject to certain ceilings.

10.4 Concerted efforts should be made to ensure that the irrigation potential created is fully utilised and the gap between the potential created and its utilisation is removed. For this purpose, the command area development approach should be adopted in all irrigation projects.

11. Water rates should be such as to convey the scarcity value of the resource to the users and to foster the motivation for economy in water-use. They should be adequate to cover the annual maintenance and operation charges and a part of the fixed costs. Efforts should be made to reach this ideal over a period, while ensuring the assured and timely supplies of irrigation water. The water rates for surface water and ground water should be rationalised with due regard to the interests of small and marginal farmers.

12. Efforts should be made to involve farmers progressively in various aspects of management of irrigation systems, particularly in water distribution and collection of water rates. Assistance of voluntary agencies should be enlisted in educating the farmers in efficient water use and water management.

13. Both surface water and ground water should be regularly monitored for quality. A phased programme should be undertaken for improvements in water quality.

14. Economic development and activities including agricultural, industrial and urban development, should be planned with due regard to the constraints imposed by the configuration of water availability. There should be a water zoning of the country and the economic activities should be guided and regulated in accordance with such zoning.

15. There should be a master plan for flood control and management for each flood prone basin. Sound watershed management through extensive soil conservation, catchment-area treatment, preservation of forests and increasing the forest area and the construction of check-dams should be promoted to reduce the intensity of floods. Adequate flood-cushion should be provided in water storage projects wherever feasible to facilitate better flood management. An extensive network for flood forecasting should be established for timely warning to the settlements in the flood plains, along with the regulation of settlements and economic activity in the flood plain zones, to minimise the loss of life and property on account of floods. While physical flood protection works like embankments and dykes will continue to be necessary, the emphasis should be on non-structural measures for the minimisation of losses, such as flood forecasting and warning and flood plain zoning, so as to reduce the recurring expenditure on flood relief.

17. The erosion of land, whether by the sea in coastal areas or by river waters inland, should be minimised by suitable cost-effective measures. The states and Union territories should also undertake all requisite steps to ensure that indiscriminate occupation and exploitation of coastal strips of land are discouraged and that the location of economic activities in areas adjacent to the sea is regulated.

18.1 Drought-prone areas should be made less vulnerable to drought-associated problems through soil-moisture conservation measures, water harvesting practices, the minimisation of evaporation losses, the development of the ground water potential and the transfer of surface water from surplus areas where feasible and appropriate. Pastures, forestry or other modes of development which are relatively less water-demanding should be encouraged. In planning water resource development projects, the needs of drought-prone areas should be given priority.

18.2 Relief works undertaken for providing employment to drought-stricken populations should preferably be for drought proofing.

19. For effective and economical management of our water resources,

the frontiers of knowledge need to be pushed forward in several directions by intensifying research efforts in various areas, including the following:—

- hydrometeorology:
- assessment of water resources;
- snow and lake hydrology;
- ground water hydrology and recharge;
- prevention of salinity ingress;
- water-harvesting;
- evaporation and seepage losses;
- economical designs for water rsource projects;
- crops and cropping systems;
- sedimentation of reservoirs;
- the safety and longevity of water related structures;
- river morphology and hydraulics;
- soils and material research;
- better water management practices and improvements in operational technology;
- recycling and re-use;
- use of sea water resources.

20. A perspective plan for standardised training should be an integral part of water resource development. It should cover training in information systems, sectoral planning, project planning and formulation, project management, operation of projects and their physical structures and systems and the management of the water distribution systems. The training should extend to all the categories of personnel involved in these activities as also the farmers.

21. In view of the vital importance of water for human and animal life, for maintaining ecological balance and for economic and developmental activities of all kinds, and considering its inceasing scarcity, the planning and management of this resource and in optimal, economical and equitable use has become a matter of the utmost urgency. The success of the national water policy will depend entirely on the development and maintenance of a national consensus and commitments to its underlying principles and objectives.

Chapter 14

SALIENT RECAPITULATIONS AND SOME RECONSIDERATIONS

Practically each preceding chapter was initially written as a self-contained paper that stood by itself. While rewriting it for this book, the author did keep in mind the results of the other papers written over a span of three years or so. It is now time that we take an integrated or holistic view of the salient findings of every chapter. In this pursuit, the contradictions, if any, can be ironed out, and the occasion is also used to offer a sort of postscript to the published papers that form the basis for writing this book.

Inadequate Water Bounty

We are well endowed with water resources only in very high rainfall regions like the east Gangetic plains and the Konkan-Malabar coastal strip down below the Western Ghat mountains. Elsewhere, the irrigation potential of our water bounty is rather modest if not meagre. Such spatial unevenness in our irrigation potential is inevitable for a country of continental dimensions. What is truly striking are the temporal variations in our water availability, both within the agricultural year and from one year to the next.

Whereas spatial unevenness necessitates heavy investment in long distance transfer of water from more endowed to less endowed tracts, temporal unevenness makes sizable investments in water storage works imperative for meeting our water needs on a dependable basis throughout the year. The expert assessment till recently has been that irrigation potential of our water resources would barely suffice for six-tenths of our crop area.[1] Under the New Water Policy of 1987, this areal coverage could rise somewhat, provided the new concept of water

1. Agricultural sector in India, unlike in developed countries, accounts for a lion's share in total water use (excluding water used in hydel power generation). For comparative data, see Adriant T. Mcdonald and David Kay, *Water Resources: Issues and Strategies*, Longman, U.K., 1988.

planning beyond a river basin is duly translated into ground reality. This is, however, no easy task from the political viewpoint as water is a state subject in the Indian Constitution. We need to be realistic, and be prepared for acrimonious inter-state disputes on water transfers as well as water sharing of common rivers. But entertaining visions of Ganga-Cauvery Link or of creating Garland Canals with the aid of Himalayan waters, are akin to pipe dreams divorced from technical-economic realism. Instead of Garland Canals for the Deccan plateau, this water-short region has better promise from the diversion of huge surplus waters of the west coast rivers.

Flood and Drought Management

We better reconcile to the natural cycle of rainfall which give rise to periodic floods and droughts. In other words, floods and droughts are inevitable to a large extent. At first thought, it may appear that eliminating flood waters resulting from excess rainfall is a far more feasible proposition than inducing extra precipitation in the event of a meteorological drought. In practice, containing the flood water menace is a very arduous task, more so in a chronic flood-prone area like the east Gangetic plains. Here, raising embankments along river courses is widely recognised a very questionable technique. The techno-economic feasibility of large detention reservoirs in the Himalayan catchments of these rivers does not look all that encouraging. Likewise, the indirect detention of flood waters via afforestation of the fragile Himalayas requires a very high order of mutual cooperation among the four riparian countries of Nepal, India, Bangladesh and Bhutan. And the option of flood plain zoning is of little practical value in a densely populated area having high incidence of flood hazard.

We must learn to live with the consequences of floods and droughts. The ill effects of drought, however, can be better coped with. The foremost need here is the maintenance of buffer stocks of foodgrains and edible oils, while continuing relentlessly with the enlargement of irrigation cover for our agriculture. In the latter pursuit, the goal of protective irrigation in acutely water-short regions of peninsular India, Gujarat and Rajasthan needs due recognition as well as implementation. In addition, dips in crop output during drought can be reduced through the following two-part strategy.

In the first part, we should use our stock of groundwater in drought-prone areas on the buffer stock principle. That is to say, we deliberately underexploit our groundwater resource in normal times, so that we can overdraw on our groundwater reserves for meeting our urgent needs for water during drought years. Logically, this demands greater emphasis on development of major surface irrigation works to take care of our normal irrigation requirements. This brings us to the second part of our strategy, namely, building storage works with extra capacity for storing excess inflows of above-normal rainfall years. These excess inflows are to be used like buffer stocks of foodgrains. It may, however, be noted that addition of such extra capacity to a proposed reservoir would not only add to the cost of irrigation but also mean added height to dams. Since increase in dam height usually leads to more than proportionate land submergence, this aggravates the problem of rehabilitation of dam oustees. Ours being a well settled country, the state governments already find it problematic to suitably relocate dam oustees. Thus, we face a tradeoff here: gain in drought proofing at the expense of greater uprooting of the people and increased submergence of land and forest cover in the river catchment. At the moment, the dice is loaded against bigger reservoirs, and the case for reducing the heights of major dams proposed on the Narmada river is indeed strong.

Groundwater vs Canal Irrigation

Irrespective of the type of irrigation, its development is a very costly proposition. Any one talking of developing groundwater irrigation at a small fraction[1] of the high cost of major irrigation works is misleading us by taking a partial view of costs incurred by the nation in developing groundwater irrigation in India. In developing groundwater-based irrigation, the totality of costs must be borne in mind. We are adding half a million electric pumpsets every year. The farmer bears an installation cost of about Rs 7000 per electric pumpset (much of it is financed from institutional sources). But its energisation through rural electrification programme alone costs to the nation about Rs 20,000 per pumpset (this is exclusive of the investment in power generating equipment).

Groundwater protagonists blithely ignore two more things: (1) much higher operational costs of groundwater irrigation (five to six times) than those of canal irrigation and (2) much smaller life of the investments like pumpsets and tubewells (hardly 15 years as compared

1. This fraction is reckoned between one-tenth and one-fourth by some empiricists espousing the cause of minor irrigation vis-a-vis major irrigation in India.

to at least 100 years in the case of major irrigation works). As a result of gross underpricing of electricity for rural pumps the reported operational cost of electric pumpsets/tubewells has to be viewed in resource cost terms at least if not in opportunity cost terms. Thus true cost advantage, if any, may be with major surface irrigation works, and not groundwater irrigation.

As regards the past development of groundwater irrigation, one comes across two contrary lines of criticism, namely, (1) the Indian planners have been more preoccupied with major surface irrigation development, and (2) there has been overdevelopment of groundwater irrigation, leading to groundwater depletion at several places. The issue of developing this or that irrigation is, by and large, a non-issue in the Indian context of scarcity of water resources on the one hand and their hydrological linkages on the other. The feeling, that development of groundwater-based irrigation has not received due attention commensurate with its advantage in costs or production impact, is not well founded in facts. It is a myth (based on wrong interpretation of the Plan statistics on irrigation potential and capital outlays) that the resources cost of groundwater irrigation is much less than that of major canals. Though the land productivity under groundwater irrigation is indeed higher than that under canal irrigation, a part of this difference is to be credited to public investment in canal works whose seeped-in waters improve well water yield in areas of poor availability of groundwater. In point of fact, if at all there has been any under-emphasis on any category of irrigation in Indian water planning, this has been in respect of major and medium works. Because of inadequate project funding by the state governments, both the cost and time overruns in such works have been intolerably high.

India being a country of continental diversity, a uniform policy for all regions of the country is not likely to work everywhere. If at all any special emphasis on developing one particular source of irrigation is needed, we may pursue the following policy for different regions. Since much of the unexploited groundwater potential of the nation is presently located in the high rainfall areas of the east Gangetic plains and Madhya Pradesh, groundwater irrigation may be promoted here. Elsewhere, promotional efforts should be much more directed at surface water exploitation. Here, the pace of groundwater development should be restricted to the extent of additional recharge of groundwater from new surface irringation works (via seepage route) and from other programmes (afforestation, nala bunding, percolation tanks, etc.)

Groundwater is naturally less bountiful than river water. In low rainfall regions, hardly one-fourth of the total irrigation can be based on natural groundwater recharge from rainfall. Here, development of surface irrigation works provides the key to a highly productive, amply stable and truly sustainable groundwater-based agriculture. For, these surface water works act as powerful instruments of artificial groundwater replenishment. The case of Punjab agriculture is an apt example in this regard. In this state, at least half the tubewell water used by farmers is of canal origin. But for the seeped in canal waters, the magnitude of tubewell-based agriculture here would have been far less than of today.

Conjunctive irrigation is now the watchword of the day, more so with the planners of major surface irrigation works. To put it more simply, they wish to promote groundwater development within the canal commands. Such development is expected to serve two useful purposes. First, wells and tubewells provide the much-needed drainage to the canal system, thereby minimising investments in horizontal drainage that keeps waterlogging-salinity problems at bay. Second, the seeped-in canal waters are put to good economic use, simultaneously overcoming administrative infirmities of a large canal system.

But it is now being increasingly realised that canal farmers are not likely to invest in well irrigation if they do not experience acute scarcity of water. This condition is admirably fulfilled in protective canals of northern India where private tubewell irrigation within canal commands has been booming. In nonprotective canals (loosely called productive canals), the possibility of groundwater development under private aegis is minimal. Here, two exigencies can give rise to groundwater development. One is that of farmers in the tail reaches failing to get their due share of canal water. The second one stems from the prevalence of restrictive practices in a canal system e.g., declaring dry and wet crop zones; crop zoning for annual crops like sugarcane; restricting canal flows to one or two seasons in a year, etc. Irrespective of how water scarcity comes to arise, one problem area is the small and marginal farmers. Such farmers may find it uneconomic to invest in their own wells. In this context, we need to study the rise of market in groundwater within canal commands, and see if it proves an economic alternative for the small and marginal farmers.

Preventing Groundwater Depletion

The empirical evidence on over-exploitation of groundwater resource in India is confusing. The source of this confusion are two sets of official estimates, one based on area approach and the other on volumetric approach. The area statistics of our groundwater potential and its exploitation, which are the basis of our planning, indicate high order of groundwater exploitation but without any signs as yet of over-development as per the state level data. However, the same statistics in volumetric terms, as compiled by the Central Groundwater Board (CGWB), reveal that bulk of our groundwater potential is still untapped. This mixed state of affairs is symptomatic of lack of firmness in information with regard to our groundwater data base. This should make us wary of contentious claims with regard to groundwater development in this country. In all likelihood, stories of gross over-exploitation of groundwater or its depletion are no less exaggerated than the CGWB's claims that groundwater is still a highly unexploited resource.

A tell-tale mark of groundwater resource being under pressure is continual recessionary trend in groundwater table. A declining water table is not conducive to a growing agriculture on two counts. First, groundwater resource may be redendered unfit for irrigation use if saline waters from adjacent tracts intrude into the voids created by the receding water table—this danger is more in the coastal plains and in the border regions of Gujarat, U.P., Haryana and Punjab states that lie in proximity to Thar desert of Rajasthan. Second, resource cost of lifting groundwater is an increasing function of depth to water table. It is because of such imperatives that Indian hydrogeologists have been repeatedly urging the state governments to enact suitable groundwater regulation laws. But legislative intervention is going to be of little avail in the particular conditions of small and fragmented landholdings of India. This may largely explain why no state legislature (with the exception of Gujarat) has enacted any legislation on the lines of the model bill circulated by the Centre in this regard back in 1974. This author believes that pragmatism requires recourse to indirect measures for preventing groundwater depletion in low and medium rainfall regions. Two useful instruments in this regard are: (i) abandonment of the existing policy of gross underpricing of electric power for electrically-driven pumpsets and (ii) replenishment of groundwater resource through extensive development of surface irrigation works in low rainfall areas because large fraction of such waters, supposedly lost in transit, end in groundwater table.

Unutilised Irrigation Potential

Irrigation being a capital intensive activity, any report about underutilisation of created irrigation potential causes alarm and dismay, more so in a capital short economy like ours. But since the basis for adjudging underutilisation of irrigation capacity is of a questionable merit, one should beware of simplistic estimates in this regard.

Much of the unutilised irrigation potential of major irrigation works of the nation is of a fictitious nature. This is especially true for works located in low and medium rainfall regions of the country, namely, southern and western India. Here, irrigators utilise bulk of the reservoir water for growing paddy, sugarcane and other heavily irrigated crops, especially in the upper and middle reaches of a canal system. This results in a drastic curtailment in total irrigated area—mainly at the expense of farmers in the tail reaches—giving rise to an apparent picture of underutilisation of created irrigation potential that is conventionally expressed in terms of irrigable area. The overall production consequences of this shift in crop pattern are likely to be adverse indeed because of the fact that crop productivity per unit of irrigation water is lower under heavily than lightly irrigated crops. For reasons of productivity and spatial equity in production gains, the deviation in crop pattern needs to be prevented.

The more germane problem of Indian canal irrigation is one of low production impact of each unit of irrigated area than of serious underutilisation of harnessed waters. One needs to separate myth from reality in regard to the utilisation of irrigation potential. For instance, it is sheer romanticism to assert full utilisation of irrigation capacity in the case of minor irrigation works in general and privately owned wells in particular.[1] Reliable but limited empirical evidence on the rate of utilisation of irrigation capacity in the case of minor irrigation works in the public sector (notably public tubewells and lift irrigation schemes) is very disquieting. Likewise, one must reckon with the harsh reality of project promoters' attempt to inflate the area to be benefited from a project. Such inflation helped in project clearance from the Centre as the implied capital cost per unit area to be irrigated was indeed an important determinant of project approval till the end of the Third Five Year Plan.[2]

1. To some extent such an assertion has been an outcome of an erroneous understanding of the Plan statistics on capacity and utilisation of minor irrigation works—till the Sixth Plan the utilisation statistics were computed on the tacit assumption of full utilisation of minor irrigation potential.
2. For projects meant for low rainfall areas, such inflation was achieved by visualising a crop pattern of low water using crops. For high rainfall areas, this inflation was accomplished by tilting the crop pattern in favour of kharif season crops for which irrigation was needed mainly during the drought years.

In contrast to the colonial period, the pace of irrigation development in India has been very rapid: the gross addition to irrigation capacity over the last 35 years has been more than twice the level of 22.5 million hectares in 1951. In the light of the current priority for irrigation in Indian planning, the national water resource potential for irrigation may be fully tapped during the coming 25 years. With such rapid expansion in capacity, the management problems become more onerous, especially when the managerial skills at the State level are not so well endowed. To some extent, the establishment of Water and Land Management Institutes (WALMIs) in each state over the recent period may overcome this gap in managerial skills. But the political leadership in each State should show as zealous a commitment to proper management of irrigation projects as it has shown in the matter of starting new irrigation schemes.

Sustaining Dam-Based Farming

The long-run sustainability of canal-based farming is threatened from two sides, namely, (1) excessive siltation of reservoirs backing up a canal network and (2) the twin problem of waterlogging-salinity development within canal commands. Both are very intractable problems, much less amenable to technological solutions than to organisational measures in the realm of preventive action. There is no alternative to commensurate investment in programmes of soil conservation in the catchments of the reservoirs, so as to keep the siltation rate within tolerable limits. Drainage is likewise an answer to waterlogging. But it is better to achieve this in a vertical instead of horizontal manner, that is, through wells and tubewells. Towards this end, a policy of extensive canal irrigation may induce farmers to invest in their own wells/tubewells, which would serve the twin purpose of supplementary irrigation and vertical drainage of the seeped-in canal waters.

Pricing Problems

The financial management of public irrigation works is unquestionably dismal. These works (with the sole exception of Uttar Pradesh) do not generate sufficient revenue to cover even their working costs, not to speak of recouping the high investment costs. A major factor in this is the policy of gross underpricing of canal water by every state government. Unfortunately, the political climate for bringing farm resource prices in alignment with resource costs is becoming more and more unfavourable, thanks to the gathering momentum of farmers' agitation in recent years. But do politicians realise the myopia of continual underpricing of farm resources?

However, it is a very naive expectation that raising the pitch of tariff for canal water would help in combating the problem of water wastage or over-irrigation by farmers. When tariff is presently linked to crop area only (or it is a lump sum amount as in Tamil Nadu), farmers do not gain any tariff remission by achieving any economy in canal water use. Unfortunately, in the Indian conditions of small and fragmented landholdings it is patently uneconomic to change the current tariff basis to one of volume of water actually used by a farmer. For one, the cost of metering water supply to every parcel of land in an Indian canal command is prohibitively high. For another, the administrative feasibility of such a metered water supply system is rather low. After all, the principal consideration in shifting from variable to fixed power tariff in the case of electric pumpsets in north India was the difficulty of collecting the power bills as per installed meters which were too often tinkered with by the farmers.

Over-irrigation

Both from social and private angles, irrigating fields beyond the requisite level is a detrimental thing. Over-irrigation in the case of public canals has been rationalised by some observers by drawing attention to (a) the existence of area-linked water tariff and (b) the large uncertainties of canal supplies. Likewise, over-irrigation in the case of electrically-operated, private tubewells/pumpsets in some areas has been traced to the changeover from variable to fixed (i.e. flat) power tariff in which electricity billing is linked to the horse power of the motor only. Thus "irrational" behaviour of a farmer has been explained away in terms of structure of water/power tariff, with the clear implication that the behaviour would be rational under a variable water/power tariff that links billing charge to volume of water/units of electricity consumption.

The empirical evidence on farmers' irrigation application by volume and depth of watering in each irrigation operation is scanty. The limited survey data that one comes across is usually unsatisfactory on two counts. Either information only on number of waterings for a crop is gathered from respondent farmers, or volume of irrigation water used is inferred from the reported expenditure on irrigation and the volumetric water tariff in force. Our examination of some survey data reveals the following picture.

S.S. Prihar and S.S. Grewal report an average of 32 waterings of paddy crop by a sample of 40 Punjab farmers during 1983-84 as against the recommended level of 24 waterings. In the case of 84 Punjab farmers owning electric tubewells, Gurcharan Singh found over-irrigation to the extent of one-fifth above the recommended level. In contrast, V.K. Sharma found significant under-irrigation in the case of 230 private electric tubewells in Uttar Pradesh. This result is in agreement with the NCAER and NSS survey data for U.P. for the mid-seventies. From these two largescale survey data, it is found that each irrigated hectare of crop area in the mid-seventies in India received, on the average, nearly three waterings. Keeping also in mind that waterings from public irrigation works, like canals and public tubewells, were deficient in timing, this cannot be described as a state of adequate irrigation, leave aside over-irrigation. Likewise, my scrutiny of the puzzling phenomenon of over-irrigation reported by some scholars in respect of public tubewells of Uttar Pradesh which sell water by volume, reveals serious shortcomings in the methods of analysis employed by these scholars. If direct measures of estimating volume of water application were to be used, the puzzle of over-irrigation by farmers paying for tubewell water by volume vanishes. Finally, on the matter of over-irrigation we must bear in mind two things. First, Indian farmers, unlike farm research scientists, are not equipped with instruments which either measure volume of water actually applied to a field or indicate the extent of wetting in field soil profile. Therefore, one must not take a very strict view of some margin of over-irrigation by him under the actual field conditions. Second, the recommended norms for crop watering lack sanctity for an entire state to the extent these are for a given soil-climatic situation. After all, both soils and weather conditions are quite varied in each state.

Problems of High Rainfall Areas

A lingering feeling exists among agricultural economists, irrigation engineers/administrators and institutional credit disbursers for minor irrigation development that returns to irrigation are rather low in very high rainfall areas. Our limited investigation in this regard is based mainly on (1) an impact evaluation of Kal reservoir-based canal irrigation in the Konkan region of Maharashtra state and (2) three impact studies relating to private tubewell irrigation in the states of West Bengal and Bihar. Our findings are as follows.

In apparent or conventional terms, barely three-fifths of the irrigable crop area potential of the Kal project was being utilised in the mid-eighties. Such low utilisation was due to the fact that the project planners had visualised nearly two-thirds of the irrigation potential for the kharif season when in fact there was no need for such irrigation. Each crop hectare of canal irrigated area of the rabi season boosted crop output (mostly rice) by nearly 2.7 tons, a very substantial output augmentation indeed. A major part of this increase was due to steep rise in intensity of cropping which rose from 100 to 188 per cent. Though the yield of the principal paddy crop also rose by about one-third, it is imperative to grasp that increase in crop yield is not a pucca yardstick for assessing the production role of irrigation in very high rainfall regions. The policy implication is that irrigation development in very high rainfall areas should aim at rabi and summer cropping, with some inbuilt flexibility to provide one or two irrigations during kharif season in the event of a break in monsoon spell.

The incidence of poverty in the east Gangetic plains is quite high. Irrigation can eradicate this poverty to a large extent via increase in rabi and summer cropping. What militates against such eradication are the following factors: (1) historical process of continual reduction in land base of the marginal farmers, (2) the indivisibility of tubewell technology for small farmers having fragmented land holdings, (3) the dismal management of government-owned tubewells and (4) the high hazard of flood and waterlogging due to poor drainage.

BIBLIOGRAPHY

Ahmed, Akhtar U. and Sampath, Rajan K. (1988). Welfare Implications of Tubewell Irrigation in Bangladesh. Water Resources Bulletin, American Water Resources Association, Vol. 24, No. 5, October.

Afro-Asian Rural Reconstruction Organisation. (1987). Role of Irrigation in Development of Agriculture in Developing Countries. Rural Reconstruction, Vol. 20, No. 1, January.

Alagh, Y.K. (1989). Indian Economic Planning-Structural Transformation and Distribution of Gains. March (mimeo).

ARDC (1982). Minor Irrigation in Bhojpur District, Bihar. Agricultural Refinance and Development Corporation, Bombay.

Borude, S.G. and Pawar, Shobha R. (1986). Economic Impact Survey of Kal Irrigation Project, Raigad District, Maharashtra. Department of Agricultural Economics, Konkan Agricultural University, Dapoli.

Central Soil Salinity Research Institute (CSSRI). (1985). Tubewells: Guidelines for Installation. Karnal.

Central Bank of India. (1983). Minor Irrigation Scheme in Rohtas District of Bihar. Economic Intelligence Department, Bombay.

Chawla, A.S. and Sharma, H.D. (1984). Conjunctive Use Components - A Comparative Study. National Seminar on Modernisation of Canal Irrigation at Lucknow, Indian Water Resource Society, Roorkee.

Chawla, A.S. Raghuvanshi, C.S. and Anil Kumar. (1989). Economic Analysis of Lift Technologies and Access of Small and Marginal Farmers to Groundwater. Workshop on Efficiency and Equity in Groundwater Use and Management, IRMA, Anand.

Chopra, Kanchan. (1989). Land Degradation: Dimensions and Causalities. Indian Journal of Agricultural Economics, Vol. 44, No. 1, Jan-March.

Dandekar, V.M., Deshmukh, D. and Deuskar, V.R. (1979). Interim Report of the Committee to Study the Introduction of Eight Month Supply of Water on the Irrigation Projects in Maharashtra. Government of Maharashtra, Bombay.

Datye, K.R. and Patil, R.K. (1987). Farmer Managed Irrigation Systems:

Indian Experiences. Centre for Applied Systems Analysis in Development, Bombay.

Dharm Narain and Shyamal Roy. (1980). Impact of Irrigation and Labour Availability on Multiple Cropping. IFPRI, Washington D.C.

Dhawan, B.D. (1989a). Mounting Antagonism to Big Dams. Institute of Economic Growth, Delhi (mimeo.; likely to appear in EPW).

Dhawan, B.D. (1989b). Tubewell Irrigation in Bihar Plains. Invited Papers for International Workshop on Economic Resurgence of Bihar through Water Resource. Bihar College of Engineering, Patna.

Dhawan, B.D. (1989c). Production Augmentation through Canal Irrigation: Empirical Results for Ten Major Irrigation Works. Journal of Agricultural Issues, Vol. 1, No. 1 (inaugural issue).

Dhawan, B.D. (1988a). Irrigation in India's Agricultural Development: Productivity, Stability, Equity. Sage Publications, New Delhi.

Dhawan, B.D. (1988b). Irrigation Performance in U.P. in R.T. Tewari and A. Joshi (ed). Development and Change in India. Ashish Publishing House, New Delhi.

Dhawan, B.D. (1988c). Irrigated versus Dry Farming. Economic and Political Weekly, 19 March 1988.

Dhawan, B.D. (1988d). The Way Out of the Narmada Imbroglio. Economic Times, 5 December.

Dhawan, B.D. (1988e). Myth about Minor Irrigation (under 'Communications'). Seminar, Special Issue on Drought, June.

Dhawan, B.D. (1988f). Water Resources Development: Groundwater versus Surface Irrigation. Economic and Social Change, Vol. VIII, No. 3, December; also in Journal of Indian Water Resources Society, Vol. 8, No. 1, January.

Dhawan, B.D. (1987a). Water Management in the Mula Command: A Study in the Productivity Impact of Canal Waters. Indian Journal of Agricultural Economics, Vol. 42, No. 1, Jan.-March

Dhawan, B.D (1987b). How Stable is Indian Agriculture? Economic and Political Weekly, September 26.

Dhawan, B.D. (1987c). Management of Groundwater Resource. Economic and Political Weekly, 5-12 September.

Dhawan, B.D. (1987d). Agricultural Productivity of Water in India. Indian Journal of Quantitative Economics, Vol 3, No.2.

Dhawan, B.D. (1986a). Economics of Groundwater Irrigation in Hard Rock Regions, Agricole, New Delhi.

Dhawan, B.D. (1986b). Irrigation and Water Management in India: Perception of Problems and Their Resolution. Indian Journal of Agricultural Economics, Vol. 41, No. 3, July-September. Also in, Indian Society of Agricultural Economics. (1988). Agricultural Development in India: The Next Stage. Himalaya, Bombay.

Dhawan, B.D. (1986c). Output Impact according to Main Irrigation Sources: Empirical Evidence from Four Selected States. Paper in Kanwar (1988).

Dhawan, B.D. (1985). Questionable Conceptions and Simplistic Views about Irrigated Agriculture of India. Indian Journal of Agricultural Economics, Vol. 40, No. 1, January-March.

Dhawan, B.D. (1983a). Source-wise Productivity Impact of Irrigation. Institute of Economic Growth, Delhi (mimeo).

Dhawan, B.D. (1983b). Impact of Irrigation on Instability in Farm Output. Economic and Political Weekly, September.

Dhawan, B.D. (1982). Development of Tubewell Irrigation in India. Agricole, New Delhi.

Dhawan, B.D. and Satya Sai, K.J.S. (1985). Economic Linkages among Irrigation Sources: A Study of Beneficial Role of Canal Seepage. Indian Journal of Agricultural Economics, Vol. 43, No. 4, October-December.

Dhawan, B.D. and Satya Sai (1987). Productivity of Irrigated Farming: Survey Evidence from Three States. Journal of Indian Water Resources Society, Vol. 7, No. 3, July.

Dutt, D.K. (1987A). Groundwater and Conjunctive Use. Key Paper Presented at National Symposium on Hydrology, National Institute of Hydrology, Roorkee, December 1987 (mimeo).

Dutt, D.K. (1987B). Groundwater - Its Role in Drought Irrigation. BHU - JAL News, Vol. 2, No.3, CGWB, New Delhi.

Dutt, D.K. (1987C). Trends in Groundwater Development and Management. Theme Paper On Groundwater, First National Water Convention, 12-14 November 1987, New Delhi (mimeo).

Dutt. D.K. (1986). Management of Groundwater under Drought Conditions. Jal Vigyan Sameeksha, HILTECH, N.I.H., Roorkee, June.

Goldsmith, E. and Hildyard, N. (1984). The Social and Environmental Effects of Large Dams. Wadebridge Ecological Centre, U.K.

Government of India (1987). Water Resources of India, Central Water Commission, New Delhi.

Government of India (1984). Report of the Working Group on Minor Irrigation for the Formulation of the Seventh Plan Proposals for the Years 1985-90. Minor Irrigation Division, Ministry of

Irrigation, New Delhi (mimeo).

Government of India (1980). Report of the Working Group on Minor Irrigation for Formulation of the Sixth Plan Proposals for the Years 1980-85. Ministry of Agriculture, Minor Irrigation Division, New Delhi (mimeo).

Government of India (1972). Report of the Task Force on Groundwater Resources. Planning Commission, New Delhi (mimeo).

Howe, Charles (1979). Natural Resource Economics. Wiley. U.S.A.

Kanwar, J.S. (1988) (ed.). National Seminar on Water Management - The Key to Developing Agriculture. Agricole, New Delhi.

Minhas, B.S., Parikh, K.S. and Srinivasan, T.N. (1974). Toward the Structure of a Production Function for Wheat Yield with Dated Inputs of Irrigation Water. Water Resources, Vol. 10

Mitra, Ashok K. (1987). Planning and Management of Surface Irrigation in Drought Prone Areas. Artha Vijnana, Vol. 29, No. 4, December.

Moorti, T.V. (1970). Comparative Study of Well Irrigation in Aligarh District, India. Occasional Paper No. 29, Department of Agricultural Economics, Cornell University.

Murthy, B.N. (1977). Life of Reservoir. Technical Report No. 19, Central Board of Irrigation and Power, New Delhi.

NABARD. (1988A). Bamboo and Shallow Tubewells in Purnia District, Bihar. ESS No. 30, Bombay.

NABARD. (1988B). Minor Irrigation of Allahabad District - Uttar Pradesh. ESS No. 33, Bombay.

NABARD. (1987). Minor Irrigation in Muzaffarnagar District- An Ex-post Evaluation Study. National Bank for Agricultural and Rural Development, Bombay.

National Sample Survey (1984). Some Selected Results of the Survey on Use of Irrigation on Household Holdings - NSS 31st Round (July 1976-June 1977). Sarvekshana, Vol. VIII, No. 2 (Issue No. 23), October.

National Sample Survey (1985). Some Selected Important Results of the Survey on Use of Irrigation on Household Holdings — NSS 31st Round (July 1976-June 1977). Sarvekshana, Vol. IX, Nos. 1 & 2 (Issue No. 25), July-October.

Pal, S.P. (1985). Contribution of Irrigation to Agricultural Production and Productivity, NCAER, New Delhi.

Patel, S.M. and K.V. Patel (1969). Economics of Tubewell Irrigation. Indian Institute of Management, Ahmedabad.

Prihar, S.S. and Sandhu, B.S. (1987). Irrigation Requirement of Wheat. Proceedings of First National Water Convention, Vol. III, Central Board of Irrigation and Power, New Delhi.

Prihar, S.S. and Grewal, S.S. (1988). Improving Irrigation Water Use Efficiency in Rice-Wheat Cropping Sequence — Technical and Policy Issues in J.S. Kanwar (ed.) (1988).

Operation Research Group (ORG). (1986). National Cropping Pattern Study in Irrigated Command Areas. (in two volumes; unpublished).

Rajput, R.K. (1988). ICAR Coordinated Projects on Water Management in India, in J.S. Kanwar (1988).

Raju, K.C. B. (1987). Groundwater - Assessment and Monitoring. Proceedings of First National Water Convention, Volume II, Central Board of Irrigation and Power, New Delhi.

Rath, N. and A.K. Mitra (1987). Economics of Irrigation in Water Scarce Region: A Study of Maharashtra. Gokhale Institute of Politics and Economics, Pune.

Sangal, S.P. (1987). Minor Irrigation and Groundwater Development. Proceedings of First National Water Convention, Volume II, Central Board of Irrigation and Power, New Delhi.

Sarkar, B.B. (1989). People's Participation in Groundwater Management Process in C.A.D.C. - An Experimentation. Paper presented at Workshop on Efficiency and Equity in Groundwater Use and Management organised By IRMA at Anand during January 30 to February 1.

SBI. (1980). Development of Minor Irrigation in West Dinajpur. State Bank of India, Central Office, Bombay.

Sharma, V.K. (Chairman). (1984). A Study of Electric Power Consumption in Agriculture U.P. Agricultural Production Commissioner, Government of U.P., Lucknow.

Singh, Gurcharan (1987). Correlation of Unit Draft of Electric Tubewells and Irrigation Requirements of Crops in Selected Areas of Punjab — A Case Study. Proceedings of National Symposium on Hydrology, Vol. II, National Institute of Hydrology, Roorkee, December.

Singh, R.P. and Vijayalakshmi, K. (1987). Management of Disaster Areas. First National Water Convention Proceedings, Vol. III, Central Board of Irrigation and Power, New Delhi.

Stone, Ian (1984). Canal Irrigation in British India. Combridge University Press, Cambridge (U.K.).

Tyagi, S.S. (1988). Walidpur: Agricultural Transformation in Two Decades. Agro-Economic Research Centre, University of Delhi, Delhi (mimeo).

Varma, S.C. (1985). Human Resettlement in Lower Narmada Basin. Narmada Valley Development Authority, Government of Maddhya Pradesh, Bhopal.

Water and Land Management Institute (WALMI) (1984). Evaluation Studies of Mula Irrigation Project. Aurangabad, Maharashtra.

INDEX

afforestation, 15, 200, 227, 229
Afro-Asian Rural Reconstruction Organisation, 73
Agricultural Prices Commission (APC), 137, 158, 177-78
Agricultural Refinance and Development Corporation (ARDC), 202-05
agriculture, Asian, 149; groundwater based, v, 3, 39, 46, 70, 81-92, 142; intensive, 10, 83, 95, 144n; market-oriented, 81; modern, 81, 97; subsistence, 81; under-irrigated, 6, 56
agronomists, iv, 10, 11, 136, 140, 143, 174
Ahmed, Akhtar U., 197
Alagh, Y.K., 194n
area, approach, 4, 39, 231; effect, 122; irrigable, 4, 7, 8, 25, 232; net sown, 25, 27; per well, 86, 143-46, potentially irrigable, 5; submerged, 146; statistics, 4
Arravalis, 36
Aurangabad, 136

balanced development, 2, 69
Bangladesh, 194, 197, 214, 227
Barak, 21
Beas, 216; — Sutlej link, 216
benefits, incidental, 103, 104, 109-14; income, 103-05
benefit-cost, analysis, 119; ratio, 5, 44, 67, 119n, 128, 129, 135 147, 147n, 204, 206, 212, 213; results, 204, 205
Bhakra Nangal, 77, 150, 150n, 179-88, 190, 192, 193
Bhalla, G.S., 194n
Bhutan, 214, 227
big dam controversy, iv, v
Bihar, north, 194, 196, 206, 213; south, 194, 202
Borude, S.G., 119-23, 125-27, 125n, 129, 131
Brahamputra, 21, 201, 217
bribes, 58; and kickbacks, 14
British rule, 6n, 30, 62, 82, 117
'boro' paddy, 198, 198n, 211
buffer, groundwater as a, v, 19; stocks of foodgrains, 19, 30, 227, 228; stocks of foreign exchange reserves, 19; stock principle, 227
buyers of water, 197, 203, 204

canal, authority, 141, 141n, 143; capacity, 8; conveyance losses, 81, 86; lining, 12, 28, 65, 81, 107; functionaries, 142; productive, 82, 109; protective, 17, 95, 98, 109; public, v, 52, 55, 91, 95, 97, 98, 156, 188; seepage, 10, 47, 65, 81, 86, 90, 143, 179, supply, 7n; system, 7, 99, 232, zoning, 164, 234
canal command, 8, 82, 84; of Mula project, 84, 86-88; head reaches, 3; lower reaches, 3; middle reaches, 184, 232; tail reaches, 3, 10, 83, 109, 184, 232; top reaches, 3, 184; upper reaches, 83
capital, costs, 3, 74, 81, 86, 104-06, 108, 113, 115-16; output ratio, 129 129n, 207
Captain Dastoor, 216
Cauvery, 21, 23
Central, Bank of India, 99; Board of Irrigation and Power, 64n; Government, 15, 144n; Groundwater Board (CGWB), 2, 24, 36n, 39, 40, 72, 93, 94, 231; Soil Salinity Research Institute (CSSRI) 18n, 43; U.P., 54, 59; Water Commission, 24, 39, 69, 72, 93, 95n

Centre, 8, 116, 30, 41, 46, 64n, 168, 231, 232
channels, feeder, 46; field, 4, 12, 98, 143n, 147, 163, 171; lining of, 72; piped, 28, 45
Chaturvedi, M.C., 21n
Chawla, A.S., 99, 101, 107
Cherrapunji, 218
Chopra, Kanchan, 10n
Chotanagpur hills, 200
Command Area Development, 4, 12, 179
comparative, analysis, 69, 71, 176; benefits, 69; costs, 68-80, 100, 101; investments, 73; performance of irrigation, 167-70, 175
Comprehensive Area Development Corporation, 197
Concept of, cost of cultivation, 127; surplus water, 217
conjunctive irrigation, iv, 10, 16, 82, 83, 97, 153, 156, 158-60, 167, 169, 230
consumptive use, 1, 151, 151n, 219
correlation, coefficient of, 181, 183, 212; matrix, 183; corruption, 15
cost, advantage, v, 229; disruption, 216; effectiveness, 1; incidental, 100; of pump energisation, 73, 228; water-lifting, 42; working, 233
Costs and Agricultural Prices Commission, 86, 177
created irrigation potential, 1, 14, 176, 182, 183, 188; basis for computing, 4; underutilisation of, 4, 232
critics of water planning, 63, 70, 76, 77
crop, aggregation, 123, 137n, 158; diversification, 119; root zone, 11, 12, 16, 36, 37, 47, 151n, 171, 201
crop pattern, 44, 162, 177-78, 181, 209, 232; actual, 5, 54; change in, 211; deviation in, 5, 232; effect, 118, 122, 135, 159
crop output per watering, 164, 174
crop yield, irrigated, 6, 17, 35, 87, 91, 139, 140, 144, 144n, 145, 148; of foodgrains, 140; in Far East, 6; according to irrigation intensity, 165
dam, big, 15, 62, 76; builders, 15, 64, 64n; check, 47, 224, dead storage of, 15, 73; ill effects of, 62, life of, 15, 64, 73, 73n; rock filled, 66; safety, 219, siltation of, 15, 64, 73; sites 15, 200; small, 15
dam height, 67, 68, 228; and area submerged relation, 67, 68; reduction in, 64, 66, 67
dam oustees, 64, 66, 67, 77; composition of, 66; demands of, 66; rehabilitation of, 64, 66-8, 228
Dandekar, V.M., 22
'dark' groundwater blocks, 41
Datye, K.R., 58, 59, 61
Deccan plateau, 8, 11, 25, 27, 41, 85, 89, 138, 153, 181, 184, 186, 189, 216, 226
deforestation, 15, 64
demand, agricultural, 1; for farm products, 15; for fertilisers, 156; for groundwater, 31, 46; for irrigation, 1, 118; for labour, 134; for water, 1,7n, 31, 35, 219, 220
dependability of irrigation, 3, 8-11, 19, 22, 23
depth of watering, 52, 58-60, 160, 172n, 234
Dharm Narain, 159, 159n
Dhawan B.D. 1, 6n, 7, 8, 10n, 32, 34n, 55, 56, 58, 62n, 68n, 81n, 87n, 95, 96, 102, 136n, 143, 150n, 155n, 158n, 159n, 172n, 176, 176n, 194n, 196, 198
Director of Irrigation Research, 86, 145
dissavings, 127, 127n
distribution, of income gains, 129-31, 135; land holdings, 7; of output gains, 102, 103, 135; network, 3; system, 9

districts of India: Ahmednagar, 84, 86, 92, 145n, 147; Aligarh, 58, 61, 92; Amritsar, 52, 53, 93, Bhojpur, 195, 202, 203; Birbhum 201; Bulandshahr, 92, 94; Burdwan, 201; Coimbatore, 39, 84; Dharamapuri, 89; Ghaziabad, 92, 99; Gurdaspur; 93; Hoshiarpur, 52-4, 93; Jullundur, 52, 53, 93; Karnal, 39; Lucknow, 59; Meerut, 34, 58, 92, 99, 101; Mehsana, 39; Mursheedabad, 201; Muzaffarnagar, 84, 91-3, 98, 99, 104, 105, 107; Purnia, 196, 213; Raigad, 119; Rohtas, 99; Ropar, 53, 54; Sangrur, 52, 53; Saharanpur, 99, 101; Saharsa, 213; West Dinajpur, 196, 206
drainage, 10, 65, 72, 82, 180, 194, 199, 200, 214, 230, 233, 236; cost of, 65; cross, 65; horizontal, 82, 107, 109, 180, 230, 233; vertical, 32, 65, 87, 107, 180, 233
drinking water, 30-2, 34, 35, 219-23
drip irrigation, vi, 28
drippers, 16, 28, 45, 65
drought, v, 6n, 7n, 10, 10n, 18, 19, 23, 29, 30, 35, 37, 50, 204, 218, 227, 228; in catchment area, 10-19; of 1979-80, 30, 37n, 88; proofing, iv, v, 10n, 19, 228; prone areas, v, 19, 218, 224
dryland farming, 62, 68n; experts, 9n; pogramme, 68
dugwells, 9, 39, 45, 71, 79, 80, 95, 96, 142
Dutt, D.K., 31, 36n, 37
Dyneshwar, 138

earthquake, 65, 66; proofing, 66
east, Gangetic plains, vi, 32, 45, 59, 76, 194-99, 204, 226-27; U.P., 27, 40, 54, 194, 196, 199
ecological, consequence, iv; degradation, 1; matters, 63; system, 218;
economic value of water, 81
Egypt, 65n
employment-output elasticity, 134-35
environment, 106, 219
environmental, angle, 64, 65; groups, 179
environmentalists, 63, 67
equity, 2, 219; and social justice, 219; in irrigation, 6-8; spatial, 7, 8, 32, 47, 174, 232
equivalence among crops, 137
estimates of, basin-wise flows, 21, 23; exploitable flows, 21, 218; groundwater potential, 23, 25, 38, 38n; groundwater recharge, 23, 24; operating irrigation costs, 70-80; number of waterings, 54-58, 58n
external, economies, v, 11, 86, 136, 143; effects, 142

Far East, 6, 194
farm, economy, 35; ponds, 9n, 68; product markets, 49; research stations, 155, 155n, 235
farmers', agitation, 97, 105; participation, vi
farmers, asset poor, 196, 197; behaviour, 48, 59; land poor, 195; large, 7, 206, 208-12; medium, 206, 208-12; small; vi, 7, 53, 197, 206, 208-14, 230, 236; marginal, vi, 195-97, 203, 204, 206, 208-14, 230, 236; rationality, 48; resource poor, 184; tail-end; 7, 8; top-end, 3, 7, 8
federal structure, 2
field-to-field irrigation, 12, 164, 171
financial, losses, 3; management, 233; performance, 13
First Indian Irrigation Commission, 22
First National Water Convention, 64n
Five Year Plan, 2, 8, 68, 71; Second, 17; Third, 232; Fifth, 70, 74, 75; Sixth, 39, 219, 232n; Seventh, 22, 26, 39, 72

flat power tariff, 48, 111, 114, 115, 234
flood, and drought management, 227, 228; and drainage, vi, 202; control, 16, 194, 195, 200, 201; plain, 224, 227; protection, 200, 201, 224; waters, 19, 36, 200, 214, 227
forest, cover, 62, 64, 70, 77, 228; lands, 64, 64n; problem of vanishing, 64
Forest Act of 1980, 64n,
full utilisation, 5n, 182, 232, 232n

Gandak, 178, 180, 182, 183, 184, 185, 186, 188, 192, 217
Ganga, 22, 23, 62, 91, 92, 98, 202
Ganga-Cauvery link, 216, 227
Garland Canals, 216, 227
Ghosh, Arun, 72
Godavari, 21, 23
Gokhale Institute of Politics and Economics, 136, 137n
Goldsmith, E., 62
green revolution, 95, 109
Grewal, S.S., 51, 52, 61, 234
groundwater, artificial recharge, 11, 31, 32, 46, 81; availability, 26, 27, 35; depletion, iv, v, 3, 15, 34, 37-39, 96, 106, 107, 227, 229, 231; dimensions, 36, 217; directorates, 24, 39; experts, 36; exploitation, 39, 40; investigation organisations, 40; mining, 42; over-use of, 34, 54; over-exploitation, v, 34-47, 34n, 37n, 38, 41; quotas, 42; versus canals, 228-30
Groundwater Directorate, U.P., 107
Groundwater Estimation Committee, 38n, 87
growth rate of, agriculture, 194, 195; crop output 194; population, 194
gur making, 104, 110; economics of, 110, 111

HYV, crops, 196; paddy, 199; seeds, 8, 10, 202; technology, 9, 10; wheat, 187, 199, 202.
Hildyard, N., 62
Himalayan, catchments, 227, flows, 20; rivers, 20, waters, 227
Himalayas, 36, 50, 66, 200, 227
Howe, Charles, 63
hydrogeologists, 16, 41, 46, 85, 96, 231
hypotheses about irrigated farming, v, 55, 156

impact per watering, 163-70, 174
income, concept, 127, 129; elasticity, 15; gains, 7, 14; growth, 47
Indian Constitution, 41, 218, 227
ICAR, 34
Indian National Academy of Engineers, 95n
Indian sub-continent, 82, 95, 117, 195, 197, 198
Indian water endowment, 18-32
Indira Gandhi Canal, 179
indirect output augmentation, 92, 142-47
Indo-Gangetic plains, 25, 36, 45, 95, 196, 203
Indus, 21
inefficiencies, 3, 15
inequality, v
inequity, 3, 7, 8
instability in agricultural growth, v
institutional, credit, 23, 235; finance, 39, 44, 46, 74, 104, 109; rate of interest, 109; support, 117.
intensity of, cropping, 44, 101, 128, 135, 159, 202, 205, 209, 210, 236, cropping effect, 118; floods, 224; fertiliser use, 160, 163, 167; irrigation, 6n, 159, 168-70
inter-basin water transfer, 22, 27, 215-17
inter-linking, idea, 19; Indian rivers, 19
Iraq, 65n
irrigation, administrators, iv, 13, 49, 81,

118, 235; authority, 14, 15; bureaucracy, 69; capacity, 8, 17, 21, 22; cover, 227; delta, 58, 149, 150n, 171, 172n, 179, 182, 185; depth, 13, 13n, 52; development, 16, 17; engineers, iv, 69, 81, 83, 118, 235; frequency, 52, 57; gap; 154; life saving, 9n, 32, productive, 10, 197; public, 6, 232, 235; ratio, 7, 117, 157; release, 149, 149n; sector, 18
irrigation impact, its measurement, 120 121; crop enterprise, 127, 128; crop output, 121-26, 135; crop yield, 139-41; on dissavings, 127, 127n; on Indian economy, iv; on labour absorption, 133-35; on labour income, 131; on paddy output, 121, 122, 163-70; on sugarcane output, 103
irrigation management, iv, 1, 2, 3, 16
irrigation planning, v, 69, 82, 97, 223
irrigation potential, v, 69, 177, 226; created, 1, 14, 70, 176; definitional deficiencies of, 17
irrigation requirements of, arhar, 50; bajra, 50, 190, 191; barley, 50; cotton, 50, 149, 190, 191; crop-wise, 177, 190-92; crop group wise, 192-93; fodder, 50; gram, 50, 190-92; groundnut, 50, 190, 191; lentils, 50; paddy, 52, 53, 134, 190-92, 198n; potatoes, 50, 187, 191-92; sugarcane, 50, 149, 190-94; wheat, 10, 50, 51, 87, 88, 149, 190-92, 198n
issues, iv, v, 48-50, 62-80

Japan, 194
Jayakwadi project, 139n, 150, 179, 180, 182, 183, 185-88, 191, 193

Kal project, 118-35, 235
Kanwar, J.S., 72, 75
Kay, David, 226n
Khosla, 23
Konkan, v., 20, 32, 85, 118, 216, 226, 235
Koyna dam, 66
Krishna river, 21

labour, opportunity cost of, 106, 108; overuse of, 48; productivity, 149; use, 133, 134
land, base, 194, 208, 209, 214, 235; consolidation, 106, 196; degradation, 65; fragmentation, 43, 106, 196; prices, 125, 126; productivity, 7, 34, 56, 89-91, 125, 126, 141, 161, 180-83, 189, 209-11, 229; resources, 15, 76, 197; subsidence, 37; submergence, 23, 62, 64, 70, 228; true cost of, 70; and water management, 63
landless groups, 197, 214
lowering of water table, 16, 37, 38, 96
Luni river, 21

Madan, T.N., vi
Mahanadi, 21; Delta project, 178, 180-88, 192
Mahatma Phule Agricultural University (MPKV), 140, 151
Mahi, 21
maintenance, funds, 14; preventive, 14, 79; work, 14; and repair, 13, 78, 79
major irrigation, 46; cost of, 2, 69, 70, 228; opposition to, 63; vis-a-vis minor irrigation, 68, 69; works, 7, 62, 68, 69, 179, 229, 230
Malabar, 20, 32, 119, 216, 226
market in groundwater, 106, 110, 196, 197, 208, 230
Mayurakshi, 178, 180-85, 188, 192, 201
Mcdonald, A.T., 226n
mhot, 43n
Middle East, 65n
Minhas, B.S., 49n, 122

Minhas – Vaidyanathan, 122
minimum farm size, 196
Ministry of Agriculture, 78
minor irrigation, 17, 68, 69, 98, 99, 232, 232n; cause, 68, 69, 228n; cost of, 2, 68, 70, 71; cost structure; 71; indirect investments of, 74, 75; myths about, 69, 70; promoters of, 2, 69; superiority of, 68, 69
Mitra, Ashok, K., 137n
monopolistic exploitation, 197, 204
monopoly surplus, 197
monsoons, 37, 82, 88; break in, 9n, 38, 124, 236
Moorti, T.V., 58, 61
Mughal days, 88
Mula, v, 84, 86-88, 92, 136-54, 180
multiple regression, 176
multipurpose river projects, 13, 77, 78
Murthy, B.N., 73n
myth, v, 69, 229, 232

Nagarjuna Sagar, 77, 150, 150n, 179-83, 185-88, 191, 193
Narmada, 21, 23, 67, 68; Bachao Andolan, 76n; dams, 62, 68, 228; Development Authority, 66; imbroglio, v; Sagar, 64, 67, 77; Valley Projects, 66, 67
National Bank for Agricultural and Rural Development (NABARD), 39, 71n, 91, 93, 97-108, 110-14, 117, 201, 205n, 213, 214
National Commission on Floods, 219
National Council of Applied Economic Research (NCAER), v, 55, 56, 58, 61, 156, 157, 173, 235
national, demonstration plots, 6; income generation, 118, 119, 130, 132
National Sample Survey (NSS), 55-58, 61, 235
National Water Resources Council, 215
natural resources, 2, 34
Nepal, 214, 227
New Water Policy, vi, 30, 215-26
non-consumptive use of water, 1
number of waterings, 51, 52, 55, 58n, 60, 155, 161-167, 171, 172, 172n; actual, 172; normative, 172, 173; observed, 173; requisite, 173; shortfall in, 55; statewise, 57; for maize, 54; for paddy, 54, 56, 60, 234, 235; for sugarcane, 54, 56, 102; for wheat, 51, 54, 56, 102; per crop, 54, 61, 235

Operations Research Group (ORG), v, 150n, 177-79, 201
operational costs, 13, 14, 70, 75-80; expenditure, 13, 78
opportunity cost, concept of, 48; of family labour, 106, 108
output gains, 102, 103, 135; distribution of, 126
output impact, 176, 178-80, 183, 188, 189, 198; direct, 179, 181-83
over-exploitation, areal extent of, 38-41, claims of, 38; concept of, 36-38, of groundwater resources, 35, 38, 44, 45, 222, 230; of natural resources, 34, 43; stories of, 38, 231
over-irrigation, iv, 1, 12, 13, 48-61, 171-73,. 234, 235
overruns, 2; cost, 2, 15, 219, 222, 229; time, 2, 7, 15, 219, 222, 229

Pakistan, 11n
Pal, S.P., 157-59
Pantnagar Agricultural University, 54
Parliament, 63
Patel, K.V., 58, 61
Patel, S. M., 58, 61
Patil, R.K., 58, 59, 61
Pawar, Shobha R., 119-23, 125-27, 125n, 129, 131
Pennar river, 21
people's participation, 46, 47
persian wheel, 43n, 88

pipe dream, 216
pitfalls of capital costs, 71-75
Planning Commission, 24, 39, 39n, 67, 94; Task Force of, 88
policy, of buffer stocking, 30; of gross underpricing, 13, 14, 231, 233; of extensive irrigation, 174, 233; of intensive agriculture, 174; of low cost irrigation, 48; of subsidising electricity, 1, 96; for sugar mills location, 144n; of under-irrigation, 7
political, compulsions, 3; considerations, 218; economy, 7; leadership, 17, 233; pressure, 44
politicians, 8, 69, 234
polity, 2
potential yields, 141, 147, 152, 199, 202
poverty, alleviation, 195, 198, 209, 214; eradication, 194-214; incidence of, 236; line, 194, 195; ratio, 198; rural, 195
power famine, 195, 202
Pravara Canal, 143n, 144n, 145
price, inflation, 137, 177; premium 122; of water, 204
pricing, of electricity, 43, 44, 79, 229, 231; problems, 233, 234
Prihar, S.S, 49n, 51, 52, 61, 234
Prime Minister, 215
private tubewell, vi, 39, 55, 56, 58, 88, 91-3, 180, 195, 197, 202, 213, 214, 235
production function, macro, 49; water-related, 49n
productivity, of canal irrigation, 109, 136, 147-52, 181; of foodgrains, 184-87, 189; gains, 7; impact, 179, 182; of irrigated farming, 155-75, 177, 181, 182, 193; of limited resources, iv; of non-foodgrains, 184-87, 189; of water, v, 174, 176, 214, per unit of water; 147-52, 155 165, 185, 186, 232
protective, benefit of irrigation, 18; canals, 17, 95, 98, 109, 230; cover, 6n; goals, 18; irrigation, 30, 32, 197, 198, 227; motive, 18; role of irrigation, 18; value of irrigation, 22
public tubewells, 14, 45, 49, 58, 59, 196, 214, 232, 235; over-irrigation under, 58-60, 61, 235
Punjab Agricultural University (PAU), 49n, 52, 88

quality of irrigation, 9, 10, 14, 99, 208, 211

rainfall, 20, 85-7, 89-93, 106, 107, 117-19, 138, 178-80; effective, 151n; infiltration, 35, 36, 85, 87, 89-93, 106, 107
Rajadhyaksha Committee on Power, 79
Rajasthan Canal, 150n, 179-83, 185-88, 190, 192
Rajput, R.K., 51
Raju, K.C.B., 23
Randhawa, N.S., 34
Rao, K.L., 22
rate of return, 86, 92, 105, 108, 109, 143, 147; internal (IRR), 205, 214
recurring cost advantage, 75, 76
regions of India: eastern, 20, 26, 28, 40, 54, 200, 216; western, v 26, 28, 31, 34, 40, 41, 65, 81, 232; northern, 17, 26, 40, 41, 81, 82, 200, 230; southern, 26, 31, 40, 65, 81, 82, 232; Central, 26, 28, 40; north-western, 7, 10, 20, 96, 153
reservoirs, 62-80, 198, 200; big, 200, 208; detention, 200, 201, 227; lands submerged by, 179, 216, 217; village submerged by, 66
resource, cost, 3, 14, 16, 78, 79, 231, 233; crunch, 3
returns to, investment in well irrigation, 11; irrigation investment, 118; tubewell investment, 107, 108, 202
rice equivalence, 158, 177, 178

river, catchment, 228; diversion, 62; embankments, 199, 200, planning, 67; names, 21;
role of irrigation, 197-99, 236
romanticism, 232
Roy, Shyamal, 159, 159n
rural electrification, 23, 43, 74, 75, 79, 97, 101, 106, 108, 117, 228

Sabarmati, 21
safe yield, concept of, 37n; principle, 36
sale of tubewell water, 103-06
Sampath, R.K., 197
Sangal, S.P., 25, 40, 89, 93, 94
Sarda Sahayak, 179-93
Sardar Sarovar, dam, 66, 76, 77, height of, 68; project, 67n
Sarkar, B.B., 197
Satya Sai, K.J.S., vi, 32, 55, 81n, 87n, 96, 155n
Saurashtra, 37n, 39
seismic angle, 65, 66
Sethi, Mrs Rama, vi
Sharma, H.D., 107
Sharma, V.K., 54, 55, 61, 235
Sidhu, D.S., 101
siltation, problem, 15; process, 15; rate, 233; of reservoirs, 15, 233
Singh, Bharat, 64n
Singh, Gurcharan, 50, 53, 54, 60, 93, 235
Singh, R.P., 23
soil, alkalinity, 81; conservation, 68, 233; erosion, 15; mapping, 144n; salinity, 10, 15, 16, 37n, 62, 65, 81, 109, 142, 146, 179, 230, 233;
scientists, iv, 171
Sone, 202
spirinklers, vi, 16, 28, 44, 65
State Bank of India (SBI), 206, 207, 209
State Electricity Boards, 78
Stone, Ian, 99
subsidy, 97, 101, 107, 108, 115, 117, 128
sugarcane cultivation, 8, 82, 86, 91, 102, 141, 142, 175
surface irrigation works, 9, 10, 31, 45-47, 218, 230
sustainability of irrigated farming, 3, 15, 16, 81, 96, 97, 233

tanks, 18, 19, 31, 47; cost of percolation, 86; evaporation, 46; in Tamil Nadu, 19; maintenance of, 46; percolation, 46, 47, 70 85, 229; system, 19
Tapi, 21
Tawa, 179-81, 183-90, 192
Tehri dam, 62, 66
Tikait, 105
transfer of water, 2, 226
tubewell, bamboo, 213, 214; borings, 196; capacity utilisation, 203; community, 196, 214; cooperative, 196; diesel, 97, 100, 101, 104, 105; electric, 97, 100, 101, 104, 105; government, 196; indivisibility, 195-97, 214, 236; investment, 96, 97, 99, 100, 207; minimum farm size for, 105, 106; running hours, 107, 110; technology, 45, 95 96
Tungabhadra, 150, 150n, 179-83, 185-88, 191, 193
Tyagi, D.S., 194n
Tyagi, S.S., 99
type of irrigation, 157, 158, 168, 174, 228

uncertainties of, canal supplies, 234; price, 49, 187; weather, 49
under-irrigation, 10, 51, 52, 55, 59, 61, 172, 173, 235
underutilisation, of created irrigation potental, 4, 182; of irrigation capacity, iv, 3, 4, 6, 17, 118, 134, 137-39; phenomenon of, 3-6; of new projects, 4; of surface irrigation

potential, 136, 152; of water resources, 4
ultimate, irrigation capacity of our rivers, 21, 22, 26; groundwater potential, 25, 26, 38, 40, 217, 218
unit capital cost, 71-75
U.S.A., 9, 42, 63, 216
unutilised potential, 4, 17, 231, 232
Upper Ganges Canal, 98
U.P. Land Development Bank (ULDB), 91, 98, 102
utilisation, capacity, 3, 176, 181-83; rate of, 4, 176, 182, 232; of groundwater resources, 4, 38, 40, 89, 92, 94; of irrigation potential, 17, 40, 90, 138, 139

Varma, S.C., 64n, 66, 67n, 68
Vijaylakshmi, K., 33
Vindhyas, 36, 200
violation of canal regulations, 83, 86
Vohra, B.B., 63, 96, 153

warabandi, 7
water, allowance, 6, 10; conveyance efficiency, 1, 11, 11n, 28, 143, 143n; disputes, 216; duty, 6; endowment, v, 8; intensive crops, 4; storage efficiency, 1; stress, 9, 10, 204; surplus, 217; unexploitable, 217; wastage of irrigation 3, 11, 13, 171;
water conveyance losses, 4, 81; in Ganges canal system, 91; in Mula project, 86, 143
water management, experts, 12, 49, 140, 147, 153; problems of, iv, 2; research, iv, 28; scientists, 50, 155
water rate, 13, 104, 113, 114, 135, 142n, 234
water resources, 8, 15, 18, 23, 28, 215, 217, 226; area potential of our, 27; complex nature of, 217; exploitation of, 4; exploitability of, 20; our bounty of, 19-29, 226-27; romanticism about, 32
water sharing, 7n, 227; principles and problems of, 216
water table, cyclical changes in, 37, 38; decline in, 16, 34, 231; depth to, 16, 37, 43, 43n, 231
water tariff, 60, 234; in public tubewells, 58, 59
water use, economy in, 28; efficiency, 149, 151, 153, 154
water yield, 11, 70, 84, 136, 143n, 145, 146, 229
waterlogging, iv, 6n, 10, 15, 47, 62, 65, 81, 82, 109, 153, 179, 180, 201, 230, 233; and flood damage, 195; and flood hazard, 199-201, 236; area under, 142; loss of output due to, 136, 142, 146; phenomenon of, 37; statistics of, 65, 146
watershed, 43; management, vi, 46
wells, within canal commands, 82-84, 86, 88, 144; outside canal commands, 86, 88, 143n, 144n, density of, 84; masonry, 73, 98; mutual interference among, 38, 42; spacing between, 43; traditional, 42, 79;
well-managed irrigation system, 5, 9
west U.P., v, 46, 54, 58, 82, 84, 91, 92, 98, 99, 106, 195
western Maharashtra, v, 84-6, 92
wheat, region, 179, 188; threshing, 103, 105, 112
Walidpur, 99
WALMI, 86, 87, 136, 136n, 137, 143, 144, 147, 233
Western Ghats, 11, 20, 32, 216, 226
World Bank, 30, 59, 143n

Yamuna, 91, 92, 98
yield, crop-wise, 190-92; crop group wise, 192-93; coefficient of variation, 181; deficiency, 151, 152; differential, 162, 186, 198; effect, 118, 122, 159; gap; 141, 151, 154; per watering, 162-67, 174, 175; per unit of water, 185, 190-93
Yojana Bhawan, 69

INSTITUTE OF ECONOMIC GROWTH, DELHI

Studies in Economic Development and Planning

1. *The Role of SmallEnterprises in Indian Economic Development* by P.N. Dhar and H.F. Lydall, 1961. (Asia Publishing House, Bombay).
2. *Indian Tax Structure and Economic Development* by G.S. Sahota, 1961. (Asia Publishing House, Bombay).
3. *Agricultural Labour in India* by V.K.R.V. Rao, 1962. (Asia Publishing House, Bombay).
4. *Foreign Aid and India's Economic Development* by V.K.R.V. Rao and Dharm Narain, 1963. (Asia Publishing House, Bombay).
5. *Agricultural Production Functions, Costs and Returns in India* by C.H. Hanumantha Rao, 1965. (Asia Publishing House, Bombay).
6. *Resource Allocation in the Cotton Textile Industry* by Dharma Kumar, S.P. Nag and L.S. Venkataramanan, 1965. (Asia Publishing House, Bombay).
7. *India's Industrialisation and Mineral Exports* by V.P. Chopra, 1965. (Asia Publishing House, Bombay).
8. *Taxation of Agricultural Land in Andhra Pradesh* by C.H. Hanumantha Rao, 1966. (Asia Publishing House).
9. *Some Aspects of Cooperative Farming in India* by S.K. Goyal, 1966. (Asia Publishing House, Bombay).
10. *Demand for Energy in North-West India* by P.N. Dhar and D.U. Sastry, 1967. (Asia Publishing House, Bombay).
11. *Some Aspects of the Structure of Indian Agricultural Economy 1947-48 to 1961-62* by P.V. John, 1968. (Asia Publishing House, Bombay).
12. *Wages and Productivity in Selected Indian Industries* by J.N. Sinha and P.K. Sawhney, 1970. (Vikas Publishing House, Delhi).
13. *Inventories in Indian Manufacturing* by K. Krishnamurty and D.U. Sastry, 1970. (Academic Books Ltd., New Delhi).
14. *Buffer Stocks and Storage of Major Foodgrains in India* by A.M. Khusro, 1973. (Tata McGraw Hill Publishing Company Ltd., Bombay).
15. *Bangla Desh Economy: Problems and Prospects* edited by

V.K.R.V. Rao, 1972. (Vikas Publishing House, New Delhi).

16. *The Economics of Land Reform and Farm Size in India* by A.M. Khusro, 1973. (Macmillan Co. of India Ltd., Madras).
17. *Technological Change and Distribution of Gains in Indian Agriculture* by C.H. Hanumantha Rao, 1975. (Macmillan Co. of India Ltd., Madras).
18. *Investment and Financing in the Corporate Sector in India* by K. Krishnamurty and D.U. Sastry, 1975 (Tata McGraw Hill Publishing Company Ltd., New Delhi).
19 *Land Reforms in India: Trends and Perspectives* by P.C. Joshi, 1975. (Allied Publishers Private Limited, Bombay).
20. *Cost Benefit Analysis: A Case Study of the Ratnagiri Fisheries Project* by S.N. Mishra and John Beyer, 1976. (Hindustan Publishing Corporation, Delhi).
21. *Livestock Planning in India* by S.N. Mishra, 1978. (Vikas Publishing House, Delhi).
22. *Rice Marketing System and Compulsory Levies in Andhra Pradesh* by K. Subbarao, 1978. (Allied Publishers Private Limited, Bombay).
23. *Farm Size, Resource-Use Efficiency and Income Distribution* by G.R. Saini, 1979. (Allied Publishers Private Limited, New Delhi).
24. *Class Relations and Technical Change in Indian Agriculture* by Sipra Dasgupta, 1980. (Macmillan Co. of India Ltd., Delhi).
25. *Conglomerates and Multinationals in India: A Study of Investment and Profit* by N.S. Siddharthan, 1981. (Allied Publishers Private Limited, New Delhi).
26. *Development of Tubewell Irrigation in India* by B.D. Dhawan, 1982. (Agricole Publishing Academy, New Delhi).
27. *Economic Appraisal of Irrigation Projects in India* by Basawan Sinha and Ramesh Bhatia, 1982. (Agricole Publishing Academy, New Delhi).
28. *Economic Planning for Iron Ore in India* by Gopal Kadekodi, 1982. (Hindustan Publishing Corporation, Delhi).
29. *Oilseeds Economy of India* by Uma Kapila, 1982. (Agricole Publishing Academy, New Delhi).
30. *Dry Farming Technology in India: A Study of its Profitability in Selected Areas* by P. Rangaswamy, 1982. (Agricole Publishing Academy, New Delhi).

31. *Planning for the Petroleum and Fertilizer Industries: A Programming Model for India* by Ramesh Bhatia, 1983. (Oxford University Press, Delhi).
32. *Studies in Social Dynamics of Primary Health Care* by Ashish Bose and P.B. Desai, 1983. (Hindustan Publishing Corporation, Delhi).
33. *Rural Development Planning: Design and Method* by S.N. Mishra, 1984. (Satvahan Publications, New Delhi).
34. *Cotton Mill Industry in India* by D.U. Sastry, 1984. (Oxford University Press, Delhi).
35. *Economics of Agricultural Credit* by Arun Kumar Bandyopadhyay, 1984, (Agricole Publishing Academy, New Delhi).
36. *Slowdown Global Economic Maladies* by A. Brody, 1985. (SAGE Pblications India Private Limited, New Delhi).
37. *Public Expenditure, Inflation and Growth: A Macro-Econometric Analysis for India* by B.B. Bhattacharya, 1984. (Oxford University Press, Delhi).
38. *Intensification of Agriculture: A Study in the Plains of Uttar Pradesh* by S.K. Ray, 1985. (Hindustan Publishing Corporation, Delhi).
39. *Productivity Growth in Indian Industry* by B.N. Goldar, 1986 (Allied Publishers (P) Ltd., New Delhi).
40. *Cold Hearths and Barren Slopes: The Woodfuel Crisis in the Third World* by Bina Agarwal, 1986. (Allied Publishers (P) Ltd., New Delhi).
41. *Rural to Urban Migration and the Urban Labour Market by Biswajit Banerjee, 1986.* (Himalaya Publishing House, Delhi).
42. *Economics of Groundwater Irrigation in Hard Rock Regions: With Special Reference to Maharashtra State* by B.D. Dhawan, 1986. (Agricole Publishing Academy, New Delhi).
43. *Agricultural Price Policy and Income Distribution in India* by Alain De Janvry and K. Subbarao, 1986. (Oxford University Press, New Delhi).
44. *The Economics of Inequality in Education* by JBG Tilak, 1987 (SAGE Publications, New Delhi).
45. *Nutritional Planning in India* by Rajaram Dasgupta, 1989. (Navrang Publishers & Book Sellers, New Delhi).
46. *Irrigation in India's Agricultural Development* by B.D. Dhawan, 1988 (SAGE Publications, New Delhi).
47. *Unstable Agriculture and Droughts: Implications for Policy* by C.H. Hanumantha Rao, Sushanta K. Ray and K. Subbarao,

1988. (Vikas Publishing House, New Delhi).

48. *Fertility in India* by S.C. Gulati, 1988 (SAGE Publications, New Delhi).
49. *Planning for Coal Sector* by G. Kadekodi, 1988. (B.R. Publishing Corporation, Delhi).
50. *Marriage Age in India* by R.P. Goyal, 1988. (B.R. Publishing Corporation, Delhi).
51. *Redistributive Taxation and Public Sector Pricing* by M.N. Murty, 1989. (Commonwealth Publishers, New Delhi).
52. *Participatory Development: People and Common Property Resources* by Kanchan Chopra, Gopal K. Kadekodi, M.N. Murty, 1989. (SAGE Publications, New Delhi).